Over Here

Also by Edward Humes

School of Dreams

Baby E.R.

No Matter How Loud I Shout

Mississippi Mud

Mean Justice

OVER HERE

How the G.I. Bill Transformed the American Dream

Edward Humes

Harcourt, Inc.
Orlando Austin New York San Diego Toronto London

www.HarcourtBooks.com

Library of Congress Cataloging-in-Publication Data
Humes, Edward.
Over here: how the G.I. Bill transformed the American dream/
Edward Humes.—1st ed.
p. cm.
Includes index.
1. Veterans—Services for—United States. 2. United States—Armed Forces—Demobilization—History—20th century.
3. World War, 1939–1945—Veterans—United States.
4. War and society—United States.
5. Suburban life—United States. I. Title.
UB357.H76 2006
362.86'820973—dc22 2006006904
ISBN-13: 978-0-15-100710-3 ISBN-10: 0-15-100710-1

Text set in Minion
Designed by Lydia D'moch

Printed in the United States of America
First edition
A C E G I K J H F D B

This book is dedicated to the memories of
Edward Aloyisius Humes and Shirley Humes,
children of the Depression, the War, and the G.I. Bill

Contents

PROLOGUE
Troop Movement Unlike Any Other

Allan Howerton had never seen anything like it—which was saying a lot.

He had swapped a job hustling White Castle burgers on the graveyard shift in Rahway, New Jersey, for action in six bloody, crucial battles in France and Germany, surviving some of World War II's most deadly months on the ground. By his own calculation, he was one of only eighteen out of 570 infantrymen in his company to make it through every one of those battles without being wounded, captured, or killed—which meant, he would later joke, he was either good, lucky, or foolish. Or a bit of all three.

Still, Howerton felt nothing he had faced before—not the deadly and constant thudding of artillery, not the endless slogging through the mud of Roer and Rhine, not even the sight of death and hope and fear mingling on the faces of enemy and friend alike along the Siegfried Line—had prepared him for this latest massing of men, for this unprecedented mission with no guarantees.

Howerton stood on a packed tramcar, thick with the smell of Winston and Pall Mall and the familiar waiting sounds of shuffling, coughing, murmuring. The troops had been gathering for weeks, arriving first by the dozens, then the hundreds, and, finally, they began moving in by the thousands. Now they streamed toward the city and headed for the high ground, an emerald hilltop near the urban core with a commanding view and easy access by road and rail—idyllic, quiet, underpopulated, waiting to be taken.

And so the most remarkable, least predictable action of World War II began to play out, a movement of more Army, Navy, Marine, and Air Corps forces than has ever been attempted before or since. Howerton's was just one location in a worldwide endeavor—a coordinated effort of such magnitude that it would shape the future of America and the world in a way that would eclipse almost every battle of the war, even the Normandy landing and the decimation of Hiroshima. The men in Washington who had conceived this audacious plan virtually as an afterthought, almost killing it a half-dozen times before finally setting it in motion shortly after D-Day, had in no way foreseen what this moment would look like—nor did they envision the long reach of its impact, still resonating to this day. In time, all America would feel its effects, from city to suburb to farm, from classroom to boardroom, doctor's office to Oval Office—an unintended juggernaut.

The tram doors creaked open and the men rushed into the thin morning sunlight, freed from the coffinlike confines of the old trolley. Howerton, his thick brow knitted in momentary confusion, struggled in the jostling crowd to get his bearings on this unfamiliar turf, this grassy knoll with its old brick and granite buildings stretching out before him, gnarled trees, singed by autumn, obscuring the horizon. Then he heard someone say, "This way," and Howerton turned and saw the sign pointing to their objective:

UNIVERSITY OF DENVER: OFFICE OF THE REGISTRAR

He took a deep breath and headed off to sign up for his freshman classes, a nervous eagerness roiling his stomach, a far different unease from the sort he came to know during his time in war-torn Germany. The fears no longer involved bullets and bleeding and death, but professors and textbooks and midterms—and contemplation of a future that was no longer simply about surviving to see the next day, but about envisioning a new century, building a career, a life, a country.

On that creaky trolley car in Denver, in a moment replayed in cities and towns throughout the nation, the age of the G.I. had drawn to an end. And the age of the G.I. Bill had just begun.

☆ 1 ☆

The Greatest Regeneration:
The Accidental Remaking of America

Although he had no idea at the time, Allan Howerton's journey to Denver began two years earlier, on January 11, 1944, when two very distinct road maps to postwar America landed on Congress's doorstep.

One vision for "winning the peace" came wrapped in the pomp and ritual of the president's annual State of the Union address. The other was scrawled by lobbyists a mile from the Capitol, on hotel stationery, then hastily typed up for public consumption.

One represented nothing less than President Franklin Delano Roosevelt's plan to expand the Founding Fathers' original vision of a just America: giving every citizen the right to a rewarding job, a living wage, a decent home, health care, education, and a pension—not as opportunities, not as privileges, not as goods to which everyone (who could afford them) had access, but rights, guaranteed to every American, from cradle to grave. He called it a "Second Bill of Rights."

The other plan, courtesy of the era's most powerful veterans organization, the American Legion, advanced a more modest goal, or so it seemed: to compensate the servicemen of World War II for their lost time and opportunities, offering 16 million veterans a small array of government-subsidized loans, unemployment benefits, and a year of school or technical training for those whose educations had been interrupted by the draft or enlistment. The Legion called this a "Bill of Rights for G.I. Joe and Jane."

The first plan promised to reinvent America after the war.

The second offered to put things back to where they were before the war.

As it turned out, neither plan's promises ould be kept. FDR never got the chance to remake America. Instead, the G.I. Bill did.

This was not by grand design, but quite by accident, as much a creation of petty partisans as of political visionaries. Yet the forces set in motion that day in January 1944 would power an unprecedented and far-reaching transformation—of education, of cities and a new suburbia, of the social, cultural, and physical geography of America, of science, medicine, and the arts. And just as importantly, the blandly and bureaucratically named Servicemen's Readjustment Act of 1944, forever remembered as the G.I. Bill of Rights, would alter both the aspirations and the expectations of all Americans, veterans and nonveterans alike.

A nation of renters would become a nation of homeowners. College would be transformed from an elite bastion to a middle-class entitlement. Suburbia would be born amid the clatter of bulldozers and the smell of new asphalt linking it all together. Inner cities would collapse. The Cold War would find its warriors—not in the trenches or the barracks, but at the laboratory and the wind tunnel and the drafting table. Educations would be made possible for fourteen future Nobel Prize winners, three Supreme Court justices, three presidents, a dozen senators, two dozen Pulitzer Prize winners, 238,000 teachers, 91,000 scientists, 67,000 doctors, 450,000 engineers, 240,000 accountants, 17,000 journalists, 22,000 dentists—along with a million lawyers, nurses, businessmen, artists, actors, writers, pilots, and others. All would owe their careers not to FDR's grand vision, but to that one modest proposal that was supposed to put the country back to where it had been before the war.

There was never anything like it before.

There is nothing like it on the horizon.

It began with a simple question: *Now what?*

WHILE president, lobbyists, and Congress debated how best to "win the peace," Allan Howerton and the other members of K Company went off to finish the war, sailing from New York Harbor aboard a converted luxury liner, the HMS *Stirling Castle,* as a military band stood dockside and played, "The Boogie Woogie Bugle Boy of Company B."

Howerton had always imagined sailing off to the sounds of a stirring march, not the latest Andrews Sisters swing, though in truth, he had never expected to sail off to war at all. The Army initially had placed him in a college-based engineering program, with the promise of a billet rebuilding Europe after the war. He spent his first year in the Army at Drexel University in Philadelphia, marveling at his good fortune, basking in a college education he had never expected to be available to him.

Then he found himself unceremoniously transferred to the infantry when frontline casualties mounted, and warm, able bodies became far more important to the Army than engineering degrees. The military had abruptly canceled most of its college programs and dumped several hundred thousand soft college boys into boot camp, then shipped them overseas. Howerton bunked in the converted luxury liner's emptied swimming pool as the jam-packed *Stirling Castle*'s long convoy zigzagged to Europe, dodging German U-boats, or so they all hoped. He spent the voyage writing his girlfriend, Mary, and dreaming of his return to her and to his old life.

Sixteen months later, with the war won and the occupation and reconstruction of Europe begun, another vessel crammed with servicemen carried a very different Allan Howerton home. After ten days on a stormy Atlantic Ocean, the cry, "New York!" rang out, and along with hundreds of other uniformed men he dashed to the rails and the upper decks for a first glimpse of home. There was no convoy this time, no zigzagging to avoid the deadly bite of torpedoes, no band waiting on the pier—just the coppery green shimmer of the Statue of Liberty, a distant, unreal skyline, and, closer by, the oily New Jersey shoreline, with its modest homes and warehouses looking strange to eyes grown accustomed to the ruined grandeur of Europe. Howerton felt exhilarated, relieved . . . and uneasy.

After a few weeks, Howerton mustered out of the Army at Fort Dix, still in his uniform, his future, a path once seemingly so clear and certain, now invisible to him. Damningly, mystifyingly, frustratingly, the uneasiness he initially dismissed had not faded but had taken firm root in his gut and grown. His civilian clothes felt strange and wrong; he could not wear them for any length of time, and so he stayed in uniform, as did many newly discharged G.I.s, caught between two worlds, neither soldier nor citizen. At the Fort Dix gate, a wild impulse seized him to reenlist, to return to the security of barracks and friends he trusted with his life, to orders and orderliness—to avoid that most awful question lurking out there in the open air: *Now what?*

"Never before or since," he would later write, "have I felt as alone."

That moment, the *Now what?* moment, multiplied 16 million times over, could either presage a terrible crisis or present a unique opportunity. "These men will be a potent force for good or evil in the years to come," predicted Harry Colmery, the former American Legion commander who had scrawled the first real version of the G.I. Bill on stationery from the Mayflower Hotel in the Nation's Capital, and who had warned Congress not to repeat past mistakes with this new group of veterans. "They can make our country, or break it."

Either way, America's leaders seemed to realize by 1944 that they could not put off planning for that *Now what?* moment until the end of the war. If they waited for the day Allan Howerton glimpsed the Jersey coast, it would be far too late. The numbers of returning soldiers were just too great.

In the jaded early twenty-first century, the sum of 16 million hardly seems fantastical, given that the concept of a million—in home prices, small-town school budgets, weekly lottery winnings, 401k-plan targets—is now all but routine. But it was and is a huge mobilization of men and women unprecedented in our history and unimaginable today, as a much smaller military groans and strains to meet far more modest recruitment goals. To put this mobilization in perspective: Fly over contemporary Southern California, gaze down during the long, slow approach to LAX, observe the unbroken waves of urban sprawl, concentric circles of houses stretching in all directions mile after mile after mile, the endless grid of streets and freeways denuded of nature and filled with humanity and a flowing river of cars as far as the eye can see. Then imagine every man, woman, and child inside that concrete sea of homes and roads abruptly lifted away and marched off to war, and the inconceivable magnitude of harnessing 16 million souls to do *anything* snaps into sharp, incredible focus.

Then consider, as the president and Congress did in January 1944, what would happen when that mass of humanity abruptly returned home and found old careers, opportunities, relationships—everything—gone or changed or reinvented. The postwar plan, whatever it turned out to be, would hold immense power simply by virtue of this startling number: One out of every eight Americans would serve in the military by the end of the war.

The "total warfare" mobilization that the United States had managed in the first year of the war, public-private partnership at its best, was nothing short of an economic miracle, literally pulling the country out of twelve years of depression, massive joblessness and crippled industries. In place of a staggered, humbled nation with a puny armed forces, disillusioned populace, and hobbled markets stood a new America of full employment, record-high wages, thriving research communities, burgeoning corporate profits, and a massive military—in short, a superpower on the rise. War had done what Roosevelt's heartfelt, humanitarian New Deal had never quite managed to accomplish: It ended every vestige of the Great Depression. And it sparked, ironically, an optimism in the face of adversity that had been missing for a very long time from the national psyche. Americans at war had never been better off—except those who had been sent off to do the actual fighting.

But this superpower was a one-trick pony—a war machine, an America that had stopped manufacturing cars, washing machines, and refrigerators in favor of bombs, tanks, and planes; that rationed its gasoline, its vegetables, its nylons, and its electricity; that had the government running manufacturing plants more efficiently and honestly than private enterprise; and that introduced bikinis, tight skirts, and vestless men's suits, not as fashion statements, but as a means of conserving cloth and energy ("patriotic chic," one department store magnate quipped). So the end of war would not be simply about discharged soldiers. Ideally there should be a plan for bringing the civilians "home" as well—for recreating a peacetime society.

Everything would change once those soldiers, sailors, airmen, and Marines stepped off the troop ships and once again became civilians. They would stride down the gangplanks to flood the market for jobs and homes and futures—men and women filled with questions, ambition, angst, and need. They had been yanked from their workplaces, homes, and families, many of them fresh out of high school, then forced to endure hardship, peril, and unspeakable violence, committed against them, committed by them. Without a plan in place for those millions of returning men and women, the nation's economy, culture, even its democracy could fall apart, with many an eager demagogue waiting in the wings to capitalize on a supremely vulnerable national moment.

So it had been in Germany after World War I, the crippled Weimar Republic crumbling as Hitler's Third Reich rose to fill the vacuum with its powerful, heady cocktail of hatred, pride, and purpose—a chain of events that, early on, might have been altered at relatively little cost had not the world chosen to avert its gaze from demigods and death camps. Now the price of stopping evil was called World War II.

Yet this was a perilous time for the president and Congress to openly discuss the aftermath of World War II. An Allied victory seemed imaginable, even likely, by January 1944, owing primarily to immense German losses to the Red Army—bought at the unthinkable cost of 27 million Russians dead by the end of the war, a sacrifice nearly seventy times greater than that of the United States. Yet triumph still remained far from certain two long years after the shocking wake-up call of Pearl Harbor thrust America into a conflict the public, until then, had overwhelmingly wished to avoid. As Roosevelt delivered his tenth State of the Union address, American forces were only just massing for a surprise amphibious assault on the beaches of Anzio, a crucial first step in taking Italy. The Pacific War was at its bloodiest stage, the lines advancing island by island, airstrip by airstrip, with another six months to go before a sustained bombing campaign against the Japanese homeland could even be contemplated. The Normandy Invasion, meanwhile, and the subsequent year-long drive toward Berlin, still lay six uncertain months in the future. If any of these bold moves were to falter, the war effort would be set back many months, perhaps years. Perhaps entirely. Talk of winning the peace would be pointless if the United Nations, as the Allies were then known, lost the war.

Even so, the risks of raising the subject of postwar planning early on paled in comparison with the dangers of ignoring it. Most Americans expected high unemployment, political upheaval, and, in all likelihood, renewed recession or depression once peace arrived and demobilization began. *The New Republic*'s TRB column warned that the country would face an epic economic disaster, "a Pearl Harbor of peace, not of war." Roosevelt knew, as did the American Legion, that preparing for that moment was not merely a matter of rewarding the G.I.s, of doing the right and good thing. They knew that failure to have jobs and homes and hope awaiting those millions of battle-hardened veterans invited disaster. Poor, jobless, and disgruntled veterans of the last world war had formed the core of initial support for the Nazi movement, the fascist movement, the Bolshevik Revolution—and similar veterans' woes had led to unrest and fear of revolt throughout American history as well.

Even politicians as enlightened as the Founding Fathers had to learn the hard way that training a large group of men to kill, then stiffing them once the combat ends, is a dangerous game: In 1783, hundreds of impoverished, angry soldiers surrounded and occupied Philadelphia's Independence Hall—then the nation's capital—after promises of long-overdue back pay and pensions were broken by the fledgling, cash-strapped government. While the

Continental Congress met inside, the jeering troops poked their rifles and bayonets through the windows of the very room where the Declaration of Independence had been signed, menacing the likes of John Jay, Thomas Jefferson, and Alexander Hamilton. The rulers of the new nation finally fled, humiliated but unharmed—which explains why the Constitution was signed in New York, and why original plans to place a permanent capital in Philadelphia were abandoned in favor of the new, safe "federal town" of Washington, D.C.

Forty-nine years would pass before Congress finally paid its debts to Revolutionary War veterans—an empty gesture, as most had died by then. Fewer than 3,000 of the nearly quarter-million Revolutionary War veterans ever received a penny promised them.

After initially suffering a similarly mean fate, veterans of the Civil War fared better—two million soldiers (with two million votes) were a force to be reckoned with, as several ousted congressmen and an ex-president soon learned. But the overgenerous pension plan finally approved by a cowed Congress quickly became mired in fraud, graft, and patronage, until it absorbed a larger portion of the federal budget—40 percent—than any other single expense. The scandals that followed led to considerable public disdain for veterans, and the Civil War pension program ended up scrapped at century's end.

As a result, the five million veterans of World War I came home from the new technological horrors of mustard gas, machines guns, and aerial bombardment to find next to nothing awaiting them. The wounded and disabled received care, and families of the war-dead received pensions—that much has always been granted America's veterans, dating back to the Pilgrims at Plymouth and their battles with the Pequot Indians. But the first million doughboys still on their feet went home with nothing more than their medals and uniforms. They received no consideration for their lost income, lost jobs, and genuine financial sacrifices, and the belated mustering-out pay authorized by Congress for the last waves of soldiers discharged—sixty dollars and train fare home—seemed more insult than help.

In contrast, the wartime economy had boomed for civilians, enriching almost everyone else. While veterans earned one dollar a day in the trenches, war department employees received twelve dollars a day at their comfortable desks, federal civil servants pocketed $240 annual bonuses, assembly-line workers saw their wages double, and defense contractors received millions in government bonuses intended to spur production even as their profits broke all records. World War I veterans got ticker tape parades but they missed the boom times, arriving home to postwar recession. Unemployment was a third higher for veterans than for the general population—stark evidence that they really had been disadvantaged by their service.

Veterans—primarily through the newly formed American Legion—soon began to call for compensation in the form of a cash bonus, but it took six years, three presidential vetoes, and innumerable bitter debates about patriotism and civic duty before Congress acted (with the chief opposition arising from the same industrialists who raked in wartime bonuses of their own). In 1924, the World War I veterans finally received payments of up to $625 each (the equivalent of more than $7,000 in 2006). There was a catch, however: The bonuses came in the form of government bonds that took twenty years to mature, although veterans could borrow up to a fourth of the face value to tide them over until 1945.

The compromise came unglued in 1929 when the Great Depression hit. A quarter of all workers lost their jobs, poverty became endemic, factories closed, banks went belly up, and veterans, once again, found themselves bankrupt, massively unemployed, and reduced to selling apples and pencils for nickels on street corners. Loans and bonds were no good to them then. Veterans demanded the cash bonus they had originally sought, and petitioned to have their bonds paid off immediately.

A majority in both houses of Congress seemed receptive to the idea, but President Herbert Hoover, faced with economic upheaval and crippling deficits, dismissed the idea, promising to veto any bonus legislation within ten minutes of its appearance on his desk. In response, a few dozen laid-off veterans in Portland, Oregon, decided to travel across the country on foot and by rail to plead their case in person in Washington. Everywhere they went, more unemployed veterans joined them, and their march soon became a media event, sparking extensive print, radio, and newsreel coverage. Within a few weeks, a grass roots movement had caught fire, as groups of veterans across the country decided to launch their own marches to the capital, joining up en route to form a massive plea for immediate bonus payments.

Within a month in the spring of 1932, more than 40,000 veterans would participate in at least a portion of the march, with 20,000 making it all the way to the capital—an astonishing mass protest that set a record at the time and set teeth on edge in official, bow-tied Washington. The veterans set up a makeshift shantytown of old crates, boxes, scrap metal, and wrecked cars within a half mile of the Capitol grounds—a massive Hooverville, as thousands of similar communities of the homeless were known at the time, named for the president most Americans bitterly blamed for prolonging and worsening, if not actually causing, the Depression.

Though they had as a spokesman the Marine Corps' most decorated war hero-general, plus widespread public support, Hoover refused to even meet with the leaders of the Bonus Army, much less accede to their demands—showing the same, almost psychotically stubborn streak that led him to repeatedly promise the nation that prosperity was just around the corner even as the Depression deepened and poverty conquered the land. Angry and humiliated by the Hooverville on his doorstep, the president became obsessed with the protestors, who took to serenading him with choruses of "My Bonus Lies Over the Ocean" and "President Hoover, He's a Bum." Hoover's aides would later recall that the subject of getting rid of the protestors came to dominate the president's conversations, and he eventually stopped appearing in public, fearful that he was surrounded by "assassins"—his term for the marchers. In the end, the president falsely accused the veterans (many of whom were accompanied by their wives and children) of being Communists plotting to overthrow the government. Then he used a brawl with police officers outside the encampment to justify calling out the military to forcibly oust them after nearly three months of mostly peaceful protest.

And so one of the last cavalry charges on American soil was launched not on some dusty prairie battleground in the bloody Indian Wars, but within view of the White House, replete with bayonets and sabers and the thunder of mounted warriors driving thousands of protesting veterans of World War I from an indignant president's sight. This ignominious end to the Bonus March was personally supervised by a trio of future military legends (one of them a future president): Douglas MacArthur, George Patton, and Dwight Eisenhower. Amid clouds of tear gas and a massive show of force that included tanks and infantry troops in full battle gear, the unarmed veterans were beaten, driven off, or arrested, their encampment burned to the ground. One of the enlisted men injured in the cavalry charge had saved George Patton's life during World War I.

It was neither the U.S. Army's nor Herbert Hoover's finest hour. The image of the desperate veterans being driven from their shanties at bayonet point and of families fleeing burning hovels as their American flags were consumed in flames haunted Hoover for the rest of his disastrous presidency.

The next morning the White House issued a defiantly hollow statement that read, in part: "A challenge to the authority of the United States Government has been met, swiftly and firmly."

Roosevelt, then a presidential candidate, awoke in the New York governor's mansion the next day, took one look at the papers, and reached an equally terse conclusion: He told his aides that Hoover had just handed him the election.

Hoover had done much more than that, however. The Bonus Army may have failed in its immediate goal—the doughboys trudged home more impoverished than ever—but Hoover's harsh tactics ensured that their plight would mark a turning point in the history of America's relationship with its veterans. For the first time, the dirty secret of veteran mistreatment had been splashed across newspaper front pages, evoking revulsion at what the government had done—and also fear of what the next crop of veterans might do. Perhaps next time it wouldn't be thousands of angry warriors marching on the capital. It could be millions. And then torches and the rattle of sabers might not be enough to turn them away. Even George Patton would later observe that had the marchers chosen to take up arms and resist that cavalry charge, there could have been a massacre. And who knew where that would have led?

Far from being an act of pure gratitude and altruism, the G.I. Bill emerged from the wreckage of the Bonus Army firmly grounded in fear—fear of the next march on the capital. Fear of that *Now what?* moment.

When FDR won in a landslide and launched a national austerity plan in 1933 that cut, rather than increased, veterans' benefits, the doughboys again marched on Washington. The new president did not summon the cavalry, however. He sent his wife, Eleanor, out to greet the protest leaders and to offer them tea.

HOWERTON lingered outside Fort Dix for a few moments, then shook off the feeling of loss and foreboding, making his way to the train station, to New York, where Mary waited, where Mary had a plan, where Mary knew what would come next.

While he was away, his girlfriend had gone to work for the phone company, a solid job with good pay. Her sister, a manager at Bamberger's department store, had an executive trainee spot waiting for Howerton. He could go to night school, earn the degree he had hoped for before the Army reneged on its promise. Their two salaries would bring them a spacious apartment, furniture, security. Eventually they'd save enough for a house of their own. But even as she spoke and smiled and exulted in these plans, Howerton's unease grew. They were good plans, he knew, all the bases covered, except for one: The young man Mary had loved before the war, who had used his memory of her to carry him through the worst of times, was gone. And this lanky stranger with the furrowed brow who had come home from the battlefields, from the Siegfried Line, from the march through Germany, would not fit so easily into those lovely plans; would not fit at all, in fact.

He said nothing at first. They went to dinner that night, excellent food, excellent wine, a special occasion. He knew what was expected of him: a proposal, the marriage they had both assumed would launch their new, postwar life. They chatted and she leaned close, waiting for the question that did not come. He could not face that now, did not want night school or department stores or a tidy apartment with children on the way or to see the disappointment on Mary's face when he simply asked for the check instead of her hand. He did not want a wife, not yet, anyway. What he wanted was to say good-bye, and so he did, and then tried to figure out what should come next.

"Freedom from fear is eternally linked with freedom from want," Roosevelt told the nation in January 1944, leaving no doubt about what he believed should be next. "It is our duty now to begin to lay the plans and determine the strategy for the winning of a lasting peace and the establishment of an American standard of living higher than ever before known."

In a speech long on vision but devoid of any nuts and bolts, Roosevelt set out his bold proposal to end poverty, democratize the economy, and guarantee full employment, housing, health care, education, and retirement income for all. He promised a specific benefits package for veterans as well, but as part of a larger strategy to lift up all Americans. He promised to protect "the right of every businessman, large and small, to trade in an atmosphere of freedom from unfair competition and domination by monopolies at home or abroad." Finally, he prescribed a method to pay for a job, a home, a doctor, and a pension for all: He would tax—heavily—all "unreasonable" profits, corporate and individual, taking from the rich to eliminate poverty and want. Roosevelt didn't define "unreasonable" in his speech, but there was no question that he intended to make taxation a tool to narrow the gap between America's haves and have-nots. And these were the days before CEOs were routinely paid multimillion-dollar compensation packages even while presiding over failed companies—wages Roosevelt (and a majority of American voters of the era) would have considered not merely excessive, but anti-democratic and un-American.

Here was the essence of the New Deal vision that FDR had first brought to the presidency, casting government not only as an essential guarantor of American security and liberty, but as the ordinary man's buffer and protector from corporate abuses, from the power and influence of a wealthy elite, and from the tendency of free markets to reward accidents of birth as if they were no different from genuine hard work, intelligence, and creativity. Without enhanced economic protections and rights, Roosevelt asserted, the country might well return to the unbridled, Gilded Age, laissez-faire world of the twenties that had ended with global economic disaster.

"Even though we shall have conquered our enemies on the battlefields abroad, we shall have yielded to the spirit of fascism here at home," he concluded. "People who are hungry and out of a job are the stuff of which dictatorships are made."

Roosevelt's extraordinary proposals, while they resonated with many ordinary Americans who had just weathered the Depression years, met with indifference or outright hostility in an increasingly conservative Congress. Many congressmen, Republicans and Democrats alike, had tired of Roosevelt's autocratic style and resented his power and popularity, the only chief executive in the nation's history to break the traditional two-term limit that had been observed (occasionally by choice, more often out of necessity) by every president since George Washington. A coalition of minority Republicans and anti–New Deal, prosegregation Southern Democrats had formed a new bloc in Congress that frequently frustrated Roosevelt's goals, and his new economic bill of rights seemed almost designed to infuriate both ends of that coalition. When the president's favorite New Deal agency, the Natural Resources Planning Board, produced two lengthy reports setting out the details of Roosevelt's new bill of rights, Congress responded by killing the planning board and shelving its reports. This came as part of a wholesale dismantling of the New Deal "alphabet soup" agencies, from the famed Civilian Conservation Corps (CCC) to the Works Progress Administration (WPA), both of which had provided thousands of jobs and much-needed public works programs during the worst years of the Depression.

Predictably, then, congressional attention focused not on Roosevelt's postwar ideas, but on the more specific veterans' proposals, advanced by the reliably conservative American Legion, for education, home loans, job training and placement, and unemployment compensation—though these, too, had to compete with several hundred rival bills, all aimed at currying the favor of World War II veterans and their millions of votes. The whole idea of postwar planning then quickly devolved into a congressional squabble over philosophy and pork, opportunity versus assistance: Should there be a lump sum bonus for the veterans—three hundred dollars, five hundred, five thousand? Or, instead of a bonus, should their salary simply continue for three months after discharge? How about a full year? Or would it be better to focus on jobs and training instead of cash payments? Money gets spent, after all, but an education lasts a lifetime. And whatever the approach, who, exactly, would benefit? All veterans? Or, if it came to college or specialized training, just a deserving elite, chosen by . . . whom? And what about women in the military? And black veterans? This was still the era of Jim Crow and poll taxes. Giving all G.I.s benefits meant giving black G.I.s the same benefits—and the chairman of the veterans committee in the House of Representatives was a man who refused to sit next to the two black congressmen in office at the time; who had adamantly opposed efforts to get voting ballots in the hands of U.S. soldiers overseas (because a side effect of a simple federal ballot would be to circumvent Southern practices long designed to suppress black votes); and who praised, in open session of Congress, the Ku Klux Klan as a grand American institution.

FDR had anticipated this. The president was the master politician and orator of his age, and he had to know the opposition to his progressive ideas would be enormous in what the legendary columnist, I.F. Stone, labeled "the cantankerous Congress." Roosevelt's speech was intended mainly as an opening salvo against a Congress more concerned, in the president's terms, with passing "tax relief for the greedy not for the needy"—an opinion shared by large numbers of editorial writers of the era. The president intended to use his notion of a new economic bill of rights in his upcoming campaign for a historic fourth term in office, and then, once World War II had been won, to make its passage the linchpin of his final four years in office and his ultimate legacy—thereby defining what America would look like in the last half of the twentieth century. He had already begun that task with his epochal Social Security Act, the New Deal's greatest triumph, and now he was looking for both momentum and a cudgel to help him complete his vision.

In the meantime, having staked out the high ground, he was mostly content to let Congress and the American Legion take the lead in the battle over a more veteran-specific postwar plan, something he had long supported. In fact, his broad suggestions about veterans' education, employment, and training, presented to the nation during one of his fireside chats a year earlier, had formed the basis of the American Legion's proposal. The difference was that FDR intended to use any new veterans' benefits as a first step in establishing a larger employment, training, disability, and housing program for all Americans, rather than craft legislation, as the Legion advocated, that made veterans a class unto themselves.

Neither side anticipated that it would wind up working the other way around: that the veterans' benefits would have an immense ripple effect, reaching a far greater segment of the American citizenry and landscape than anyone had ever imagined. In the end, the policymakers who crafted the G.I. Bill really had no idea they were about to unleash that which they had hoped to avoid: the accidental remaking of America.

ALLAN HOWERTON had dreamed of going to college almost as long as he could remember—knowing it was impossible. There was no money for such an extravagance. His father was a sharecropper-turned-factory-worker who had uprooted the family in western

Kentucky when Allan was two, moving them to nearby Evanston so that he could take an assembly line job at the Vulcan Plow Company.

When the stock market crashed and the Great Depression hit, farms began dying by the thousands, and the plow factory, like so many others, was shuttered. The Howerton family went back to rural Kentucky as Allan's father searched for work, moving from job to job.

Allan's mother died of cancer when he was nine, and his father found a new career as a Baptist preacher, leading to a far stricter religious upbringing than Allan had ever known—and one from which he could barely wait to stray. Allan's aunts raised him, more or less: an introspective boy who threw himself into his studies and graduated from Union County High School in 1941 as class salutatorian. He still longed to go to college, but there were no college recruiters appearing with scholarship offers at his little Kentucky high school. Instead, there were recruiters from the White Castle chain of hamburger stands, the forerunner of the fast food business. The recruiters announced that there were openings at a new White Castle in Elizabeth, New Jersey, and Howerton decided at age eighteen to go for it. He had never been to the East Coast, had never seen New York City or a real skyscraper. And then there was the bottom line: The one thing children of the Depression wanted most was money in their pockets, and so Howerton decided if he couldn't go to college, why not get on a Greyhound bus and see another part of the world?

The money was pretty good—Howerton started at $18.50 a week, but soon gave up the salary in exchange for doing curb service and working for tips, which proved more lucrative. By taking the late shift and catering to generously juiced customers who came by after the two A.M. bar closings, Howerton found he could often make in a day or two what he had previously made in a week. In his spare time he took a course in radio announcing and tried to break into the business by applying, without success, for a job as a page at Radio City Music Hall.

The graveyard shift mostly meant sleeping during the daytime. He remembers clearly that it was just after four in the afternoon that he woke up on December 7, turned the radio on, and learned that Japan had bombed Pearl Harbor, changing his and almost every other American's world for good.

When the draft notice came a year later and he reported for duty, a man at the induction center looked over Howerton's stellar high school record and gave him a choice: go into training as a medic, or join a new program the Pentagon had just launched called the Army Specialized Training Program. When Howerton gave him a blank look—he had never heard of this ASTP—he got a quick explanation. Top students were being selected to cram four years of college into two, mostly in engineering and medicine, after which they'd get their degrees and their officers' commissions. Then, if they were lucky and the Axis had been destroyed by the time they graduated, they would get to rebuild Europe without having to dodge bullets. A million guys would be sent to college by Uncle Sam for all sorts of specialized training through the ASTP, Howerton learned.

He thought that sounded pretty good: He could go to college as he had always wanted, plus he'd have a decent shot at avoiding getting killed while still serving his country.

"Can I think about it a couple days?" Howerton asked.

"I'll give you ten minutes," the recruiter answered.

The unlikely figure behind the most far-reaching and egalitarian Big Government social program in the history of the nation was a dyed-in-the-wool racist, anti-Semitic, Red-baiting, New-Deal-bashing future Dixiecrat—a diminutive brawler with a shock of reddish hair, a drawling sarcasm, a tendency to throw punches at fellow congressmen twice his size, and a gift for parliamentary maneuvering that made him both a formidable adversary and a sometimes necessary, if loathsome, ally.

Many have received or claimed credit across the years for fathering the G.I. Bill, from FDR to the American Legion to a sizable list of senators and congressmen—no fewer than six different politicians have been eulogized as the father of the G.I. Bill, along with one mother, most of them possessed of reputations for vision and gentility. But in keeping with the accidental nature of the G.I. Bill's greatness and reach, it was a volatile bigot, Representative John Elliott Rankin of Tupelo, Mississippi, who served as the primary force behind the version of the bill that actually got passed into law.

And Rankin was also the force that almost killed it.

"A little man with bushy hair and a hallelujah voice," the journalist and author Allen Drury called Rankin in 1944, while *Time* magazine described him as "rancorous," a "demagogue," and an "angry mosquito." The crusading columnist Drew Pearson wrote that Rankin was a leader of Congress's "hate group," a prominent early player on the House Un-American Activities Committee, where he detected Communist foul play seemingly everywhere while blocking all attempts to investigate crimes by the Ku Klux Klan. Rankin was immortalized by name in an otherwise fictional Hollywood blockbuster, *Gentleman's Agreement*, a 1947 film based on the Laura Z. Hobson novel, which had exposed rank anti-Semitism in colleges, restaurants, clubs, home sales, and throughout American society. Rankin once took the floor of the House to describe famed gossip columnist Walter Winchell as a "little kike," openly advocated a "race war" against anyone of Japanese ancestry, and later defended the honor of Nazi war criminals during the Nuremberg trials while assailing attempts to bring the death camp creators to justice.

Still, Rankin had clout. His colleagues more than once had arisen to deliver standing ovations to his racism-tinged orations. ("To listen to his harangues on the floor became, for me, an agony," wrote Congressman Emanuel Celler of Brooklyn, one of two Jewish members of the House at the time; the other, Michael Edelstein of Manhattan, collapsed and died of a heart attack moments after responding to one of Rankin's racist jeremiads.)

A veteran of World War I, Rankin had come to Congress in 1921 and had risen to the chairmanship of the House Committee on Veterans Legislation—putting him directly in the path of the postwar planning efforts. His power, standing, and outrageous behavior underscored the major political conflict of his time: the uneasy combination within the ruling Democratic Party of liberal Roosevelt New Dealers, who sought social, civil rights, and economic reforms through federal programs, and Southern states'-righters, with their absolutist opposition to any legislation that threatened segregation, America's apartheid. Rankin had long been one of the latter group's leaders. Though he had been an early supporter of Roosevelt and the New Deal, particularly when they worked together on rural electrification and the massive Tennessee Valley Authority public works project, the president's concern for civil rights drove a fatal wedge between the men. Rankin's specialty then became joining forces with conservative Republicans to thwart Roosevelt and preserve what he called, "the natural order of things." This alliance voted to block the creation of a special federal vote for soldiers for the 1944 elections, intended to address the logistical impossibility of getting individual absentee ballots from fifty different states delivered in time to millions of soldiers worldwide. Republicans, assuming (correctly) the G.I.s would vote overwhelmingly for Roosevelt, appeared happy to disenfranchise them, while Rankin and his cronies feared the hundreds of thousands of votes that would be cast by black soldiers, who otherwise could never get past the gauntlet of poll taxes, citizenship tests, and poll-watching thugs they faced at home. It was a shameful episode: Even during the Civil War, Union troops got the chance to cast ballots in their presidential election, but during World War II fewer than 85,000 of the 11 million soldiers serving overseas on election day had the opportunity to vote. Likewise, Social Security, crafted by Roosevelt to be scrupulously color blind, was modified under pressure from this conservative coalition to exclude two classes of employees from enjoying its benefits—farmworkers and domestic workers. It was no coincidence that these were the two most common occupations for black Americans at the time. Twenty years would pass before a remedy arrived for that exclusion.

Yet Rankin was the man the American Legion chose to carry forward its vision of the G.I. Bill: Whatever his warts, Rankin chaired the right committee, he had always wholeheartedly supported the Legion, he was vociferously pro-veteran in his past votes, and, as for his views on blacks and Jews, well, the Legion practiced segregation itself.

A committee of Legion notables, led by a former governor of Illinois, had sketched out the main benefits they sought—housing, education, training, job placement, and unemployment compensation—mirroring the general proposals FDR had made a year earlier. They would seek no bonus this time, having learned from the Bonus Army debacle that outright petitions for cash compensation turned off politicians and public alike, making veterans vulnerable to claims of greed and lack of patriotism. Instead of money, they wanted to focus on opportunity. Never mind that the cost would be greater for their programs than some of the conventional bonus legislation other veterans organizations favored—the psychology of the Legion's proposal was entirely and purposely different. It would be government aid on an unprecedented scale, directed at a select group, but it would wear a palatable disguise, something that could be portrayed as a hand-up instead of a handout. Harry Colmery, the affable former Army pilot, lawyer, and past president of the Legion, had urged this approach, and he was given the task of pulling a loose collection of ideas together into a coherent legislative draft, famously scrawled on hotel stationery and destined for display many years later at the Smithsonian Institution. With the exception of the Legion's innovative idea for subsidized home loans for veterans, Colmery's sketch of an omnibus veterans bill (which the head of the rival Disabled Veterans of America organization soon began calling "the ominous bill") mirrored earlier suggestions by the Roosevelt administration. Rankin, torn between his genuine pro-veteran feelings and his hatred of all programs that sought "social uplift," agreed to introduce the Legion's proposal, but on his terms. He made the bill as small and restrictive as possible—a package equipped with a bit of something for everyone, but with very little chance of having a life-changing impact or altering the social fabric of the nation.

In Rankin's bill, unemployment payments were to be limited to twenty-five dollars a week for up to year—a sum later lowered to twenty dollars (after the war, the five million veterans receiving this aid while seeking work were said to be members of the Fifty-two/Twenty Club). Even this small amount bothered Rankin, who felt it could damage the southern economy by making it hard to get black farm workers for the scandalously low wages offered them at the time. He consoled himself by insisting that veterans employment programs be overseen by locally appointed (that is, reliably segregationist) veterans officials, and by inserting an anti-union provision that would make any veteran who went out on strike ineligible for Fifty-two/Twenty Club payments.

Home, farm, and small business loan benefits also remained rather niggardly in Rankin's bill, with mortgage guarantees capped at $2,000 and sporting a high interest rate (for the times) of 6 percent—too little money and too much interest for most vets to buy a home. Rankin engineered the defeat of amendments that sought to raise the loan amount and lower the interest, and Roosevelt's New Deal proposal to add direct housing aid to the bill, rather than simply guaranteeing bank loans, was swatted aside as well.

Rankin reluctantly included college and other schooling in the bill, despite his belief that institutions of higher education were basically un-American enclaves of Jews and Communists in which "good" Americans, particularly his southern constituents, would likely have little interest. Tuition payments of up to $500, book allowances, and stipends of $50 a month would be offered ($75 for married vets)—barely enough to cover a modern college book bill, but more than enough in 1946 for a free ride to Harvard, Yale, or any other college, technical program, acting school, or chef's institute in America. The apparent generosity, however, was limited to only those veterans whose higher education was interrupted by military service—a limitation Rankin insisted upon, knowing that those eligible would represent a relatively small percentage of the overall Army, Navy, and Marine population. As introduced by Rankin, the G.I. Bill further limited the college benefit by covering only a single year's tuition and fees. Additional years could be covered by the government only for a select few who had demonstrated extraordinary abilities in their chosen fields.

Critics decried these restrictions as elitist and unfair, creating "a richman's son" bill that served only the relatively small number of veterans already on the college track before the war. The Senate Committee on Education and Labor chairman, Elbert D. Thomas of Utah, a New Deal liberal, led the charge for a rival version of the G.I. Bill's education benefit, pushing for the government to cover a full four years of college or other training for all veterans with nine months of active duty under his or her belt. Whether it had been interrupted by war or not, Thomas wanted to make higher education widely available to all vets, as a means of providing them new opportunities, and of creating for business and industry a new professional class of workers—a truly revolutionary proposal in an era in which colleges were considered inappropriate for the common man, and federal support for college attendance remained essentially nil. Expansive education benefits, Senator Thomas argued, could also provide a cushion against the likely postwar unemployment crisis by delaying veterans' entry into the labor pool, while giving New Deal planners the chance to use the power of the purse to direct veterans toward occupations where they would be most needed in the postwar economy.

Many leading college administrators, however, expressed horror at this approach—they preferred Rankin's exclusivity provisions, which, not coincidentally, gave the colleges, not the federal government, complete autonomy on which veterans to accept and how to educate them. The same Ivy League that had existed so long as an aristocratic enclave, where academically unqualified legacy admissions all too often triumphed over merit, suddenly cast itself as the champion of academic standards when faced with the possibility of a horde of blue-collar G.I.s at the gate. Harvard University President James Conant predicted a disaster if Thomas's version won the day, claiming it would lower the quality of college education by failing to "distinguish between those who can profit most by advanced education and those who cannot." The usually progressive president of the University of Chicago, Robert Hutchins, was even more blunt, predicting that a G.I. Bill with a wide-open education benefit would turn colleges into "hobo jungles" filled with veterans interested not in education, but in a monthly stipend. Most colleges in the country, with budgets and enrollments devastated by the war, would accept every veteran they could, qualified or not, he said. "Educational institutions, as the big-time football racket shows, cannot resist money," Hutchins morosely warned.

Congressional debate about this, if heated at times, rarely penetrated the public awareness or the front pages—the national focus, naturally, stayed on the daily advances, setbacks, and genuine horrors of the war, not on the political jockeying over postwar benefits or how many vets could go to Harvard. Rankin had a point: College simply wasn't on the radar screen for most Americans at the time; for many it seemed merely a costly delay to job opportunities, not a path to greater ones. Fewer than half the G.I.s who served during World War II had even graduated from high school much less contemplated college, and only about a quarter of adult Americans overall had a diploma at the start of the war. In the end, Congress and the military concluded it wouldn't much matter which version of the education benefit was adopted, as they estimated that only roughly 7 percent of veterans—somewhere between a half million and one million G.I.s—would wish to take advantage of the education benefit, a sizable but thoroughly manageable number.

As it turned out, just about all such estimates and predictions—about veterans' academic prowess, their interest in college, the ability of planners to coax them into certain professions, the dire predictions of postwar economic problems and needs—proved wildly off base, grossly underestimating the veterans' desire to better themselves through education, while completely overestimating the likelihood of recession in the vibrant new economy of a victorious America. Far from turning into hobo havens, America's colleges would experience a renaissance, ceasing to be bastions of elitism and becoming the better for it. Government planners' desire to influence college majors and career choices also proved to be a pipe dream—after weathering drill sergeants and D-Day, no one was going to push these G.I.s anywhere they didn't want to go.

Still, even if the conclusions proved erroneous, discussion of the bill's impact on education at least took place in Congress. Other aspects of the G.I. Bill seemed to pass through with little meaningful discussion at all. When it came to the most unprecedented benefit of the G.I. Bill, its home loan benefit, the focus was on *how much*, not *what if*—with almost no consideration given as to how such a benefit, made available to millions, might affect home ownership and home construction in America. There were the usual anti-New-Deal arguments about excessive government intervention in economic matters, and some questioned the wisdom of giving veterans loans when everyone believed the economy would tank after the war, with bankruptcies and defaults inevitable. But Congress seemed to have no inkling of the truly significant impact of the G.I. Bill's home loan provision: that it would trigger a historic housing boom in unexpected places, creating new communities while dooming others—that it would remake the American landscape with the force of a bomb. During the rush to craft a G.I. Bill, that subject just didn't come up.

Instead, some of the most heated and lengthy debates revolved around unemployment benefits and the rules governing G.I. Bill eligibility and administration. It was during this phase that Rankin seemed to become more obstacle than oracle for the G.I. Bill, at one point calling the very proposal he had introduced "half-baked," then adding, "I see the most violent discrimination against that strong, virile, patriotic, determined man who goes into the Army to fight for his country and comes back and says, *I don't want anything. I am going back and going to work and that is what the rest of you ought to do* . . . At the same time I see a tremendous inducement to certain elements not to try to get employment."

The head of the American Legion, Warren Atherton, bristled, calling the idea that veterans would willingly forgo a good job to earn a measly "pork-and-beans check once a week" an insult. If the bill is half-baked, he added, "Perhaps we need a new baker."

Atherton would be proved right after the war, though his was the minority view at the time. Rankin and his allies assumed the unemployment benefits would be the largest and most costly aspect of the G.I. Bill, and so Congress spent much of its time and energy on what would turn out to be the bill's least significant (and, in the case of unemployment payments, least utilized) provisions. While many veterans would take advantage of the benefit, very few in the end would use up their entire year "on the dole," as Rankin had feared—eighteen weeks in the Fifty-two/Twenty Club would turn out to be the average. But Rankin, notorious for his own long lunches, short hours, and numerous absences during the House workday, argued strenuously that this benefit needed to be as limited as possible, or it would create a generation of loafers.

Eligibility provided the greatest controversy—who could go to college, who could get a loan, who could get unemployment compensation and job placement services. And who would decide? The debate was not limited to whether the education and training benefits should be narrowly available only to those whose schooling was interrupted by war (as the American Legion advocated); or to veterans who showed the greatest academic aptitude (as the colleges wished); or who had been wounded and required retraining for a new career (as the Disabled Veterans of America argued); or who chose to major in a subject deemed useful to the nation and the economy (as Roosevelt and his New Deal central planners believed). The debate was also very much about race.

Though the Serviceman's Readjustment Act was, on its face, race and gender neutral, making the G.I. Bill potentially an important advance in civil rights legislation, Rankin made sure to include a poison pill. The bill specifically limited benefits to only those servicemen who had received honorable discharges, a diabolically simple ploy designed to have the same effect on black veterans as the exclusion of farm workers and domestics from Social Security had on black retirees. The military, at the time still rigidly segregated, had adopted an unwritten policy of granting other-than-honorable discharges to black servicemen in disproportionately high numbers. The innocuous-seeming requirement for honorable discharges, Rankin knew, would confer G.I. Bill benefits to the vast majority of white veterans, while denying them to the majority of nonwhites. By also insuring that staffing and oversight would be controlled at the local level in veterans employment and training programs, Rankin felt sure that "the natural order of things" in his home state would remain undisturbed.

Rankin stretched out hearings and debate for months, turning back almost all attempts in the House to make his bill more generous. Rival veterans organizations, snubbed by the American Legion in crafting the original G.I. Bill proposal, begged Congress to reject the legislation outright, arguing it would bust the federal budget and degrade essential core services to wounded and disabled veterans and the families of those killed. The Senate, meanwhile, with little dissent, took a third of the time to adopt the bill's more progressive version, dispensing with the honorable discharge requirement, making education benefits available to all veterans for a full four years, and providing a more generous home loan program than Rankin's bill—one that would actually let veterans of modest means purchase a home at low interest and with no down payment, a critical provision.

When Rankin's bill finally passed the House and the time came for reconciliation with the Senate's version, it became clear he would rather have no G.I. Bill than see a more liberal version become law. The conference committee charged with marrying the two versions of the bill in early June 1944, found itself deadlocked, with three favoring a compromise that favored the Senate bill, and three, including Rankin, opposed to it. The seventh and tie-breaking vote belonged to a Georgia Democrat, John Gibson, who had returned home because of illness, giving his proxy vote to Rankin to cast as he saw fit. That would have doomed the bill, except that Gibson had second thoughts after arriving home. He telephoned Rankin with instructions to cast his proxy in favor of the Senate bill.

Rankin, however, declined to do so—without telling Gibson. Whether this was sheer mendacity or simply a strict implementation of voting rules is open to interpretation, but either way, the wily parliamentarian knew that in the event of a tie he would prevail: The G.I. Bill would die on the table for lack of a compromise. Rankin was already thinking about throwing the whole thing out, anyway, in favor of an enormous bonus bill. (He eventually would propose and push through the House a leviathan pension plan for veterans of all wars—$90 a month for each veteran, whether he or she needed it or not, beginning with his own doughboy generation, with regular adjustments for inflation. His idea, had it become law, would have cost the nation a staggering 200 billion of that era's dollars—more than two trillion in 2006 currency.)

With the deadline about to expire on the G.I. Bill, frantic supporters reached Gibson at home, having recruited a local telephone operator to call him every fifteen minutes until he returned from a hunting trip. When he got home and learned the bill would be doomed if he could not get to Washington by ten the next morning, he agreed to race back in time. A military motorcycle escort guided him through a raging, nighttime thunderstorm to an airfield ninety miles from his home. There, an airplane chartered by the American Legion stood waiting to whisk him off to Washington. He arrived at the Capitol just in time to break the tie, much to Rankin's dismay. The G.I. Bill then passed both houses of Congress with many of Rankin's restrictions dropped and the remainder eliminated a few months later by amendment, passage coming easily once the dam Rankin had erected was breached.

On June 22, 1944, President Roosevelt signed the G.I. Bill into law, confident that he would be able to use the bill as a starting place for his grand vision of a new bill of rights. There would be so many veterans receiving these benefits, how much harder would it be to extend similar provisions to all, and how much better would the country be for it? "Apart from these special benefits, which fulfill the special needs of veterans, there is still much to be done," he promised the nation.

But FDR would be dead within the year, never seeing the world war victory he had helped engineer, nor the chance to keep his promise. His successor would have neither the clout nor the political will to see his vision through, as the country took an entirely different direction after the war, away from the New Deal and toward the politics of Cold War, anti-Communism, wrenching civil rights battles, and a new breed of proxy wars in Asia.

Yet if Roosevelt considered the G.I. Bill a mere beginning, what a beginning it turned out to be. It ended up driving many of the housing, employment, and education reforms the president had sought in his Second Bill of Rights—and which men like Rankin had so adamantly opposed, even as they unwittingly paved the way with what turned out to be the most successful piece of socially uplifting legislation the world has ever seen.

WITH ten minutes to settle his future, Howerton jumped at the chance to attend college on Uncle Sam's dime. After that, it seemed he had it all—school, a girlfriend, life in the big city. Yet he remained a part of the war effort—and a clean, safe part at that.

But the last phase of the war had begun to chew up too many men for Howerton and the other military college students to keep their spots on campus. The Army yanked him and the other pasty-faced students in his class and sent them to boot camp as privates, not officers, unceremoniously thrown in with the real soldiers. A few months later, however, there was no way to tell them apart, and Howerton found himself wading ashore at Omaha Beach, the Normandy landscape so familiar from the D-Day newsreels he had watched while in training. He came ashore at the very place where battle had raged just a few months earlier, the abandoned German pillboxes still standing sentinel on the cliffs above the sand where G.I.s had scrambled for cover or died trying. Now it was a dead place, utterly quiet, empty except for the twisted debris of war.

The Red Ball Express—a wild convoy of trucks that carted a constant stream of fresh troops to the frontline on the French-German border—brought him to the war.

He passed through a landscape of destruction pocked by bomb craters and the ubiquitous *Kilroy Was Here* scrawls American soldiers invariably left behind, a national calling card, balm and punch line rolled into one. The feelings he shared with his fellow troops as they crammed into that bumping, high-speed caravan were odd and bittersweet, an optimism that the Allies would ultimately prevail, mixed with uncertainty about individual survival.

He would take part in most of the major battles in the rest of the war in Europe, driving toward Berlin as most of his comrades fell, wounded or killed, along with their replacements, and their replacements' replacements. Blood and death and terror and bravery and fear, the mainstays of any war, became his constant companions. And then, one day it was over—sudden quiet, astonishment, relief, celebration, a long journey home, and an unease he could neither name nor dismiss.

When he found home didn't work anymore, that the old plans and dreams could not make him whole, the one thing that gave him purpose, that let him answer the question *What now?* was the G.I. Bill. It saved him, he would later realize. It put him back on course. With it, he could return to college once again.

And this time, he'd finish.

☆ 2 ☆

Cold Wars, Hot Rockets, a New American Dream

Bob Booth had a problem.

The USS *George Washington* would soon be ready to sail, the nation's first nuclear ballistic missile submarine. The new sub had been developed in record time, as if the nation were at war rather than enjoying the most prosperous and peaceful period in U.S. history. Yet a shiny new attack sub had been hurriedly cut in half, and a fresh center section bristling with eighteen missile-launch tubes dropped in the open space—the sort of engineering-on-the-fly that usually happens only during war. The sub crew nicknamed the new complex of missile silos Sherwood Forest.

Which is where Booth and his problem came in: There were no "trees" for the forest—no missiles to give the hastily reconfigured submarine purpose, or rival superpowers pause. The young engineer with the G.I. Bill degree was supposed to figure out why the new Polaris missiles intended to fill that forest of launch tubes kept blowing up right after launch. And then he was supposed to fix them.

Before Booth joined the project at Lockheed Aircraft Corporation in the late 1950s, the Polaris tests—all ground launched up to that point—had not gone well. One early, errant test missile not only tumbled out of control, but the destruct button did nothing more than click ineffectually when pushed by the range-safety officer. Instead of blowing up harmlessly out over the ocean, the prototype plowed into its launch site, obliterating the Cape Canaveral cafeteria, with loss of life avoided only through sheer luck—mealtime had ended and no one was inside.

After the accident, the commander at Cape Canaveral, which was hosting the run-up to the historic Mercury flights at the same time, thought it prudent to evacuate the rebuilt cafeteria every time the crew from Lockheed had another launch. "It was quite embarrassing," Booth recalls with a laugh. "But motivating."

Back at the new Lockheed Missile Systems plant in Sunnyvale, California, Booth began puzzling out the Polaris flaws, experimenting with rocket engines mounted on rails until he finally identified why the Polaris engines kept melting shortly after takeoff, sending the missiles out of control. Months of brainstorming, experimentation, and laboratory trial and error had led him to a novel, if not heretical, solution, and he flew out to Florida just before the next test launch to hastily install his unorthodox remedy.

When the launch manager came charging over to his gleaming missile and saw what Booth had done to it, he became enraged.

"I've been a base manager since you were in diapers, and if it comes to putting crap like that on a plane to make it fly, I'm gonna quit," the launch boss shouted. "Better than that, get the hell out of here and go back to Sunnyvale."

Booth slunk back to California, certain he had been right about the remedy, but fearing for Polaris's future—and his own—if the surly executive at Canaveral had his way. Polaris was said to be vital to the nation's security, yet Booth's findings were being ignored as the ravings of an upstart.

As the day of the next launch approached and the pressure for a successful test built to a fever pitch, all he could do was wait.

Sometimes, Bob Booth would later reflect, it seemed the war never ended.

There had been decisive victory, of course, celebration, and an end to shooting and dying, at least for a few years. America remained the only combatant left standing—the one major participant in the war whose landscape, infrastructure, morale, and economy had not been devastated by bombs, death, and privation. Indeed, alone among Allies and Axis combined, America ended World War II as the sole country whose economy had improved since 1941, and whose standard of living actually had increased throughout the war, with wages, productivity, stock markets, and employment all making vast gains. America found itself king, as the postwar peace and prosperity turned the 1950s into an economic miracle moment unlike any in history—one many mistook for a permanent blessing.

Yet, paradoxically, few Americans felt secure, as if the wartime mind-set had become permanently ingrained in politicians and public alike, as if the nation needed an enemy to give it continued purpose. An almost frantic urgency soon fueled the nation's postwar economic growth—particularly when it came to a continued peacetime military build-up and the development of new, even more terrible technologies of destruction, of which Polaris was only one of many. The drive to increase America's military might barely diminished from the wartime footing that followed the bombing of Pearl Harbor. If anything, in terms of dollars spent and engineering talent committed to the task, the business of defense grew dramatically—and grew in importance to the economy—*after* the world war ended.

Those postwar years proved a peculiar and pivotal moment in U.S. history, so unlike the wake of World War I, which swept the country into the 1920s with a new pacifism, isolationism, near disarmament of the military, and, finally, the nation's most bruising and long-lived economic depression. This old pattern had been the expected course of events, but this time American society, government, and enterprise took a wholly different turn, a looking out rather than within, as the country refashioned itself as nation-builder, free-market apostle, and, most of all, global cop armed to the teeth. It would be the G.I. Bill and the veterans who used it that would lead the country in this new direction, becoming the foot soldiers, leaders, innovators, and political supporters of a new, seemingly unending war that gave America a new purpose in life—the Cold War. This battle against global Communism soon elevated a foreign ally that had never attacked America to a greater perceived threat than the Axis powers that had declared war on the U.S. and bombed its shores. The G.I. Bill and the Cold War would become the two dominant forces of the age then, and men like Bob Booth seemed made to order to serve its cause. It would define their lives and their era, and dictate the American political, economic, and cultural landscape to this day.

Born in Omaha three years before the Great Depression began, Robert Booth grew up a middle child with two sisters and a fondness for working with his hands. His father supported the family with a milk business, supplying dairy products to restaurants. By twelve, the younger Booth started washing dishes in the same restaurants, earning fifty cents a day to supplement the family's meager budget.

Like many kids of the day, Booth became fascinated with flight, concocting airplane models out of scraps and dreaming of becoming a pilot. The Wright Brothers, after all, had only just conquered the air a handful of years earlier, and Orville Wright remained a living, breathing hero throughout Booth's childhood. The rapidity of aerodynamic advances since the Wrights' 1903 first flight exceeded even the 1990s' rapid advances in computer technology. In just two decades, the science of flight had moved from puddle jumps lasting barely a minute at speeds of little more than a horse's gallop, to flights that circumnavigated the globe with high-performance aircraft. Booth, whose teachers had observed his knack for building, designing, and math, had dreamed early on about a career involving ailerons, stabilizers, and cockpit dials.

In his sophomore year in high school, the Booth family moved to Novato, California, just a few months before the bombing of Pearl Harbor brought America to war. Booth's dreams shifted gears then, as he fantasized of becoming an ace of aces, intent on joining the Army Air Corps as soon as he got his diploma in 1943. Three of his high school friends—together, the top four students in their class—decided to enlist together. One ended up graduating nearly a year earlier than the others, however, and he joined up first, earning his wings in the Air Corps. Before the other three could even finish school and try to catch up, Booth heard the bad news: His friend had been killed over Africa.

When it came time for Booth to enlist, his high school football coach and math teacher intervened, literally dragging him from the Air Corps sign-up line to a nearby Navy recruiting office, where they talked him into enlisting in a special program called V-12. This was the Navy's equivalent of the Army Specialized Training Program that had snared, then abandoned, Allan Howerton. V-12, created for rapid training of cadets for specialized duties during the war, would cram two years of college courses into one—after which graduates could choose from a number of assignments, including Naval aviator. Booth reluctantly agreed with his teachers and signed up for V-12.

"They were convinced I'd get killed, too," recalls Booth, who would become a civilian pilot in later life, and who was still flying his own small plane as his eightieth birthday approached. "I guess I'll never know. 'Course, I fly all the time now, and I do all right. But in a way, that decision did save my life—because it set me on the greatest of paths, one I'd never have taken otherwise."

His family's move to northern California proved especially advantageous then: Booth's V-12 training would come at a world-class school, the University of California–Berkeley. He attended two semesters there—intense, exhausting, inspiring—until the Navy abruptly ended V-12 along with all the other military college programs, transferring Booth unceremoniously to war duty before he had finished his studies.

Even so, Booth had spent enough time in college to realize he loved it, something he had never expected to experience given his family's lack of financial resources and the fact that no Booth had ever before strolled a university campus, much less attended one. And in those engineering, physics, and math classes the Navy made him attend, Booth realized something else: Glamour and romance aside, his real love was not flying airplanes, but designing them, figuring out how they worked—and how to make them work better. When his naval instructors asked him where his interests lay, he didn't hesitate: "I want to be an engineer."

With the V-12 program ended, however, his studies gave way to six months of sea duty. He pulled an assignment on a sub chaser in the Atlantic Ocean, mostly boring work with little action, punctuated occasionally by tense, cat-and-mouse games with elusive German U-boats. Every time his little ship managed to close in on an enemy target, however, a powerful destroyer would race up and take over the chase and the glory. Mostly, though, his duties consisted of mind-numbing routines, with the only bright spot being a quicker-than-expected conclusion: One month before completing his tour of duty, the war ended, as did his training. He never even got his officer's commission.

The gangly high school student had by then transformed into a tall, broad-shouldered young man with an uncertain future and no real prospects. His hope of an education and career in the Navy had been short-circuited by the needs of the military and the end of the war; the last real job he had held, while still in high school, was cutting hay for a few dollars a day in the farmlands surrounding Sacramento. And so he returned to Novato, where his father had done well during the wartime boom years by trading his dairy deliveries for a carpentry business, which in the peacetime building boom had just begun to take off.

The younger Booth found work repairing tractors and engines, his love of machinery and cleverness with his hands providing a reasonable living. By then he had a wife to support and the first of five children on the way. Like many servicemen, he had experienced a whirlwind wartime courtship with a young woman he had met at a USO dance—introduction, wooing, and wedding all in a matter of months, their actual time together in the same room measured in hours before they began a life together. When Booth left the Navy, the newlyweds found they hardly knew each other and had little in common beyond their children. Work is where Booth found his greatest satisfaction.

Eager to learn more about his mechanic's craft and still pining for his school-time experiences in the Navy, he asked one of his old high school teachers if he had ever heard of any classes on engine theory, something that might help him better understand how they worked.

"I want to know more about them," he explained a bit lamely when the older man just stared at him.

"Son, you're a veteran, aren't you?"

Booth nodded.

"You ever heard of the G.I. Bill?"

Booth shook his head. The landmark legislation had received low-key press coverage when it passed, drowned out by more pressing news of blitzes and beach landings, and while the various branches of the military made a concerted effort to inform their discharged troops of the benefits they had earned, it was a chaotic time of discharges and mass troop movements. Some units were better at spreading the word than others—with one base erecting elaborate displays with information booths and counselors on hand, while the next might do little more than ask a sergeant to toss a few G.I. Bill pamphlets into a bunk room or barracks. Booth hadn't gotten even that much.

The teacher handed him a business card, jotted a note on it, and said, "Go on over to Berkeley and show 'em this card. They'll take care of you."

The following Monday, Booth enrolled at the University of California–Berkeley—as an engineering student with full credits from his V-12 days, all expenses covered. The full ride offered by the G.I. Bill, the deference shown veterans at the time, the informality and subjectivity of college admissions in those days, and his existing excellent record on campus from his Navy training combined to give Booth as easy an admissions experience as could be imagined (and one that, sixty years later, prospective applicants to the highly competitive Berkeley campus can only envy). Booth could barely believe a law that not only paid for his education, but brought him $90 a month to support his family, had been passed by Congress in the midst of the war.

"I can say this honestly—I'd never have gone to college without it," he would recall many years later. "I'd have stayed on the farm, fixing tractors. So many of us wouldn't have gone to school."

Bob Booth graduated in 1949, just as the Cold War shifted into high gear. Russia had been conducting nuclear tests. The newly divided city of Berlin, meanwhile, had become a tense flash point, with the Soviets staging a blockade and the U.S. launching an airlift of food and goods to counter it. America rapidly became obsessed with the threat of Communism at home and abroad, a cudgel that conservatives began to use with great effect against the "soft" liberals of the FDR era—a brilliant political tactic that succeeded in depicting as weaklings the very leaders who had built up the U.S. military (over conservatives' objections) before Pearl Harbor, then engineered a victory in World War II. The political dynamic of the country began an epochal change then, as America placed itself on a war footing that would span four decades.

As school basements and other underground facilities became fallout shelters marked with ominous yellow and black signs, and the Pentagon began planning scenarios for when the Cold War turned hot, there would be no higher calling for a young engineer than to come to the aid of his country—to work, as Booth saw it, at keeping America safe while tackling the engineering questions that fascinated him. He could scarcely believe his good fortune, to have been born with the chance to make history, when previously he had hoped merely to survive it.

This transformation seemed almost inconceivable to the men and women of Booth's generation, children of the Great Depression conditioned to expect the worst and the least. Most veterans simply hoped to come home from the war and get on with their interrupted lives: If military duty had taken them from the farm or a small city apartment, a job fixing engines or driving a truck or flipping burgers, then most didn't expect much more than the chance to return to the old way of life, although their experiences overseas left many craving something better. Their horizons had been expanded immeasurably, but given the privations they had experienced before and during their service, hopes for a different, better life were tempered by an assumption, well grounded in history, that hard times lay ahead as part of the price of peace.

The end of 1941 certainly looked like the end of the world to them, with the possibility that war might come to the shores of the U.S. mainland a realistic fear, even as coastal patrols and civil defense squads hastily geared up. A year into the war, beachgoers in Miami watched as German U-boats sank American freighters within miles of shore. That America survived world war not only intact, but in many ways healthier and more prosperous than before despite the many sacrifices the country had made for the cause of victory, was a giddy, stunning relief to the returning soldiers, airmen, sailors, and Marines.

They had left a nation still suffering the lingering effects of the Great Depression. Eight million American workers remained jobless in 1940—a steep unemployment rate of close to 15 percent. The middle class was insignificant in size, upward mobility mostly a fairy tale. Disenchantment with free market capitalism had reached a zenith in the poverty-stricken thirties, with national and business leaders fearing a populist or socialist revolt. Charismatic radicals such as Father Charles Coughlin and the legendary Louisiana governor and senator Huey Long had captured the public's imagination—and capitalized on its anger. Long's socialist campaign slogan, "Every man a king, but no one wears a crown," had caught fire with voters, just as it terrified corporate leaders and led his one-time ally, President Roosevelt, to label Long as "one of the most dangerous men in America." Long's assassination in 1935 cut short his presidential bid.

During the war, the conditions that made Long a compelling candidate evaporated. For all practical purposes, unemployment vanished, replaced by worker shortages. Wages rose significantly to spur production. Shuttered factories roared to life, a new ship steamed from America's shipyards at least once a day (when previously only a handful of ships had been launched all year), and at the height of the war effort a new airplane rolled off the assembly line every five minutes. Women flooded the workplace to take over for the men who departed for war, forcing a long-avoided update to age-old notions about jobs and gender roles. Marginal family farms, meanwhile, bellied up by the thousands, farmers selling out to cost-efficient agribusinesses as fifteen million rural residents packed off to urban areas in search of more lucrative work. America's capacity to produce reached historic levels by the end of the war, with workers' earnings at their highest. Support for populist and socialist movements disappeared in a wave of economic good times as the country took a hard tilt to the political right.

Then the war ended, threatening to undo it all. Instead, at this crucial postwar moment—the point when things began to fall apart after the First World War—two factors made all the difference: the G.I. Bill and the Cold War.

First, the G.I. Bill, as Congress had foreseen, provided a buffer against unemployment. But it wasn't the predicted half million veterans or so who postponed entering the job market to go to college or trade school. It was fifteen times that number. In the five years after the war, nearly 8 million veterans would use the G.I. Bill's education benefit. A similar number accepted payments from the Fifty-two/Twenty Club as they searched for work or applied to schools, most for far less than the full year to which they were entitled. And during that time, U.S. unemployment remained minuscule—under 4 percent in the immediate years after the war, shocking economists, politicians, and the public alike.

From there, those same G.I.s signed up for duty in the new Cold War economy. The jobs were there because the huge industrial capacity created during the war was not mothballed along with the excess planes and ships pulled from combat. Much of it remained in place to fight the Cold War, as well as the three-year, less-than-decisive conflict in Korea a mere five years after the end of World War II. Once again, America was transformed by war, though this one had a distinctly different strategy and a language all its own. This wasn't the "Total Warfare" of World War II; the Cold War featured "containment" of Communism coupled with "nuclear deterrence," a strategy that would eventually be known by the all-too-appropriate acronym MAD, for mutually assured destruction. No country would be mad enough to risk annihilation by launching a nuclear first strike, the war planners supposed—a theory that presumed adversary nations would always act rationally, an odd and shaky belief given the behavior of the just-defeated German führer. Yet it was America's primary defense policy across four decades.

Home bomb shelters, Emergency Broadcast System warning tones, and schoolhouse duck-and-cover drills became the hallmarks of this era—multigenerational paranoia as a way of life. First graders didn't just practice fire drills or tornado drills or earthquake drills. There were atomic bomb drills. Soldiers, sailors, and Marines were sent on maneuvers at atomic test sites, marching, flying, and sailing—literally—into mushroom clouds, so certain were Pentagon planners that the war of the future would be fought on the nuclear battlefield. Battalions of scientists and technicians educated on the G.I. Bill stood by to measure the effects of blasts and radiation on man, equipment, and tactics. Many years later, the data would be covered up and falsified as thousands of veterans grew sick and died from radiation-related illnesses the government claimed could not exist.

Of course, there were Cold War policies that had far more benevolent aspects and effects, the justly celebrated Marshall Plan to aid war-ravaged Western Europe the most notable example. The plan, officially known as the European Recovery Program but named for the general-turned-secretary-of-state who conceived it, George C. Marshall, expended 13 billion dollars (the equivalent of 140 billion in 2006) to rebuild allies and former enemies alike. Like the G.I. Bill, the Marshall Plan was not merely an altruistic helping hand: American companies provided much of the materials, brainpower, and manpower for the reconstruction, and the American economy reaped enormous benefits from the revitalized markets and consumer demand that a restored, democratic Europe generated. The Marshall Plan, like the North Atlantic Treaty Organization that followed, was sold not as a good deed so much as a good investment, one that would use capitalism at its best to make communism as unattractive as possible in comparison—containment and altruism combined, with spectacular success.

In theory, the Soviet Union was invited to accept Marshall Plan aid as well, and had the offer extended in 1947 been genuine, the history of the world might have been very different, with trust and cooperation sown instead of fear and conflict. The Cold War might have been an historical footnote instead of a multitrillion-dollar enterprise. But Soviet General Secretary Joseph Stalin was highly suspicious of the offer and wanted it on his high-handed terms, while the U.S. attached conditions to the aid for oversight and democratization that the bloody Soviet tyrant would never accept. And even if Stalin had called the bluff and accepted those terms, everyone knew the U.S. Congress, where John Rankin's coalition still held sway, would never have gone along. In the political climate of the era, Congress likely would have killed the entire Marshall Plan before sending a Communist country a dime, no matter how many of them had died in the war to defeat Hitler's Germany. The path to Cold War was irrevocably locked in place.

While the Marshall Plan proved as much a boon to the U.S. economy as to Western Europe's, providing a raft of jobs and opportunities for returning veterans and G.I. Bill college grads, it was the ever-expanding military spending of the Cold War era that helped drive U.S. prosperity forward. The federal government's workforce had increased fourfold and its budget tenfold during

World War II, from $9 billion to $98 billion, and continued astronomic defense spending in peacetime would drive it even higher before the end of the fifties. The gross national product increased by half in the 1950s, fueled in large part by all that defense spending, which soon absorbed half the peacetime budget. Figures of no less stature than the president of General Electric urged "a permanent war economy" as the route to permanent prosperity, a path strongly supported by the suddenly powerful American labor movement, which reached its zenith in the fifties with more than a third of American workers onboard. In contrast to the Gilded Age and the excesses of the Roaring Twenties (and, for that matter, the first decade of the Twenty-first Century), when the nation's growing prosperity was spread primarily among a wealthy elite while most Americans' incomes stagnated, the prosperity of the postwar years proved historically egalitarian. Factory workers saw their wages rise 50 percent. The ranks of the middle class swelled fourfold. Homeownership skyrocketed. New suburban communities sprang into existence as the postwar baby boom created enormous demands for housing, consumer goods, schools, teachers, doctors—everything. Nearly 30 million American babies were born in the 1950s, as America's birth rate in those years matched India's. Major corporations responded by providing increasingly generous medical and retirement benefits to lure and reward blue- and white-collar workers alike, sometimes because of union pressures and demands, at other times simply out of enlightened self interest and the laws of supply and demand.

Before this era began, economists had always described income distribution as a pyramid, with most of the people dwelling at the bottom where incomes were low, while at the top, a few enjoyed fabulous wealth. But after the war, economic distribution in the U.S. began to resemble a diamond: relatively small numbers of poor and rich at either end, with a big, fat, middle class at the center.

At that time, a young veteran could expect to hire on at a company—Boeing, Bell, General Motors, RCA, IBM—and stay there a lifetime, with room for advancement, opportunities for in-house training and education, and retirement security. Mass layoffs as an accepted and even praiseworthy fix for ailing bottom lines—business as usual in the late twentieth century—were unheard of in this era. These companies needed the talent and the educated workforce to create new products and designs, from transistors to toasters to pinball machines to jet engines to nuclear warheads, and they paid a premium for it, rewarding loyalty and, in return, being rewarded with productive, loyal employees. These were companies building new technologies, new armies, new worlds—their thinking was not limited to the next fiscal quarter but to the next quarter century. All this was far from perfect—the new prosperity skipped whole segments of society, thanks to rampant race and gender discrimination that would require decades of unraveling—but in comparison to eras before and since, this moment proved for many Americans, particularly the veterans, to be an economic golden age.

Little of this would have been possible without the hundreds of thousands of engineers, designers, physicists, and technicians trained through the G.I. Bill's education benefits, and the millions of homes built, sold, and financed on the G.I. Bill's guarantees. The vast majority of the workers who powered this new economy of perpetual warfare were the veterans who fought so hard to end the last war. And the money flowing to and from the burgeoning defense industry gave Americans far more to spend on consumer goods, travel, cars, swimming pools, and entertainment—leading to booms in virtually every industry and business sector.

Along the way, the G.I. Bill ended up driving a redefinition of the American Dream. No longer would it rest on the Founders' noble abstractions about liberty and civil rights, nor on nineteenth-century agrarian ideals of the yeoman farmer. After the war, Americans came to long for a more tangible and material dream, one of home ownership (preferably in the suburbs), a new car, job security and benefits, and a television set. This vision of the American Dream as commodity, the antithesis of the empty cupboards and bank foreclosures of the Great Depression, became over time more than merely iconic. It formed a potent cultural weapon in the us-versus-them mind-set of the Cold War, reaching even into the interplay between White House and Kremlin, sometimes to the point of absurdity.

In 1959, Vice President Richard Nixon traveled to Moscow for an exhibition in which America showed off its industrial prowess and high standard of living with a state-of-the-art model American kitchen. The occasion led to an impromptu debate between Nixon and Russian Premier Nikita Krushchev, who poked and prodded the prosaic world of toasters and garbage disposals even as they held forth on the world-shaking question of which system of government was most likely to prevail and outlast the other, communism or capitalism.

Americans were not amused by the barely polite repartee of "The Kitchen Debate," especially when Krushchev proclaimed, "America has been in existence for one hundred fifty years and this is the level she has reached. We have existed not quite forty-two years and in another seven years we will be on the same level as

America. When we catch you up, in passing you by, we will wave to you. . . . You don't know anything about Communism except fear of it."

Despite Krushchev's bluster and exaggerated boasts (the Soviet Union's economic output and overall technological capabilities never came close to matching America's), he was right about one thing: Fear based largely on ignorance had become a pervasive part of the Cold War, even amid the peacetime prosperity and the can-do spirit that still permeated American society in the wake of World War II victory. The mushroom clouds of the Soviet's Siberian bomb testing, the new Sputnik satellite speeding overhead before America had figured out how to get its own machines into space, the grim division of Berlin—all were seen as ominous challenges to American supremacy and exceptionalism that had to be met, and met firmly.

In a world where a dishwasher or the General Motors brand could become just two more weapons in a nuclear-powered ideological tug of war, anything that smacked of Big Government, populism, or socialism suddenly seemed suspect, possibly dangerous, certainly unpatriotic—and far too similar to the nation Americans saw as a dangerous adversary and repugnant moral opposite: the Soviet Union. Ironically, a majority of World War II veterans—the recipients through the G.I. Bill of the largest program of special-interest largesse in U.S. history, including subsidized education, health care, housing, and business loans—took this view to heart, supporting it with their leadership, their wallets, and their votes. In that climate, President Truman's attempt to pursue FDR's dream of a second bill of rights—a housing, schools, and jobs program he called the Fair Deal—never had a chance. The New Deal plan to attack the problems of universal health care, poverty, and education that continue to bedevil American society today, died with the only politician who had the remotest chance of seeing it through, as Roosevelt succumbed to a fatal stroke just twenty-six days before Germany's surrender. And so the G.I.s became not only the engine that enabled America to fight the new Cold War, they also became the principal political supporters for opposing the extension of G.I. Bill–like benefits to a broader segment of American society.

It is impossible to know now, sixty years later, what America and the world would have looked like had the U.S. taken a more historically typical posture after World War II, returning to its traditionally isolationist ways rather than marching forward as a new superpower, engaging in ideological warfare and proxy armed conflicts in Korea, Vietnam, Africa, Latin America, and elsewhere. What if the Fair Deal had passed, if Roosevelt's original proposal for a second bill of rights had been adopted along with the G.I. Bill of Rights, if Americans and Soviets had chosen détente and cooperation in the 1950s instead of waiting until the 1980s, and if all the money and talent that fueled the Cold War and its ever-more ingenious weaponry had been channeled instead into inventing new sources of energy, new medical treatments, new educational reforms?

Where would we be now if the Bob Booths of the world had not felt compelled to serve their country by devoting their creativity and genius to the arms race with the Russians, and instead had pursued more peaceable research? Would it have mattered if both sides had resisted the xenophobia of the Cold War, if the Russians had understood that America had no intention of launching a first nuclear strike, and if the U.S. had, in turn, understood Russia's deep-seated, historically based fear of invasion and attack? This

Russian paranoia had been stoked by World War II casualties almost beyond imagination, and it led to one misunderstanding after another that repeatedly brought both nations to the brink of destruction. To the U.S., the expansion of communism to other nations posed an unbearable threat; to the Soviets, it was America's unrivaled influence and power and its willingness to prop up even the most wretched dictators so long as they were on the political right that threatened world peace. To the U.S., the Cuban Missile Crisis would be an intolerable provocation and imminent danger; to the Soviets, putting missiles in Cuba was a predictable response to America's own Jupiter nuclear missile squadrons already planted on Russia's border in Turkey, as well as to the new threat posed by Bob Booth's submarine-based Polaris missiles, which Soviet technology was then years away from matching.

Would communism have failed even without the wildly expensive, budget-busting defense spending America pursued across the last half of the twentieth century? For a long time, the ravenous defense budgets contributed to economic good times—but then deficits soared out of control and Americans learned that every citizen, newborn to retiree, suddenly owed a twenty-five-thousand-dollar share of the national debt. Would a different path after the war have brought us to a safer, better world today, or a more dangerous, less prosperous one? Would America be stronger or weaker?

It's impossible to know, although popular and expert opinion then, as now, suggests the path America followed was the only sane and properly cautious one. Still, it is somewhat astonishing in hindsight to consider that America's reaction to decisive victory in World War II and to unprecedented peace and prosperity at home was to ramp up, not slow down, military research and spending, thereby helping launch forty years of tense and potentially devastating brinkmanship and conflict with one of our main World War II allies—the very same Russians who had liberated tens of thousands of American prisoners of war a scant few years earlier.

But that, for better or worse, was America's path, one that few questioned at the time. It brought Bob Booth to Lockheed Aircraft and the Polaris missile program—and then to a discovery that would have far-reaching benefits not just for Polaris, but for America's fledgling efforts to conquer space.

The month Bob Booth graduated from Berkeley, Boeing recruited five hundred top engineering students to come to Seattle to work for the aircraft and weapons giant. Virtually all of the new hires were G.I. Bill graduates. Booth's assignment was to work on upgrades to the B-29 Superfortress, the last of the propeller-driven heavy bombers, introduced late in the war and used to drop the atomic bombs on Japan. He was thrilled and eagerly made the move from California with his family.

"I still have the letter on my wall offering me the job," Booth laughs. "I earned two hundred fifty dollars a week. And I thought it was a fortune!"

But one Wednesday, after he had been at Boeing a few weeks, a manager pulled aside Booth and the fourteen other engineers on the B-29 project with some unusual instructions: Take the rest of the week off, then come back on Monday using a "devious" route. Their manager spoke so quietly the engineers had to huddle close to hear his instructions. When someone asked him what he meant, the manager said only, "Make sure no one is following you."

Their boss offered no further explanation, but the novice engineers knew the score. Concerns about Russian industrial and military spying had reached a fever pitch at the start of the new decade, so this sort of warning did not seem all that strange to Booth and his colleagues. Boeing had a plethora of sensitive national security projects in the works—all the major contractors did. However, Booth doubted that his little group's modifications to a World War II B-29 bomber, an airplane already badly obsolete, could generate much interest for either Soviet spies or American spy catchers. He guessed something else was up, and he was correct.

On Monday, he felt a bit silly about the circuitous route he took and his constant gazing in the rearview mirror. But when his team assembled, they found two FBI agents standing there with them, watching expressionlessly as Booth and the others were told they'd been assigned to a new project: the experimental and as-yet only imagined B-52, a new jet-engine bomber intended to fly faster, farther, and higher while carrying more bombs than any plane in history.

The B-52's original requirements from the Pentagon called for a bomber that could fly 5,000 miles with a 10,000-pound bomb load at altitudes of up to 35,000 feet and speeds of up to 450 miles an hour—capabilities the B-52 would exceed when it finally flew in 1955, but which at the time seemed as unreachable as the moon.

"No one had any idea how to build a plane to meet those requirements—it had never been done," Booth recalls. "We worked day and night on just getting the wings strong enough to support their own weight."

When the eight-engine jet bomber ended up flying much faster and higher than the original specifications demanded, it was rushed into production even as testing and further modifications continued—a wartime urgency in a time of peace. No expense was spared, Booth says, for it was understood that money was no object when it came to besting the Soviets.

The B-52 quickly became one of the mainstays of America's 1950s Cold War strategy, with a force of the nuclear-armed bombers in the skies twenty-four hours a day, refueling in midair and ready to strike in the event of an attack on America. These were strategic aircraft, far more delicate compared to the sturdy bombers of World War II, which could take a horrific pounding from guns and fighters and still stay aloft. Still, the B-52 proved so adaptable and capable—converted over the years to fly ground-hugging, radar-evading courses, to drop millions of pounds of conventional bombs high above Vietnam, and to launch cruise missiles far from an adversary's shores to elude modern anti-aircraft defenses—that it remains to this day one of the Air Force's main strategic and heavy bombers. Though most of the original production run has been mothballed—the planes hauled to the Arizona desert and chopped into scrap metal as part of arms control agreements with the Soviets—nearly one hundred of the new models remained in service more than half a century after the last B-52 rolled off the assembly line. The Air Force has suggested it could fly these remaining B-52s through the year 2040.

"No one ever imagined it would still be flying after all these years," Booth marvels today. "We knew the B-52 could never stand up to the sort of combat that bombers encountered in World War II—it would be torn to pieces. But it does the job it was designed to do very well, even after fifty years."

The accomplishment is unheard of in the world of aerospace engineering—fifty years is an eternity in aircraft design. Fifty years before the Pentagon contracted for the B-52, there were no airplanes at all.

Booth loved the B-52 design phase at Boeing: the challenge, the arguments, the give-and-take. He'd pull out reams of butcher paper and hang it on the walls, drawing different solutions to the same problem, crossing out and revising and starting over, until he found one he felt would work best. He was a mechanic at heart, a tinkerer, which fit the times—this was an age long before computer simulations (or computers of any useful sort), and engineering meant getting your hands dirty, at least the way Bob Booth practiced it.

But once the B-52 had gotten off the ground, the main problems solved and production started in earnest, he lost interest—time, he realized, to begin looking for another job. Not everyone at Boeing was sorry to see him go: Booth had a habit of irritating his superiors, either by criticizing them openly or, worse yet, telling them they were wrong, then proving it. As Booth saw it, that was his job: to provide the best engineering assessment he could, not to avoid stepping on egos and toes. But with a healthy ego of his own in play, it also meant having to pack up and leave on occasion.

Chasing the design challenges as he would throughout his career, Booth left Boeing for Hiller Aircraft, where he worked on designing a new breed of helicopters—the familiar two-place H-23 flying bubbles that became a mainstay of the Korean war and the early years of conflict in Vietnam. He also designed the first helicopter with ramjets on the end of the rotor blades—the prototype is now in the Smithsonian Institute—and worked on an experimental version of the first tilt-wing, vertical-takeoff-and-landing troop-transport plane, a forerunner of the Marine Corps' Osprey aircraft.

After Hiller was bought out, Booth next moved to Lockheed's new missile systems division in Sunnyvale, California, which had just won the Polaris missile contract.

By the time Booth joined the project, Polaris was in trouble. The pressure to succeed—and quickly—was enormous, but so were the technical challenges: Lockheed had been charged with developing a nuclear missile that could be fired from a submarine and carry its warhead at least a thousand miles to its target, a weapon radically different from any other rocket yet produced. No missile had ever been launched from under water. No missile had ever used the solid propellant planned for the Polaris—the liquid fuel systems commonly used in rockets at the time were too volatile for the confines of a submarine. Even launch methods had to be reinvented, using compressed air to propel the missile from the launch tube before the engines fired up, as there was no safe way to channel the intense exhaust heat while the missile was still inside a submerged submarine. And everything was complicated by the intense secrecy imposed by the government, as well as a constant pushing forward of deadlines.

When the project started in 1957, Lockheed had been given ten years to go from concept to production. Within a few months, the time allotted shrank to five years, then three, as U.S. war planners, not to mention the public, felt panicked by the Soviet's successful Sputnik launch in October 1957. It did not matter that the first successful artificial satellite posed no actual threat. The capability Sputnik represented was the sobering part to the Eisenhower administration, and it desperately sought an immediate counter to Russian nuclear missile capabilities, a far more formidable threat than a mere beeping satellite. The Cold War policies of containment and deterrence required the U.S. to have a credible nuclear force that would survive any attack by the Soviet Union.

But before Polaris, the U.S. had no nuclear forces guaranteed to survive a first strike. The B-52 bombers Booth worked on were an important part of that defense, but they still could be shot out of the sky before reaching their targets or obliterated while on the ground in a sudden first strike. Land-based missiles would be even more vulnerable, easily targeted in an initial, massively destructive attack. Only a submarine-based missile could be counted on to elude detection and attack—it would be, as it remains to this day, the ultimate stealth weapon, capable of creeping undetected to enemy shores, then firing its deadly cargo at point-blank range. If Polaris could be perfected, the Pentagon believed, no enemy would dare launch a first strike against the United States.

Which, given the Cold War paranoia and anti-Communist fervor of the era, explains the urgency of the program and the accelerated design and production schedule that rivaled anything undertaken during the pressures of World War II, when the U.S. had actually been attacked. Brand new nuclear submarines were being chopped in two and refitted with missile tubes, and the first would be ready to begin patrols by the end of 1960. The missiles had to be ready to fill those tubes. No secret military program had higher priority at the time or commanded more free-flowing dollars from Congress than Polaris—the only problem being that none of the systems needed to make it work existed at the time those deadlines were shrinking.

"Basically, we had to figure out how to get twenty-three tons of missile from what amounts to San Francisco to Omaha in three and a half minutes," Booth recalls. "And it had to launch from a submarine. No one had ever done anything like it. And we had three years to do it, which wouldn't have been that bad if not for the fact that the things kept blowing up."

After the disaster at the Cape Canaveral cafeteria, Booth found himself assigned to troubleshoot the thermodynamics of the Polaris's solid-fuel engine. The rocket-sled tests he set up to test fire the engines on the ground revealed an unexpected problem with the direction of the exhaust gases. As the missile reached supersonic speeds, air flow behind the motor reversed, and blindingly hot gases leaving the engine nozzles beat back against the base of the rocket motor. Under the motor's thin metal skin lay critical hydraulic controls, which melted in moments after the exhaust reversed, causing the rocket to fail and fly out of control.

"Supposedly I was some kind of genius in thermodynamics," Booth says dryly. "And if I wasn't, I needed to become one in a hurry. They said we had to turn the Polaris into the phoenix—you know, rise from the flames."

Identifying the problem proved to be the easiest task facing Booth. Fixing it was another matter, once again calling for hands-on engineering. Redesigning the entire motor was out of the question in terms of time, cost, and difficulty. So that meant adding some sort of insulation—metal, ceramic, or some other material—to the bottom of the motor. But that created another set of problems: Too much insulation would create a size and weight penalty that would affect the missile's ability to reach its target. Safety is always desirable, but a completely safe aircraft would be too heavy to fly, Booth knew. It's one of the first rules an aircraft designer must acknowledge.

They had to find something light yet heat-resistant to protect the bottom of the rocket. It only needed to last three minutes. Exhaust temperatures could go as high as 6,000 degrees Fahrenheit—hot enough not just to melt steel, but to vaporize it—so whatever they used had to be very, very tough.

Experimentation to find this material was no simple matter. Booth and his colleagues first had to find some way of simulating the temperatures reached by the rocket exhaust without setting fire to their lab or blowing up their entire work area. Booth finally hit on the idea of banding together a half-dozen acetylene torches, lighting them all at once, and concentrating them on a single steel plate mounted on concrete. Temperature sensors underneath the plate recorded the success—or the failure—of whatever insulation they tested on the steel.

And they tried everything: plastic wood, dental cement, tailpipe blankets. Nothing worked. Quarter-inch steel disks sizzled into vapor in six seconds under the blaze of those torches.

Then one night Booth had an inspiration while lying awake thinking about the problem, and he came in early the next day with a suggestion: silicon rubber. His plant had a large supply of the stuff, which was used to coat rivet heads to make an airtight surface wherever the fasteners pierced the metal skin of a missile. It went on like a soft, malleable modeling clay, then dried to the consistency of a pencil eraser. And silicon had proved to be surprisingly durable. "Let's fire up some of this," Booth said.

The rest of the team members shrugged: Why not? It seemed an unlikely choice, but there was little to lose. Nothing else had worked.

Booth applied the goo to their test bed, let it cure, then turned the torches on it for a good, long blast. When the smoke cleared, everyone stared: Nothing seemed to have happened—the silicon was still there, charred but intact. Then someone announced the temperature readings beneath the steel—the place where the missile's hydraulics would be on a real Polaris. "Something must be wrong—we're showing only a ten-degree rise."

But nothing was wrong—the readings proved to be correct. They did the test again, and then a third time, with the same low-temperature result. The silicon had succeeded where other harder, seemingly stronger materials had failed. A simple coat of this material slapped on the weak underbelly of the missile could put Polaris back in business.

At ten thirty that same morning, Booth boarded a plane bound for Florida with twenty-three gallons of silicon rubber coating as his luggage. And the next day he was crawling around under the Polaris missile prototype, smearing the stuff on with tongue depressors, only to have the launch director at Cape Canaveral come charging out in a rage, then boot him from the premises for putting "crap" on his missile.

The flight back home to Sunnyvale was miserable for Booth. But the next day back at work in California, his boss looked at him with a puzzled expression. "What are you doing here? Why aren't you in Florida?"

That's when Booth learned that the launch had been a complete success, the first triumphant test of a Polaris prototype, and a complete vindication of Booth and his smeary solution. His reputation was made after that, and he has been credited with discovering the insulating properties of silicon rubber, which soon found its way onto the first Mercury space capsule to achieve Earth orbit, the gaps and seams in the reentry shield sealed with the stuff, keeping astronaut John Glenn safe in his historic flight. And the next time Booth arrived at Cape Canaveral, his old nemesis, the flight director who gave him the boot, was nowhere to be found.

"People ask me all the time, *How the heck did you think of that?* and I just have to tell the simple truth: Me and God thought it up. Really, that's what I say, even when I was at a party with all the big shots and the admirals, they wanted to know, *How'd you think that up?* I just say, me and God thought that one up. Because it just came to me: silicon rubber. And before we had tested it, I just knew it was right."

The Polaris project finished on time and the first sea-based launch from the USS *George Washington* took place on schedule in July 1960. Soon there were forty such submarines armed with Polaris missiles plying the seas and lurking beneath ice packs, tilting the strategic balance far in America's favor. This made Booth a hero in Pentagon and engineering circles, though the successful fielding of Polaris had an undesirable side effect in the tit-for-tat calculus of the Cold War: It was Polaris, coupled with American nukes in Turkey, that drove the Soviet Union to construct missile bases in Cuba, leading to the missile crisis that almost touched off World War III.

Bob Booth went on to a storied career at Lockheed and other defense contractors, working on the fastest helicopter ever built—the Cheyenne, which was canceled by the Army in the prototype stage—and the Viking surveillance plane for the Navy. He designed everything from aerial refueling nozzles, to high-speed aerial cameras with rotating turbines that shot more than a million frames a second, to rotor blades that could survive punishing changes in temperature without failing. He bruised a few more egos along the way, too, because of his impolitic habit of criticizing his superiors when he was sure he was right, which continued to lead to sudden departures and career changes right up until his retirement. He laughs about them now. "It's not like I was going to change who I am," he says.

When he finally retired after a half century as a design engineer, he moved to Alaska to be close to his oldest son. He and his wife had divorced amicably after eighteen years of marriage. In

Alaska he bought an airplane that he continues to fly regularly, finally earning the wings that his old coach and teacher talked him out of seeking during the war so long before. Along the way, he took up opera—he has sung tenor at some twenty performances of the West Bay Opera in San Francisco—and he met and married his second wife, Jackie. He remains a large, imposing man, his hair and beard gone white, his days full. He still loves to work with his hands, to tear an airplane motor apart and put it back together, to make it run better than it did before.

Shortly before Christmas 2003, Booth was invited to an event in Washington, D.C. to commemorate the one hundredth anniversary of the Wright Brothers' flight at Kitty Hawk—and to unveil a new wall of honor at NASA headquarters memorializing the most significant contributors and pioneers in the history of flight and space exploration.

Booth's name is on that wall.

Later, at a signing for a book detailing the history of Lockheed, the former company chairman, Dan Tellep, spotted Booth, stopped what he was doing to shake the old engineer's hand, then called for quiet at the crowded reception. "I'd like to tell you about Bob," he told the gathering. "He and I go way back, and I'd like to tell you in two words what Bob did."

At this point, Booth, feeling a bit embarrassed at the spotlight, figured Tellep was about to say something like "kicked butt," or perhaps something less flattering, given Booth's reputation for speaking his mind whether his superiors wanted him to or not.

Instead, Tellep paused, then uttered these two words: "Contained Communism." For once, Booth was caught speechless.

Hanging on Booth's wall in his comfortable home in Nikiski, Alaska, is a letter written in 1960 by Admiral William "Red"

Raborn, who oversaw the Polaris program and would later head the CIA. Raborn, who was aboard the *George Washington* for that first successful Polaris launch, wrote: "My pride in the Polaris team is unbounded. History will record this event as a major development of weapons, ranking in importance with the advent of the crossbow, gunpowder, the airplane, and atomic weapons."

"It's just stunning, isn't it?" Booth says now. "Sometimes I still can't believe that poor farm kid could end up in college, become an engineer, spend a lifetime designing things—and enjoying it—discover the endothermic properties of silicon, and have a part in building our country after the war. It's just stunning. What could be better than that?"

☆ 3 ☆

INVESTING IN THE FUTURE: Bill Thomas and the Rise of Suburbia

Bill Thomas plunked a few nickels into the pay phone outside his one-room beach-side apartment (he couldn't yet afford his own telephone), asked the operator to connect him to his future (he hoped) wife three thousand miles east in North Carolina, and then dropped the big one.

"Well, I went and bought a house today," he announced proudly.

Silence.

Bill cleared his throat. "I used the G.I. Bill—no down payment, just 4 percent interest, only sixty-four dollars a month."

More silence.

The twenty-six-year-old ex-G.I.-turned-college-student and bookstore manager had been so proud of his real estate acumen that he hadn't fully considered that his future partner in life might want to help choose their dream house, no matter how great the deal. Given the way they had decided to get married—happy-go-lucky Bill plopping onto the couch and asking, "Hey, you want to get married or something?" and Soula, looking him sternly in the eye before flashing a brilliant smile, answering, "We'll get married or *nothing!*"—he really should have known better.

"It's going to be brand new, it's not even built yet, eleven hundred and seventy square feet. What a great deal!" And then, with a note of pleading, he added, "Don't you think?"

Eventually Soula sighed and conceded that it at least sounded okay. But Bill realized he badly needed to build his case and get his fiancée feeling more involved and invested in their new home—otherwise, it might just be only *his* new home.

So he hit on the idea of mailing her pictures every week, showing the progress of their new home construction in the as-yet nonexistent Los Angeles suburb of Lakewood. In 1950, bean and sugar beet fields on the outskirts of Long Beach, California, were just yielding to this revolutionary new housing development—which has periodically laid claim to being the first and largest fully planned suburban community in America, although many historians give Levittown, New York, the nod on scoring that achievement by a year. Not that it mattered to the tens of thousands of families who lined up each weekend at these developments on both coasts, hoping to take advantage of the no-money-down, G.I. Bill–subsidized, low-interest mortgages for World War II vets, and the chance to trade a shabby rented room or garage apartment or living with the in-laws, for their own real house with a yard and a tree or two and good, hard oak floors.

Most every weekend, Bill and some friends would take sandwiches or a bag of burgers and a few cold beers and pile into the car to drive out to the vast construction site. The farmland had been scraped down to a lunar five-o'clock shadow, rocks and stubble, flat as a griddle, ready to be seeded with new crops—row upon row of houses. They'd eat, and then Bill would get out his old Kodak and snap picture after picture of the bulldozers, lined up like the tanks and artillery pieces he had lived and fought with during the war; or he'd capture the crews moving down the street, sawing, hammering, plastering, smoothing, or painting, each crew with one endlessly repeated task, much like the old assembly line he had once worked in Detroit, though on an unimaginable scale. He would watch it for hours, fascinated at the conversion of land into city at such an astonishing rate, not one or two or three houses at a time, but a hundred. The construction swept across the packed dirt with the speed of a wildfire in reverse, as the houses rose up right before his eyes, almost as fast, he sometimes imagined, as a blaze could have brought them down.

Later, he'd drop off his film at the drugstore and pick up the last batch of developed photos, which in those days came in long, perforated strips folded into a booklet. He'd write up notes for each photo on adding machine tape left over from the bookstore. Then he folded it all up together, so when Soula opened the letter it would unravel like an accordion-style book, a sort of multimedia history of Lakewood in the making.

Soula loved these missives so much that she began posting them where she worked—which happened to be Durham City Hall, where she was a probate clerk. Sooner or later, pretty much everyone in town eventually walked by the courthouse bulletin board and gawked at those pictures of scraped earth and armies of carpenters, so alien to the lush, green world of hundred-year-old, hand-crafted brick houses of the Old South. Little did Bill know that his personal photo collection was making him something of a celebrity in Durham, North Carolina, and that the town would be watching all too closely when it came time for this invader from the land of "earthquakes and cowboys" to fetch his bride.

The story of a brash ex-G.I. with a knack for sales, and an instant community unlike any before it, are truly inseparable, an overlapping narrative of the postwar housing boom and the men, women, and children who occupied it—the new world of America's suburbs, yet another creation, both momentous and unintended, of the G.I. Bill.

Before the war, Bill Thomas never for a moment imagined a place like Lakewood, California. No one did—not the home builders whose business had all but died during Depression and war; not the lenders hungry for new mortgage holders who just weren't there during the war; not even the legislators who crafted the veterans' home loan benefits, who merely sought to reward and mollify the ex-G.I.s, not remake the American landscape. And even if Bill had, somehow, glimpsed this future of suburbs and detached homes and backyard barbecues, he certainly never would have expected to be lucky enough to land there.

Yet it is impossible today for him to imagine any other life for himself, Soula, or their three children—or any better one—just as it is impossible to imagine a modern America without the lasting footprint of suburban cul de sacs, Cape Cod homes, and concrete slab foundations, which were all but unheard of before the war.

Indeed, Bill Thomas would be the first to say that Lakewood, California, is about as far as possible in feel and fact from his hometown of Detroit and the world in which he grew up, an inner-city neighborhood of ethnic restaurants and Depression-era poverty, of houses crowded in on one another, with little green space and few trees.

His parents worked long hours—his dad behind a barber chair, his mother as a seamstress. Both had emigrated from Greece ten years before Bill's birth in 1923. Bill's father anglicized his given name—Thomaides—after serving in the U.S. military during World War I, where he grew tired of being called "Private Tomatoes."

There wasn't much money for the Thomas household in those years of chronic unemployment, though they did better than many others—more than 25 percent of workers remained jobless the year Bill turned ten. His father earned twenty-five cents for a haircut and fifteen cents for a shave, and those prices could prove a strain for more than a few customers. Bill used to shine shoes for a nickel at the shop.

He was the oldest of the Thomas kids, with two younger brothers and a sister, and he felt it was his duty to bring in more cash. So he chafed under his mother's occasionally severe household rule: She required him not only to go to public school but to Greek school, too, and to take violin lessons, an intolerable distraction from his first love, baseball, and his desire to make more money (though he concedes that to this day he is both fluent in Greek and able to read and write music, thanks to his mom).

When he got a little older, he took over a paper route for the *Detroit Times* and worked it so hard that he increased his customer list from forty-six subscribers to 107 in his first five weeks on the job. Bill was short for his age, but he was wiry and strong, and his pleasant features assumed a very grown-up look of determination when it came to work—a combination that made him a successful salesman. People would look at his earnest smile and they just couldn't say no. His Sunday paper run was so heavy he had to drape bags all over his bicycle and tow another load in a wagon behind him.

Bill's paper route exploits were good enough to win an all-expenses-paid trip to the New York World's Fair of 1939 with a crew of other newsboys—Bill's first substantial trip from Detroit and his first ride on a train. He was sixteen and thrilled to visit New York City, to see the Rockettes kick at Radio City Music Hall, and to attend showings of two new movies that debuted in 1939, destined to become classics: *Gone With the Wind* and *The Wizard of Oz.* At the fair, he found America's vision of the future, circa that far-off year of 1960—an enormous amalgam of nationalism, industrial magic, and proto-Disneyland amusements sandwiched between past Depression and future Holocaust, filled with fantastic animated dioramas of master-planned utopian communities, homes filled with robots, and a new technology called television. A web of imagined interstate highways linked all, with high-speed cars whizzing quietly by, marked (presciently enough) by a conspicuous absence of the rail and trolley systems that dominated the real world of the thirties. No surprise that these grand displays were erected by the major automobile and oil companies, who soon would make their vision a reality beginning in Southern California, with the historic postwar dismantling of the largest light-rail system in the world to make room for freeways and more cars and new suburbs.

Though he was too young for it to register at the time, and it certainly was not part of the intended design, the fair also displayed something more sinister: the growing world tensions that would soon lead to war and irrevocable change in the life of Bill

Thomas and millions like him. Germany had no direct presence at the fair, but the pavilion of the Czech Republic, annexed by the Nazis the previous year, bore an anguished banner reading, "After the Tempest of Wrath has Passed, the Rule of thy Country will Return to Thee, O Czech People." Midway through the fair's run, France found itself under Nazi occupation as well; the Blitzkrieg threatened to reduce Britain to rubble; and the Soviet pavilion, one of the largest at the fair, was razed because of Joseph Stalin's ignominious nonaggression pact with Hitler (which abruptly ended when Germany invaded Russia and the Soviets switched sides to the Allies).

Back in Detroit, Bill soon quit high school in the eleventh grade to go to work full time at a Ford plant, where he sat in a nine-by-nine metal cage and signed out tools and equipment to engineers on the assembly-line floor. He hated every minute, and after several months he left to take a job with the New Deal's Civilian Conservation Corps, where he worked for several months in the Michigan woods with forest rangers, clearing brush and maintaining trails. He liked it enough to conclude that the forest service might be a great place for him to make his career, and one of his supervisors told him he might be able to help him get hired—if Bill first went back home and earned his high school diploma, the principal requirement for rangers at the time.

So Bill went back home, fully intending to return to school, but before classes began he heard that Cadillac had job openings at a new plant that manufactured parts for the P-38 Lightning fighter planes that the U.S. was selling Great Britain—military support President Roosevelt had eked through a reluctant, isolationist Congress. Bill could make eighty cents an hour at Cadillac, a relative fortune compared to the one-dollar-a-day salary he had earned with the federally financed Conservation Corps. He let money win out over his dream, at least for the moment, and he went to Cadillac, where he became a grinder, machining connecting rods for the P-38's Allison engines.

One day a few weeks before Christmas 1941, shortly after he turned eighteen, Bill pulled a Sunday shift at the P-38 plant. As usual, the radio played loudly on the plant floor, a little music to make the time pass for the shop crew. But then the music abruptly stopped, interrupted by an announcement. The announcer's tone caught everyone's attention and, slowly, the plant fell silent as the gravity of the broadcast sank in.

At his big metal grinder, Bill noticed the reaction of his fellow workers before he comprehended what the announcer had said. He saw other workers crying, women and men alike. All work came to a stop, as people kept asking how could this happen, why would anyone do this, what's going to happen now? He heard someone ask, "Where's Pearl Harbor?" Nobody knew. It was not a place or a destination often mentioned in Motor City.

Then Bill heard the radio announcer talking again and he understood. The United States had been attacked, a base in Hawaii bombed. Many ships had been sunk. Many sailors had died.

The country, he realized, was at war—the war everyone had feared and had desperately hoped to avoid, and had known, somehow, would come knocking. And no one in that airplane plant, it seemed to Bill, knew what to say or what to do next.

Then the shift supervisor jumped on a bench and everyone's eyes were on him. "Okay, let me tell you something. You know, we've been making these airplanes for the British and we've been doing a fine job." He paused, looking around the plant. Bill still gets choked up when he remembers this moment, the sadness that gripped him, and the anger, and the pride he felt at this man's next words. "But now we have to start making them for our boys. So let's get to work."

And so they did, returning to the grinding and the welding and the assembly, suddenly feeling that in their small way they really were doing something to help. And that plant's productivity went up some 50 percent in the next few months.

The following year, when he turned nineteen, Bill and his two friends—both also named Bill, a popular name in 1923—decided to enlist together rather than wait to be drafted. They marched into an Army recruiting station and made it clear they had to be in the same unit. They were promised it would happen, but they ended up separated by the military bureaucracy, with Bill Martin destined for the infantry and an early death at the Battle of the Bulge; Bill Perry assigned to air transport, where he suffered terrible facial injuries that led to his drinking himself to death after the war; and Bill Thomas assigned to artillery. If you thought too much about fate, the only surviving Bill says, it would drive you crazy.

He began his training in February 1943, and by summer's end he set sail with the 938th Field Artillery Battalion and its massive 155-millimeter howitzers, first for Africa for final training, then to Italy. Combat duty for him began in Naples, then on the long march northward, where he took part in the war's "other D-Day," the amphibious landing and pitched battle at Anzio in late January 1944. Thirty-six thousand troops stormed the Italian beach, then dug in there for more than four months, attempting to break through German lines and drive toward Rome.

They managed to move exactly three thousand feet in four months, so determined were the Germans to hold the northern portion of Italy and, if possible, push the Americans back into the sea. The stalemate resulted when the general in command of the invasion force opted to linger on the beachhead, waiting for supply lines to be better established. They missed an opportunity to overrun the surprised Germans when the troops first pounded out of their landing boats and raced up the sand (where the diminutive Private Thomas almost drowned but for a timely tug on a towline by a team of sailors). Within a few days, the German forces had taken the high ground and began dropping artillery shells on the Americans, picking them off slowly but surely. Thomas only learned of this tactical error many years later while reading accounts of the battle; at the time, he, like all the other grunts, had no thoughts other than the need to fight, survive, and protect his buddies.

His job with the artillery battalion put him in the thick of things—not manning the big guns, but stringing telephone wire in trees, on poles, or in trenches, so spotters on the frontline could relay enemy positions and targeting corrections to the artillery crews manning the cannons to the rear. He would also climb trees and call in artillery coordinates himself once the wires were laid. This dangerous job regularly put him in harm's way, particularly when he donned his spiked shoes and clambered up some treetop or telephone pole to gaze down at enemy troops, who would have loved to have shot him on sight. He always managed to avoid detection, and his buddies soon nicknamed the thin, elusive, five-foot-seven soldier with the million-dollar smile the Mink.

The Mink lived in a bunker he and his sergeant, Mousey Reed, had painstakingly dug and reinforced with a roof of timbers, sandbags, and steel sheets. It was a strange life in combat—so close to the enemy, shot at regularly, but responding not by shooting back with his carbine, but by calling in targets for the big guns.

He rarely fired his weapon—he was there to support and protect the infantry, not be the infantry—but his exposure to enemy fire was no less than an infantryman's, and often greater. When the fighting grew particularly heavy at Anzio, Bill and his buddies had to spend weeks without adequate supplies, dug in and unable to wash or shave because water was so scarce and supplies could not get through.

When the water truck finally arrived one morning, everyone rushed to scrub up and shave off their unkempt beards and mustaches ("I probably had all of nineteen hairs on my face, I was still so young," Bill recalls with a chuckle). The Mink hung his tin mirror on a tree and smeared his face with Barbasol, preparing for a cold water shave. Moments later, a German shell smacked into a nearby tree, too distant to spray shrapnel on the troops, but close enough to cause a chain reaction of timber breaking and falling, sending one large, jagged branch crashing right into Bill's face. It knocked out four front teeth, bruising and cutting him badly.

Mousey took one look at the mix of blood and shaving cream and said, "Jeeze, you look like strawberry shortcake." No one laughed. Numb to the pain, his face swelling like a misshapen balloon, Thomas rode with friends to the nearest field hospital, where the first doctor he encountered, fresh off the boat and apparently appalled by the dirty, smelly soldiers in his office, would do little more than offer him a couple of aspirin in a hand stretched out as far as possible. "My buddies had to hold me back, or I would have been all over that guy and facing a court-martial," Bill recalls. "I remember reaching for my .45, but my holster was empty, fortunately. I was out of my head and he offers me aspirin."

Instead of arguing, Bill's friends drove him to another hospital unit, where a kindly major cleaned and stitched him up.

Bill didn't want to stay longer than absolutely necessary. The Germans often shelled the area, aiming for the local Army headquarters, but frequently falling short and hitting the field hospitals instead. During the Anzio campaign, many hospitalized soldiers were killed, along with six Army nurses, leaving any soldier capable of walking reluctant to linger at the field hospital any longer than necessary. Bill chose to return to the frontline before the novocaine had worn off and he went right back to work.

In the coming days, a troop carrier he was riding would accidentally run famed war correspondent Ernie Pyle off the road (Bill helped dust him off and chatted for a bit), and he would also bump into future Pulitzer-Prize-winning war cartoonist Bill Mauldin, who had pulled over next to a telephone pole the Mink had just climbed, awaiting the passage of a convoy. Bill yelled his thanks for the famous Willie and Joe cartoons Mauldin drew—"The guys love 'em!" he told the cartoonist—and Mauldin waved and thanked him. When your unit is sustaining a 30 percent casualty rate and you're well on your way to a near-record 565 days of active combat duty, you take your high points where you can get them, Bill recalls. (Many years later in California, with Mauldin suffering from Alzheimer's disease and nearing the end of his life, Bill tracked him down to a care facility and visited him with a group of fellow World War II veterans. Bill reminded the old cartoonist of the time they had met in Italy and how much he and his buddies had loved those cartoons in the *Stars and Stripes* military newspaper, how Mauldin managed to give them a laugh when they needed it the most. The cartoonist managed a small smile—the first time, the facility administrator later told Bill, that Mauldin had reacted at all to any visitor in a very long time.)

In April 1944, the American forces at Anzio finally prevailed when the Germans launched a foolhardy frontal assault, with the advancing troops, as far as Bill could tell, fortified to the point of recklessness by copious amounts of schnapps. The carnage was terrible, with the big U.S. artillery pieces lowered to barely clear the heads of the American frontline troops, then blasting into the advancing German soldiers at point-blank range.

Within a few weeks, Bill found himself in a liberated Rome, the Italians offering hugs and flowers, the U.S. Army offering him a few days rest and a quick set of false teeth. The days and battles blurred together after the brief respite in the Italian capital—then the march through France, the advance to the Ardennes forest during the Battle of the Bulge, then crossing into Germany. He'll never forget the stench in the air outside the Nazi death camp at Dachau, or the hoarse cheers of the gaunt prisoners in their striped uniforms, liberated by American troops. The German army at that point was so depleted that the resistance the advancing Americans encountered came mostly from the Volksturm—the people's army—which meant old men and boys with cast-off guns.

Bill remembers walking with his unit past a stockade near the death camp filled with these sad militiamen, thousands of them having surrendered in town after town, when suddenly one of them, no more than fourteen or fifteen years old, lunged at Bill and tried to grab his carbine. It was a foolish, childish impulse that drove the despondent teenager, and he was no match for the combat-hardened solider who had seen too much. Bill reacted instinctively, crashing his rifle butt into the teenager's chin and shoulder, then training the barrel on the boy, Bill's finger beginning to squeeze the trigger, all in one, quick series of motions.

Then he stopped himself as the boy fell backward, and breathing hard, he lowered his rifle and watched as the skinny kid was taken away.

As a small group of older prisoners was escorted past a moment later—men in their late forties and fifties, ragged and haggard—each one turned his head toward Bill and murmured *"danke."*

"In all that time in combat, with everything we had all gone through, that's the closest I ever got to having to shoot someone," Bill Thomas says. "He caught me by surprise and went for my gun; it would have been justified. But I'm glad I didn't."

The war in Europe ended a few weeks later with Bill's unit in Munich. After the surrender, he was sent to Camp Lucky Strike, one of the two main staging areas in France for troops on their way home, and then he returned to the U.S. for his discharge while the war with Japan entered its last days.

Back in Detroit he felt restless, moving from job to job in a country relearning how to live at peace. He took a class in servicing refrigerators and air conditioners, but the work wasn't for him. He did better at selling cookware, which had been in short supply during the war and in great demand afterward. He was seeing a young woman named Lois, who would help him make his sales presentations—preparing meals for would-be customers with the kitchenware while Bill made his pitch. He brought to pots and pans the same relentless energy and organization and easy smile that made him a contest-winning paperboy, but now he was earning up to $1800 a month in commissions, a relative fortune at the time, bringing him new cars, new clothes, new and better lodgings.

He gave it up, though—he says because "all those nights and weekends on the job infringed on my love life"—but the truth is, he had gotten nervous at Lois's talk about marriage, and he broke it off, too young for the commitment and increasingly concerned that the match was not the right one. During a visit to distant cousins in New York, he had met and spent a little time with the daughter of his hosts' friend, a smart and attractive child of Greek immigrants named Soula. Bill could not stop thinking about this woman he hardly knew, which seemed a bit crazy, even to happy-go-lucky Bill. He and his best friend decided that the cure for all this would be to take off to see the world.

First they considered Alaska, hearing there were some good jobs available on America's last frontier. But it was the wrong time of year, they decided—too cold, they weren't acclimated, Bill had slogged through enough bad weather in Europe to last a lifetime. Then they thought perhaps South America, but no, the rainy season had just begun. Who wanted to arrive in a monsoon? Saudi Arabia sounded good, too—oil roustabouts could earn a fortune and live like kings in the desert, with nary a snowflake or tropical storm in sight. But no, guys who could be nicknamed the Mink and shimmy up poles like a cat just weren't burly enough for the roustabout trade, a recruiter told them dismissively. Which is how they ended up going with their fourth choice: a long drive through the West ending in California, where hundreds of thousands of servicemen had trained or bunked down or passed through during the war, liking what they saw and vowing to return. When Bill drove through Long Beach, he saw a sign for a Veterans Administration office and dropped in, asking about work but ending up getting—and ultimately accepting—advice to enroll in college.

He was going to give refrigerator repair another try first, but decided it wasn't for him after he went to apply for a job and found thirty far more experienced journeymen waiting in line to vie for one position. Instead, he chose to pursue a business and marketing degree at Long Beach City College, which in the late forties was bursting with ex-G.I.s. Bill worked a part-time job at the college bookstore between classes and found a room in a boarding house on Ocean Avenue, right near the water in Long Beach, then a booming Navy town, the state's fourth largest city. He paid thirty dollars a week rent on real estate that, sixty years later, would command millions but was then considered shabby, drafty, and undesirable—because it was too unfashionably *near* the beach.

Bill had never thought of himself as college material, but he loved it. The courses he chose were all practical—how to write a business plan, marketing, economics, accounting, business law. One of his classes even included mock job interview sessions, right down to what to wear and how to craft a proper résumé. This was the sort of thing many G.I.s craved, and for guys who had always worked the farm or the assembly line or the docks, it was like receiving a secret password to a white-collar world most of them had never expected to see from the inside. Bill grasped this right away—he was being offered a life in which, if he chose, he would never have to turn a wrench or run a grinder for a living again, not because there was anything wrong with this kind of work, but because suddenly the possibilities seemed so much more varied. This is why city and community colleges, law schools, business programs, and university engineering departments burgeoned in this era, their classes filled with guys with no particular interest in Shakespeare or Tolstoy, but who flocked to practical courses that were useful in making a living.

After completing his studies, Bill immediately put those new skills to work, applying to become the manager of the school bookstore, using his new business and marketing skills to win the job (notwithstanding the fact that his boss-to-be showed up unexpectedly at the erstwhile applicant's apartment, causing the job interview to begin with Bill wearing only his skivvies).

At Christmastime he visited Soula in North Carolina, where he discovered she had four Greek uncles along with a Greek father, each of whom ran a restaurant. His time there consisted of visiting one family restaurant after another with Soula, where the uncles would eye him narrowly, the aunts would stuff him with coffee and pie, and both would barrage him with questions. Bill found himself spending considerable time explaining that there was more to California than "just cowboys and earthquakes"—an opinion held firmly by one uncle who happened to be in Long Beach for the devastating quake of 1933, which knocked down so many municipal buildings and schoolhouses that it ended permanently the practice of constructing unreinforced brick buildings in the Golden State. He assured them that California was prosperous and beautiful and much changed in the past fifteen years, but the uncle kept shaking his head and muttering, "Nothing but earthquakes and cowboys."

Bill's holiday wooing ended with his now legendary marriage proposal and Soula's firmly phrased affirmative, all so spontaneous they had to use a twist of Christmas tinsel in lieu of a ring. The old Greek uncles got a good laugh, which drove Bill to visit a jeweler immediately upon his return to Long Beach so that he could mail Soula a proper engagement ring.

Not long after that, he spotted an enthralling advertisement extolling the ultramodern homes planned for a new place called Lakewood, on terms even a hardworking ex-G.I. with next to nothing in the bank could afford. And he couldn't resist.

If the G.I. Bill of Rights altered the landscape of higher education in America, it transformed the cultural and physical landscape of the country even more dramatically. The American suburban exodus of the 1950s did not simply spring into existence on its own: It is no exaggeration to say that the creation of suburbia and the resulting extension of home ownership to a majority of families in America was launched, underwritten, and paid for by the G.I. Bill.

It's what allowed Bill Thomas, with no real savings and a fairly small paycheck, to impulsively purchase a planned three-bedroom home where there was only a bean field, just as it empowered millions of other veterans and their families to do the same—transforming the nation's cities, its rural areas, its way of life, and even what Americans did on lazy summer evenings (the backyard barbecue industry owes much to the G.I. Bill).

If the bill's transformation of college in America from an elite bastion to a virtual entitlement proved revolutionary, its home loan provisions were nothing short of radical. Not since the Homestead Act of 1862 had stimulated the settlement of vast lands in the American West had the U.S. government so broadly engaged in a redistribution of wealth and property, or intervened so intensely in the areas of home construction, homes sales, and home loans.

Indeed, the G.I. Bill's primary proponent, the American Legion, almost left this provision out, fearing that the home loan benefits could provoke controversy and opposition for many of the same reasons the Homestead Act had failed to pass Congress after decades of attempts; Abraham Lincoln could sign it into law only because the states that had long opposed it had seceded, sparking the Civil War. The twentieth century's suburban version of the Homestead Act arrived additionally burdened with the political fallout of New Deal programs bitterly opposed by congressional conservatives. At stake was the longstanding tradition that elevated home and land ownership as a mark of standing and privilege. Except for ancestral properties handed down across generations, real estate required capital and income to acquire, and therefore implied and conferred a certain status and class. Typical prewar home mortgages required down payments of 50 percent and relatively short periods of time to repay the balance. Just as college was reserved for the elite before World War II, so was home ownership out of reach for a majority of Americans.

Upsetting this long-standing balance with what amounted to an enormous government giveaway and regulatory program was seen by some as bad policy that could destabilize the home and banking industries, promote the construction of slums disguised as affordable housing, and greatly increase the frequency of defaults and foreclosures. The working class (i.e., most veterans), it was said, was better off renting, leaving the complexities of property ownership to landlords. And if economic depression accompanied the end of war, as many had predicted, then issuing a passel of home loans to men who couldn't afford them was just asking for trouble, particularly when the federal government would, under the G.I. Bill's provisions, be stuck with honoring the bad loans if the economy went south.

Opposition had the usual racial component as well. Just as Southern states had voted down the Homestead Act for fear that it would add to the population and power of the free states while undermining the South's slave-powered agricultural dominance, so, too, did defenders of segregation rise in opposition to the G.I. Bill. They feared the bill would become a tool for de facto desegregation because it explicitly treated all veterans equally, regardless of race or gender—a first for federal legislation and a potentially explosive point in a nation in which housing was still largely segregated.

The proponents of the G.I. Bill home loan provisions, however, cleverly played on the fears and desires of both progressives and conservatives to advance their cause, giving all sides something to embrace. For the progressives, there was the obvious benefit of home ownership for a much broader segment of the population than ever before imagined—mortgages for the masses, bank loans even a wage earner on an assembly line could love. The image of the hoi poloi buying homes next to bankers and corporate moguls warmed many a progressive's heart.

For the business lobby, there was the simple fact that the home building and home loan industry needed a major helping hand, for they had been ground into the dust by the Great Depression and the war. The country saw home foreclosures top one thousand a day by the time Hoover left the White House and Roosevelt walked in. At that point, evictions in major cities reached double, then triple the pre-Depression rate. Half the country's mortgage debt was in default, and housing starts in 1933 were one-tenth the pre-Depression level. There had been some recovery by 1940, with housing starts climbing to a still-anemic 50,000 a month. But war the following year sent home construction plummeting even further than the Depression had, with the nadir reached in 1943, when ground was broken on a paltry 11,800 homes a month—for the entire nation. That was less than one house for every town and city in America. (By comparison, during the postwar housing boom the Los Angeles area alone would break ground on that many homes in a week.)

Even before the end of the war, the housing shortage in urban areas had become a nightmare, so no one doubted that this pent-up demand would explode when the troop ships started coming home. The notion of veterans buying new homes in droves, sparking a wave of construction—with loans guaranteed by the federal government—had the home builders and bankers all but salivating. They could see an economic rebirth on the horizon.

But kill the G.I. Bill home loan provisions, and the consequences could be catastrophic, proponents warned: If millions of veterans arrived home to massive housing shortages with no end in sight and no opportunity to find a place of their own, then the resulting unrest could make the World War I bonus march pale in comparison. Sixteen million veteran marchers—or voters—could cause a great deal of political upheaval, even revolt, it was said. And therein was a third argument, one that appealed to the growing anti-Communist factions in the country, who came to believe that home ownership—one of the great potential benefits of capitalism—would diminish interest in the socialist solutions that had gained currency during the Depression. Home ownership was said to be the best insurance policy against creeping socialism—even if it took an immense exercise in socialism to accomplish it.

For that is what the G.I. Bill boiled down to: the government transferring wealth to veterans. The bill allowed them to acquire capital without a capital investment—no down payment for a new home. It circumvented all state laws on mortgages and lending to allow normally unqualified people to buy. And then it insulated lenders from any risk for these low-interest, low-payment, high-risk loans, by guaranteeing the mortgages and assuming responsibility for each home financed, and its resale in the event a veteran defaulted. The free market, in essence, was removed from the equation to create a new middle class of homeowners who, it was thought, would inevitably become more conservative and less interested in Big Government solutions as their home equity grew. As one sociologist put it at the time, "Socialism and Communism do not take root in the ranks of those who have their feet firmly embedded in the sod of America through home ownership," a sentiment later affirmed by President Roosevelt, who observed that "a nation of home owners . . . is unconquerable."

The G.I. Bill home loan proponents were soon proved correct: The citizen-veterans of the new suburbs did become more politically conservative and less inclined, overall, to support Big Government solutions to civic problems. Even support for organized labor, which had achieved its greatest level of power and reach during and immediately after the war, began its long, slow decline with the suburban migration sparked by the G.I. Bill. Meanwhile, the wave of home ownership prompted by the G.I. Bill propelled the rapid postwar expansion of the middle class. Before the war, less than 10 percent of the population would have been considered by contemporary standards middle class in terms of income and assets; by the end of the fifties, the middle class represented a third of the nation's population.

None of the authors and sponsors of the bill envisioned the end result, however. It was assumed, when it was discussed at all, that home building would continue as it always had—small-scale construction by craftsmen-builders adding on to existing developments, with the gradual expansion of cities and towns outward from their centers. Most Americans were supposed to remain renters.

At the time, only one in six Americans lived in what could be called the suburbs. Except for a small number of prototype planned communities designed under the New Deal such as the utopian Greenbelt, Maryland, affordable-housing project, suburban construction was extremely varied and idiosyncratic. No one had ever used the term "cookie cutter" to describe suburban houses before the postwar boom. And no one expected the nation's entire panorama to be redrawn—the G.I. Bill's home loan provisions would simply get the home industry back on its feet, it was believed. It would level the playing field for the returning veterans, something the World War I vets had long sought and never really achieved.

But a builder and veteran named Bill Levitt had glimpsed a different future while working as a contractor building military housing during the war, and later, as an officer with a Navy Seabee construction battalion. In the Navy, Levitt observed for the first time the techniques of high-speed, assembly-line-style construction and use of prefabricated building elements for everything from airstrips to barracks to bridges. He was enthralled with the idea.

After the war, Levitt's genius lay in being the first to foresee the enormous profit potential sitting dormant in the combined forces of the nation's housing shortage, the millions of returning G.I.s, and the generous loan benefits of the G.I. Bill. If he could add to that mixture the sort of assembly line techniques used by the Seabees, then a construction company like Levitt's—successful but small before the war—could transform itself into something else: no longer a home builder, but a developer, a new and entirely different animal. Why build a home or two at a time when the demand (and, more importantly, the government subsidy) was there to build whole neighborhoods—hell, whole towns—all at once? Such houses would be inexpensive by virtue of volume and mass production techniques, and therefore as easy to buy as renting a home had always been.

The result of Levitt's insight was the prototype for all of America's modern suburbs as well as for the mass production techniques that created them, a name that is virtually synonymous with housing development in the 1950s: Levittown.

"This is Levittown! All yours for $58. You're a lucky fellow, Mr. Veteran," read a *New York Times* advertisement for that prototype of American suburbia a few months after the end of World War II. More than 1400 homes, to be erected on a potato field on Long Island, were sold within a day of that ad. Soon there would be 17,000 largely identical two-bedroom, 800-square-foot Cape Cod–style houses, followed by a ranch-style model to break the monotony, all planted in that field. Most sold for under $8,000, with (if you were a veteran) no money down.

In many cases, it was cheaper to buy than to rent.

As Henry Ford had revolutionized the auto industry with mass production techniques, Levitt revolutionized home building, winning a construction code change that allowed him to leave out basements entirely—all the houses of Levittown were built on concrete slabs. There would be no building of individual houses, one at a time, there. Entire blocks went up at once, one crew dedicated to pouring concrete, the next to smoothing it, the next to erecting the framing, the next to nailing, and so on—each following the other from house to house, street to street. Crews with minimal training and few skills could put up houses in this way at startling speeds.

The dark side of this tale, however, was the complete violation of the egalitarian and color-blind language of the G.I. Bill. Shamefully, Levittown, like many other heavily subsidized new suburbs of the late forties and fifties, took the concerns of segregationists to heart by adopting racial housing covenants that made these new communities white only, walling off this new American dream from black and brown veterans and any other potential buyers of color. Because the U.S. government controlled the purse strings, such covenants, which many years later would be ruled unconstitutional, could have been prevented by federal edict right from the beginning. Instead, the Federal Housing Administration, which oversaw the G.I. Bill housing program, condoned and even encouraged the creation of restrictive racial covenants. Even baseball legend Willie Mays, who moved West when the New York Giants became the San Francisco Giants in 1957, was turned away from the home he wanted to buy in a new Bay Area suburb because of such covenants. The G.I. Bill's promise of home ownership that so profoundly altered the lives of so many veterans; that raised so many low-income families into the middle class; and that could have become such a potent force to advance civil rights, equality, and desegregation, was largely withheld from black veterans.

But home builders were not looking to become conduits for social change—not unless they were forced to. They wanted to sell houses. It didn't take long for builders in other communities across the country to figure out that Levitt had discovered a gold mine of veteran housing demand and government subsidies in his Long Island potato field. Levittown-like instant communities began springing up throughout the nation (while Levitt built new Levittowns in Pennsylvania and New Jersey).

The next big one was Lakewood, California, which billed itself, in true California fashion, as bigger and better than Levittown. The houses were larger and a bit more stylish (some had three bedrooms), the lots were bigger, and unlike Levittown, the tracts had been developed around a new shopping center—an instant mini-downtown for a new suburban community, which Lakewood's developer relentlessly pitched as a distinction that made it, not Levittown, the first planned community.

The developers bought their 3,350 acres of farmland in 1949 and quickly drew up their plans. As the last harvest was picked, the bulldozers sat waiting, then immediately scraped the land to stubble, laying out the grid of the city-to-be. D.J. Waldie, a lifelong resident of Lakewood, describes the creation of this new suburb in his poetic book *Holy Land,* noting how the developers proudly displayed aerial photographs depicting their project's progress in reducing the landscape to a surreal grid: "The photographs celebrate house frames precise as cells in a hive and stucco walks fragile as an unearthed bone. Seen from above, the grid is beautiful and terrible."

According to Waldie, the future town was scraped so perfectly flat that there is less than a one-foot variation in elevation from one end of town to the other.

Crews of thirty worked their way down the grid, assembling houses with the Levitt mass-production method, completing as many as fifty a day in a development that would ultimately have 17,500 new houses. Cement trucks would line up for more than a mile waiting to pour foundations.

In 1950 Lakewood was dubbed the fastest growing housing development anywhere in the world. Mortgages started at under $50 a month for the two bedroom models; buyers could opt to have a refrigerator, washing machine, and gas range waiting for them inside for an extra $9 a month per appliance.

With one street of model homes completed, the sales office opened for the first time on Palm Sunday in April 1950. As Waldie tells it, 25,000 people showed up that weekend to tour the houses, with a crew of community college students on hand to escort them. A hundred homes sold in one hour.

The creation of Lakewood that Bill Thomas witnessed and photographed became a bellwether, but not a singular one. Developers throughout Los Angeles, and then the nation, followed the winning formula of Levitt and Lakewood: inexpensive construction and labor methods; smaller houses that used fewer materials; and government subsidies that made buying easy, selling easier, lending essentially risk free (except to taxpayers), and developer profits enormous. As one after another suburban development paved over rural Southern California, Lakewood proved to be the beginning of the end of the Los Angeles of orange groves, dairy farms, and Red Car trolleys. The prewar Los Angeles that Raymond Chandler celebrated for its vast hardness and mocked as having "no more personality than a paper cup," was soon displaced by suburban sprawl, brown smog, ribbons of freeway, and a riverbed lined with concrete to make floods—and nature—all but impossible. "Los Angeles," *Time* magazine announced in a special cover issue, "will never be like anything else on Earth."

The suburban phenomenon took off everywhere then. By the end of 1950, four houses were being built nationwide, on average, every minute. Seventy-five percent of them were in the new suburbia, as were three-quarters of America's new, first-time homeowners. Housing starts went from a wartime low of one new house per thousand Americans in 1944, to twelve new houses per thousand Americans in 1950—a phenomenal rate of home building that has never been matched. Nearly five million World War II veterans bought homes with G.I. Bill benefits, representing close to half the new homes constructed nationwide in the decade after the end of the war. In booming parts of the country such as California, veterans' mortgages accounted for a good deal more than half.

The result was the transformation of America into a nation where a majority of people live in their own houses, and in the suburbs. The quantum leap in the percentage of Americans who owned their homes in the immediate postwar era has never been matched since.

The result also was a hollowing out of our cities never envisioned by the G.I. Bill authors, but in retrospect, a fate that became inevitable the moment word got out that Bill Levitt had sold 1,400 unbuilt houses in a single day. It was unheard of and irresistible; a force had been unleashed that no one could stop, not that many tried.

That it caught the nation unawares is to put it mildly. Within a year of the end of the war, the government and private industry housing experts from the major trade organizations produced estimates on what they believed the postwar housing boom would look like: a healthy 400,000 units built a year (which represented a huge increase over anemic wartime construction), split evenly between public housing, urban renewal projects, apartment complexes, and single-family homes.

Instead, the G.I. Bill brought into being nearly 2 million new homes built in 1950 alone, 85 percent of them single-family houses, almost all in new developments. The experts never saw it coming.

The ripple effect on the economy proved electrifying: The new homes spurred the furniture, appliance, and housewares industries, along with road building, utilities, department stores, service stations, and milk and bread delivery businesses—a new infrastructure to support these new communities. New schools were built for a G.I. generation having children in record numbers, and new teachers, many of them G.I. Bill–educated, flocked to those new classrooms, then bought homes in the same suburban tracts.

The birth rate peaked for the twentieth century, with 4.3 million births in 1957 (an immense birth rate of 25.3 babies for every 1,000 U.S. citizens). That represented a 50 percent increase when compared to the birth rate of 1939. It was double the birthrate the country would experience in the year 2001.

And, finally, the result of this housing and baby boom was a new type of community, remote from the cities and linked not by readily available public transit but by automobile. At a time when most families had only one car, the new suburban lifestyle encouraged (if not required) many women, who had made so many employment gains during the war, to become stay-at-home moms.

The uniformity of the home styles, the somewhat barren landscape (the plants and trees would take years to fill out), and the dearth of cultural attractions city dwellers value made the new suburban communities easy targets for social critics: The new communities were boring, homogeneous, soulless—corporate homes for the new "organization man," it was said.

But the veterans who snapped up those new homes were coming from a different outlook, a different place—from boarding houses and cramped apartments and lives that just a few years earlier had offered little hope of college or home ownership or lasting financial security. The average income in Lakewood was about $5,000 a year in 1950. Yet now they had backyards and barbecues and streets where the kids could ride their bikes without fear of being run over. Who cared if the houses were small? They could always be expanded—the Levittown attics had room for a couple add-on upstairs bedrooms, and those Lakewood homes with their nice backyards could easily handle a tacked-on room or two. And every property owner knows that once you have a house, you can always sell it and buy a bigger, better one.

That was the truly liberating aspect of all this: Men with almost no money, who just a few years earlier had occupied trenches and PT boats and bombers while watching 400,000 of their fellows die and far more of them fall wounded—guys who had always just scraped by, paycheck to paycheck—were now property owners. The G.I. Bill gave them a ticket to the middle class, gave them security, a nest egg, a future. And once those suburbs went up, the developers realized the demand far outstripped just the number of the veterans—others could buy in as well at a cost low enough that many nonveterans of modest means could afford the down payment, which ran in the hundreds rather than the thousands of dollars. The G.I. Bill created an economy of scale that benefited a much larger population.

It was easy to forget, amid the glitzy advertisements that stressed the industrial prowess of the private developers and the hardworking veterans who had earned those homes, that all this was possible not because of the magic of free markets, but because of federal largesse on the grandest of scales, Big Government at its biggest.

Where the critics would later see blight and the ruin of cities and the exclusion of nonwhites, the new suburbanites saw a dream come true, a promised land they had never expected to find when they returned from the war, and that had never awaited any other generation of veterans.

"No doubt about it," Bill Thomas says. "I was very lucky. Still am."

When Bill next returned to North Carolina, he drove cross-country in his chrome-laden '49 Mercury. Before going to see Soula, he stopped at a department store in downtown Durham to pick up a fresh shirt, and he was surprised when the sales clerk drawled, "You're Bill, aren't you?" When he nodded, taken aback, the clerk called to a co-worker, "Here's Soula's finance!"

It got worse when he strolled into City Hall to find his fiancée. People he didn't know greeted him in the hallway. *Hi, Bill! How's the house, Bill? Loved the pictures, Bill.* Then he saw the bulletin board along the building's main corridor, with the before and after pictures of Lakewood and their new home, along with a snapshot of himself, and he blushed a bit at his unexpected celebrity.

Some, particularly several of Soula's uncles, were unimpressed by what they had seen and resumed trying to talk Soula out of the move west and the marriage itself. Bill finally won them over at a big party before the wedding, when the uncles continued to criticize California and its people as somehow shifty or unreliable. Bill told them to relax, that he actually was a Michigander by birth, a word that amused them.

"And I guess that makes you all Durmites," he continued. "You know, in California, we exterminate Durmites."

They stared at him. He continued, "So they don't chew up our houses."

The Greek uncles burst into laughter and told Bill he was all right. He soon became the stuff of family legend by showing up late for the enormous Greek wedding, having gotten stuck in traffic behind a row of slow-moving farm trucks and tractors coming to market in Durham that day. He rushed in so hastily he forgot he was chewing on a stick of Doublemint, and he had to feign a cough at the altar, moving the gum to his hand then surreptitiously dropping it to the floor. He almost got away with this little stunt—until the part in the traditional Greek ceremony where the couple was symbolically bound with two loops of ribbon, at which point they had to walk around the altar three times with the priest at their side. The priest stepped in the wad of gum and began sticking to the ground with every step. No one in the church but Bill knew why the priest appeared to be walking so haltingly, and the new groom practically had to choke himself to avoid bursting out laughing.

In the car, he and Soula giggled all the way to the reception when he told her. The priest later shook his hand and made a pointed comment about doing his best to avoid future "sticky" situations in life.

In 1951, Bill and Soula moved into their new house in Lakewood, where their family soon included two daughters and a son. Bill went to work as a salesman for a specialty envelope company, then after fourteen years changed careers to became one of the first financial planners in the area. He spent the rest of his working days introducing his fellow suburbanites to a then-novel vehicle for investing—mutual funds. Bill was an early adopter, long before the mutual fund craze began in the eighties. He felt it was an investment perfectly suited for the new suburbanites, who suddenly had earning power and equity—and responsibilities—they had never imagined. It was their money, lying fallow in savings accounts or whole life insurance policies with abysmal rates of return, that helped the mutual fund industry take off, and helped guys like Bill find their true calling, a chance to use their salesmanship and organizational skills and witty, easy manner to make others' lives better and their financial situations more secure.

Like many of Lakewood's first residents, Bill and his family soon outgrew their little "starter" home—that, too, was a new term for the era. A friend of theirs had moved from Lakewood to the nearby Orange County, California, community of Rossmoor, and when they visited one evening to play pinochle, he and Soula admired the big fireplace, the swimming pool in the backyard, the separate dining room. Suddenly their 1,100 square feet of paradise in Lakewood looked a little sparse and cramped. The children, Tim, Mary, and Zoe, were getting older and wanted their own rooms, and a swimming pool sure would be nice. And so one weekend in 1961, the Thomases visited a home for sale in the same little community their friends had chosen, tucked next to the coastal town of Seal Beach, and they bought it that same day for the then-princely sum of $24,000. It was a financial squeeze, but they got a good price for their home in Lakewood—twice what they had paid—and managed to scrape by, which, Bill says, is what his generation of World War II veterans and children of the Depression have always managed to do.

Bill and Soula still live in that Rossmoor house, on that same leafy street. At eighty-one, he is retired but still does, gratis, the occasional financial plan for friends and their children. He is active in the local post of the Veterans of Foreign Wars, writing their monthly newsletter (as well as several stories and novels based on his wartime experiences), and in 2004 he was honored by the American Legion and VFW for designing a World War II memorial plaque on display in the city of Seal Beach's oceanside park. Soula, meanwhile, has become an avid race walker who frequently competes; she recently went to Spain with her walking group for a race there.

The Thomas kids grew up in that Rossmoor house, then all went to college, and all three became teachers—two in public schools (his middle daughter, Mary, was named teacher of the year in her school district not long ago) and his youngest an aerobics instructor with her own house and kids in Rossmoor—a new generation, carrying on the dream.

"My education, my house, the life we were able to give our children, sending them to college so they could become teachers and pass it all on—all of it was possible because of that wonderful G.I. Bill," Bill says. "What an amazing thing for our government to have done for us—I had no idea it was coming while I was over there. It would have been a long time before we could have bought a house without it . . . People like to complain about taxes, about government, my generation particularly. But this was government getting it right, doing something great, building something great. Who can complain about that?"

☆ 4 ☆

Bill and Vivian Kingsley:
G.I. Tech

It was a little thing, really, but it stayed with him for years, a deeply satisfying memory. Sitting outside Harrods in London, resting after a marathon shopping expedition with his wife, the retired schoolteacher from Sun City, Arizona, heard a voice call out his name, an American midwestern twang unmistakable on a street thick with black London cabs and proper British accents.

"Mr. Kingsley! Mr. Kingsley!" A young man rushed over, his hand extended. "I just wanted to say hello. I've never forgotten your class."

They chatted for a bit, then parted, the former student with his whole life ahead of him and the retired teacher with most of his lived. The words stuck in his head, as they often did after these kinds of meetings, the pride as fresh now as ever: *I've never forgotten your class.*

Almost wherever he goes, he seems to run into an ex-student, some young man or woman he can barely place but who vividly recalls a comical dissection lesson in biology class, or the photography elective sessions he loved to teach, or the time he and his wife looked after the young woman whose mother had passed away just before the Christmas holiday. He hears it all the time, teachers and doctors and pharmacists and photographers he's met on the street or at the market or out at dinner, calling, *Mr. Kingsley, Mr. Kingsley! Remember me?* This is the reward a lifelong teacher earns, tonic for a man who went from high school dropout to G.I. Bill veteran to would-be doctor to a teacher who loved his job so much he could barely wait for vacations to end, just so he could get back to work. Back to his kids. Back to the job he never knew he'd love until he stood in front of his first class.

Bill Kingsley taught on average one hundred kids a semester, two hundred students a year. He figures somewhere on the order of eight thousand young men and women passed through his classrooms during his four-decade career in the public schools of Denver. Influenced a few kids, he figures, changed a few lives. How many jobs give you that kind of reward?

"Not a bad legacy, eh, Vivian?"

His wife, two bulging Harrods bags in hand, smiled. "No, not bad at all."

William Kingsley and Vivian Erickson met in 1944 while stationed at St. Albans Naval Hospital in Queens, New York, where she served as a nurse with an ensign's rank and he as a pharmacist's mate, the Navy's noncommissioned version of a physician's assistant. Their sprawling military medical center, built on the once-grand grounds of the St. Albans Golf Course, a favorite of such local luminaries as Babe Ruth until the Depression bankrupted its owners, had become a major arrival point for thousands of wounded sailors and Marines.

Vivian was born in 1920 in what was then rural Connecticut, near Middletown, the retirement home of her grandmother, a genuine prairie schooner homesteader who once received an apology from Sitting Bull for a red tablecloth his braves had stolen from her house. Vivian was schooled in New York City, where her father had a hardware business, but it was the Connecticut countryside she most craved. Vivian loved that old house where her grandmother had two kitchens, the summer kitchen for canning, the winter kitchen for cooking. She learned how to cook on a woodstove, learned how to can the beans her grandma grew and how to make sarsaparilla for cool summer nights, and she rarely gave thought to leaving her little slice of paradise.

But then her young beau joined the Navy and went off to war, as had all his friends and the other young men of Middletown. When torpedoes sank his boat in the North Sea, killing everyone onboard, Vivian decided to go into training as a nurse and join the Navy, eager to help with the war effort that had claimed her boyfriend. Her first posting was St. Albans, where the casualties were numerous but for the most part relatively minor—men who would be whole again. She was head nurse, never dour or brusque, but caring and warm—a smile-generator, her future husband would later call her, the sort of person whose mere presence evokes smiles, even in hospitals or grocery lines. Anywhere.

"Still lights up a room—she hasn't changed," says Bill Kingsley sixty years later. During her nightly bed checks at St. Albans, the diminutive Vivian, with her wavy, honey-colored hair, counted the wedding proposals she received from her patients by the dozen.

But it was Bill Kingsley who caught her attention.

He grew up in New York City with his father, who worked as an agent for photographers, supplementing his income by selling candy at the movies. His parents had divorced during the Depression when Bill was nine. At seventeen, his father died and Bill dropped out of school, finding a job as an office boy at the General Artists Corporation and living in a hotel near the old RKO Theater in downtown Manhattan, his future anything but promising.

The draft notice arrived in 1943. When he reported at the induction center there were two lines, one to the Army, one to the Navy. A man with a checklist looked him up and down and then jerked a thumb at the right, the Army line, but a few steps farther on, Bill impulsively veered to the left, toward the Navy, thinking, somehow, the sea would be safer than the mud.

As it happened, he was never shipped overseas. He finished boot camp, then training as a pharmacist's mate, and landed at St. Albans, where manpower was short as casualties mounted. Shortly after he arrived and watched in amazement the mixture of efficiency, kindness, agony, and heroism on display at St. Albans, he reached two decisions: He wanted to become a doctor, and he wanted to be with Vivian. He saw her intelligence, her sense of duty, her innate sense of how to work with patients and make them feel better about themselves, and decided to do all he could to forge a relationship.

"He was different than anyone else," Vivian recalls with a smile, the tall, serious young man of 1944 still vivid in her mind's eye sixty years later. "He had a patch on his sleeve. One day I put a penny under it, for luck, just as a favor. And he made me take it out—it wasn't quite cricket, he said. And I thought, this guy has something. Anyone else would have pretended to appreciate that lucky penny, just to please me. I liked that . . . I realized he had potential."

When Vivian was transferred to the Patuxent River Naval Hospital in Maryland, a major waypoint for some of the most severely wounded sailors and Marines returned from war, Bill soon followed, transferring to the naval dispensary at Solomon's Island, a short ferry ride away. "I knew it was fate, then," Vivian says. Even as they grappled with treating some of the worst wounded in the war, including a wave of casualties from D-Day—double, triple, quadruple amputees, men who would never fully recover, faces and voices still vivid in Vivian's memory—the couple found a way to continue their courtship, a source of strength, solace, and hope.

They married within the year, and their first son was born the next. After the war and their discharge from the Navy, Bill turned to Vivian and said, "I'm going nowhere without an education. I want to go back to school."

So he returned to high school—an all-girl's school in New York, which he attended at night, cramming two years of crash courses into one semester, passing all the regents exams necessary to secure his high school diploma. His goal was to use the G.I. Bill to go on to get his college degree, and then apply to medical school.

Vivian had spent time in the West and loved Colorado, so Bill applied to the University of Denver. To his mild surprise, he was accepted by the private school. When Vivian learned that the university had an advanced nursing degree program, she decided to apply with her G.I. Bill benefits, and was accepted as well. The idea was that her degree would qualify her as a school nurse, freeing her from the erratic and long hours of hospital night shifts and private nursing. She became one of about sixty women veterans at the

University of Denver at that time, attending through the G.I. Bill—a representative number, given that about 3 percent of G.I. Bill college students nationally were former WACs, WAVES, or other female veterans of the war.

In 1947, scared to death, the couple arrived on campus and found themselves in a sea of bodies, lines backed up for hours as students waited impatiently to sign up for classes. The campus overflowed with veterans, thousands more than the school was designed to handle. As they held hands and considered this strange world of philosophers and engineers and fraternities, so different from the Navy in which they had cared for the wounded and in the process grown up, Vivian and Bill had to wonder if they had made a terrible mistake.

If any school could serve as a case study of the impact, reach, and consequences of the G.I. Bill on higher education, it would be the private college that sits in the heart of Colorado's mile-high capital. The University of Denver, referred to on campus and around town simply as DU, but during the postwar years as G.I. Tech because of the enormous number of vets enrolled, was both rescued and transformed by the bill—a pattern by no means unique, but particularly dramatic at this snowy hilltop campus.

As with so many other American institutions of higher learning, there is a clear demarcation between the pre- and postwar eras at DU, a boundary that marks not the wartime interruption and peacetime resumption of normalcy that had always occurred in past times of conflict, but rather a very clear and permanent metamorphosis. There would be no return to the prewar world for America's colleges and universities. After one hundred and seventy years, college in America, long based on the European model—

traditional and elite—had evolved into a distinctly American experience—progressive and egalitarian.

DU had deep but humble roots, founded as the Colorado Seminary in 1864 by John Evans, President Lincoln's appointed territorial governor. The school began with three instructors and thirty male students studying a classical curriculum of algebra, rhetoric, French, Latin, music, and theology. A poor state economy led to closure of the school within three years, and it did not reopen until 1880, at which time the college football team was nicknamed the Fighting Parsons. Within a few years, a financial scandal gripped the campus, leaving it debt ridden and facing permanent closure. The school was rescued by Henry Buchtel, a prominent Methodist minister and friend of industrial magnate Andrew Carnegie. Buchtel went on to become governor of Colorado, but not before raising sufficient money to put the school on a firm financial footing, and building a new campus on the current hilltop location. He gave the revitalized school a new main building and an observatory with what was at the time one of the major refracting telescopes in the world. The new campus was rechristened the University of Denver.

Buchtel's reincarnated school established itself immediately as defiantly coeducational and open to all races and religions, at a time when such openness remained extremely rare. Its academic reputation grew throughout the twenties and thirties, particularly for its science instruction, its unique school of "librarianship," and, most of all, for its pioneering international studies program headed by Ben M. Cherrington, who interrupted his career at the university to join the Roosevelt administration in 1938 as the first director of the U.S. State Department's Division of Cultural Relations. Cherrington's progressive outlook—his oft-repeated credo in Washington and at DU was, "The human race ought to get along!"—led Roosevelt to tap him as a coauthor of the United Nations charter, and he helped found UNESCO (the United Nations Educational, Scientific, and Cultural Organization). His influence and contacts brought national and world leaders to the campus regularly.

The school prospered through 1928, with enrollment peaking at more than 3,500 students, then struggled along with the rest of the country's institutions of higher learning during the Depression. In the years leading up to World War II, enrollment stagnated, averaging about 3,000 students. Plans for expansion and construction on the campus stalled for more than a decade.

The retrenchment only intensified with the outbreak of war and the departure of millions of the nation's college-age men for military duty. Universities typically saw their student bodies shrink by a third or more during the war years. College enrollments nationwide had hit 1.4 million in 1939; they reached a low point of 750,000 during the war.

Remaining enrollments were heavily weighted toward women, shattering out of necessity a century of stereotypes and creating obligations and opportunities that hadn't previously existed for young women—from coveted slots in engineering programs, to practical training in auto mechanics, to the editorship of college newspapers. The numbers of women enrolled in engineering programs rose 75 percent during the war, women in pharmacy studies went up 60 percent, and journalism and architecture enrollment by women rose 12 and 14 percent respectively. Overall, however, the number of women in college dropped during the war, as enrollments in the two college subjects then traditionally dominated by women—teacher training and home economics—declined. Many women took defense industry and government work instead of opting for college, filling jobs emptied by the draft.

Law schools and small liberal arts colleges were hardest hit by the war, with total enrollment drops of 50 to 70 percent. Some simply shut down. Even the Ivy Leagues suffered, sometimes dramatically; Yale University in 1944 found its total undergraduate enrollment down to 565. The previous freshman class alone, before the war, topped 800.

Typical of the war-years declines, enrollment at the University of Denver dropped to just over 2,000 students. Even the young chancellor, Caleb Gates, who had left a professorship at Princeton University to head the Denver campus, departed to serve in the Army.

Early in the war, DU became one of many colleges pressed into service as part of the war effort, a role embraced both out of a sense of duty and out of necessity: Converting classrooms and manpower to serve the military was considered a moral necessity, but it also meant an influx of much-needed government cash that kept many a school afloat.

The transition to a wartime footing represented a sudden reversal for many students and schools, long a base of opposition to involvement in the conflict. At Denver, as elsewhere, college students, while expressing horror at the war in Europe and the depredations of Hitler, previously had little appetite for direct involvement. Indeed, in the decade preceding the war, the nation's college campuses had served as a center for antiwar rallies and protests, a movement that advocated less U.S. defense spending and a national posture of strict neutrality. Starting in 1935 and continuing for the next six years every April, college campuses across the country staged simultaneous rallies for peace, students and professors alike championing the cause. The protestors sent thousands of petitions to President Roosevelt calling for neutrality, with many of the students vowing not to participate in any war, and campus newspapers routinely editorializing in favor of the antiwar movement.

In contrast to the sixties-era college protests against the Vietnam war, antiwar fervor in the thirties was a sentiment expressed strongest at the nation's most politically conservative campuses, such as Penn State University, where campus straw polls had overwhelmingly supported Herbert Hoover's doomed reelection bid over FDR in 1932; the students there (like most of the Republican politicians they supported) proudly called themselves isolationists. Yale University was another hotbed of conservative antiwar sentiment, where a small cadre of Nazi sympathizers and a much larger number of die-hard isolationists rallied repeatedly against involvement in the conflict. When a speaker was invited to the campus and passionately argued in favor of America entering the war to protect democracy and halt atrocities, the student body listened politely, then voted firmly in favor of staying out of the war, two to one.

Even after Hitler conquered France and blitzed Britain, opinion remained decidedly mixed on college campuses; a majority of students favored material support to the British, but not the commitment of troops or even weapons. FDR's announcement in 1940 that America would nevertheless supply arms to Great Britain— "We must be the great arsenal of democracy," he told a skeptical nation—generated enormous controversy, for many considered it a provocation that would lead America to war. A poll at Ohio State University in late 1941, representative of many colleges at the time, found 77 percent of students opposed a U.S. declaration of war on Germany. Some colleges became asylums for persecuted Jewish academics—Princeton University famously "adopted" Albert Einstein, while impoverished, progressive Black Mountain College in North Carolina took great pains to offer asylum to several Jewish scholars—but others did nothing, notably Yale, which maintained strictly limited Jewish student quotas and accepted no refugee academics. Instead, Kingman Brewster, then a student at Yale and a future president of the university, helped found the America First Committee, which attracted a number of public figures and civil leaders in voicing opposition to American aid to the British, among them renowned aviator Charles Lindbergh. When Lindbergh spoke on campus against American intervention in the war, cheering students packed the Yale auditorium to overflowing.

College students were by no means out of the mainstream in their thinking. Isolationism, embraced to one degree or another by eight of out of ten Americans, remained in favor on and off college campuses right up until December 7, 1941. War was not considered inevitable until that moment.

The antiwar sentiments that preceded America's entry into the most terrible conflict in human history are often glossed over and forgotten in accounts of the era, given the incredible motivation, dedication of purpose, and national unity that transformed the country once Pearl Harbor was attacked. But there is no question that a majority of college students and teachers initially, like the rest of the country, adamantly opposed entering what many believed would be Armageddon, and that the antiwar movement was, at the time, a deeply conservative political cause.

So powerful were the isolationist forces that, in August 1941, with the military draft about to expire and the U.S. Army, as a result, about to disintegrate, the House of Representatives approved President Roosevelt's urgent request to extend the draft by a single vote—arguably altering the course of world history. Without that vote, America's already underwhelming military could never have mobilized as quickly as it did once war ceased being avoidable just a few months later. The country would have been all but defenseless. America's entry into the war, the defense of United States territory, Hitler's defeat, America's future status as superpower, and the ability of the country to sustain something so powerful, generous, and life-changing as the G.I. Bill, all came down to that one-vote margin on August 12, 1941, at a time when most Americans simply didn't believe Germany and Japan were a threat to us, or that joining the fight was worth the risk.

The surprise attack on Pearl Harbor abruptly altered that equation. Overnight, the isolationists vanished. And colleges and universities became integral to the war effort, with hundreds of thousands of students signed up as a reserve force, with the goal of training them to be platoon leaders or to fill other skilled positions once they graduated.

University of Denver students had just departed for their holiday break when news of the attack on Pearl Harbor arrived. They returned to find a starkly altered campus, with spring vacation canceled so that students about to leave for military service could finish their classes and get full credit for the year. Nationwide, it was not uncommon for colleges during the war years to confer degrees in two and half years or less, speeding up graduations—and enlistments. The University of Illinois created an entire war curriculum, while the bastion of the antiwar movement, Penn State, reversed itself with a vengeance, enrolling 1,500 men and women in more than fifty defense and military courses, including marksmanship, bomb defusing, and aerial photography. The isolationists and America Firsters also seemed to vanish at Yale, where seven of the ten residential colleges on campus were turned over to the military, and the Army opened one of its many college-based aviation schools there for churning out "ninety-day wonders"—the pilots who got their officer's commissions after three intense months of training. In Northampton, Massachusetts, meanwhile, the all-women Smith College gave over half its dormitory space to the Navy's WAVES officer training program, and used its astronomy department to train students as airplane spotters.

At the University of Denver, old Carnegie Hall—donated three decades earlier by the mogul as a library and since transformed into the student union—underwent another transformation. The university hangout became a military mess hall and post exchange.

Night school classes began at DU for training in defense jobs, and a satellite campus sprang up to accommodate the military trainees. Aviation classes formed almost overnight: Students could choose flight training or glider training. One class taught combat engineering; other classes for inductees offered crash courses in French, German, Bulgarian, Russian, and Italian. Military geography and map reading, and the mathematics of trajectories, artillery, and troop movements were rolled into the curriculum, while electronics courses were beefed up to include avionics, radar, and radio. Civil defense and first-aid classes were filled with women on campus and from the community at large. Professors became air raid wardens. Nineteen-year-old girls learned how to repair Jeeps, to apply tourniquets, and to assist in battlefield surgery should the war arrive on the U.S. mainland, as many feared. Flying contests were staged for local high school students to measure their aptitude as pilots, with the winners offered scholarships and early entry into the Army Air Corps.

Men in uniform marched across campus and filled the classrooms, then vanished after a few weeks of training as orders to some distant front arrived. Pilot cadets turned the fraternity houses and dormitories into makeshift barracks.

The carefree mixture of lofty and naïve pronouncements that had marked the school's yearbooks in the past gave way to a deeply somber, surprisingly mature tone: a reflection of a nation at war; of young people suddenly asked to grow up faster than had been expected just a few months earlier; of a conflict that threatened a way of life, and an outcome that, in the first years of the war, looked far from certain.

In 1943, the University of Denver yearbook for the first time featured an "In Memoriam" page that was not devoted to aged faculty members who had passed away, but to students who would not return from war. Twenty-one names were listed that year.

The memorial section would triple in size before the war ended.

Across America, colleges and universities made similar contributions and weathered similar losses. These ranged from the momentous—academics who fueled the Manhattan Project, who helped devise the new tactic of psychological warfare, who invented a new science of aptitude testing intended for soldiers but ultimately used on every public school student in the country—to the mundane yet no less critical job of supplementing the wildly strained basic training programs of the military.

"Wars come and peace treaties are made, but universities continue through the ages," the DU chancellor, Caleb Gates, wrote to his students, urging them to trust in the future, in the quest for knowledge, in the power of democracy. He told them how the Chinese leadership had forbidden the enlistment of scholars in the army and had relocated universities deep in the interior of the country, away from the fighting, hoping to preserve them through the war. And Gates offered a fateful prediction: "The centers of learning [are] . . . the seeds of hope for the post-war era."

V-J Day—when Japan formally surrendered and the world found itself at peace, at least for a few years—arrived only one month before the school year opened in September 1945, too soon for most returning soldiers to attend. Even so, the G.I. Bill "early adopters" already began having an impact, though what seemed at first to be a flood of veterans to the nation's colleges would turn out to be a mere trickle compared to what was to come.

The University of Denver campus newspaper, the *Clarion*, raved in its inaugural September '45 issue about enrollment unexpectedly "soaring" to its highest level since the beginning of the war, reaching 2,539 students thanks to an influx of 850 freshmen, 250 of whom were newly discharged veterans. The school immediately began laying plans to expand campus facilities and hired fourteen new faculty members, half of whom were recently discharged G.I.s themselves. At that point, one fifth of the total student body at DU was made up of veterans, with the G.I. Bill covering tuition and expenses.

By the second quarter, enrollment had shot up to 3,631, one of the largest student bodies ever at the university. The night school program doubled in size. The law school, down to fifteen students during the war, had sixty-four enrolled. Thirty-six more faculty members were hired, and the university opened a new School of Hotel and Restaurant Management, which was immediately filled to capacity. The mood on campus turned giddy as administrators finally relaxed, seeing a measure of financial security for the school, while students enjoyed, for the first time in four years, a university in which football games, dances, and exams took precedence over air raid drills and war bond drives.

After the Christmas break, enrollment at the school reached a new record, 4,697, and school officials began to worry about what to do with all the new students. Veterans comprised half the student body by then, about fifty of whom were women. The periods between classes had to be lengthened to give students enough time to press through the crowds, the organic chemistry lab had to accommodate 120 students at a time with facilities for only sixty, and double and triple bunking in single dormitory rooms became commonplace. Bulldozers trundled onto the campus and cleared an empty adjacent lot, soon filled with trailers leased from the federal government, providing housing for sixty-two veterans and their families—a first for the campus, where married students and students with young children had been all but unheard of before. Those trailers did not begin to meet the existing demand for family housing for veterans who had started both their college educations and new families—the waiting list had more than 200 families on it, and that was just the beginning.

Denver was not alone; a similar flood of veterans swamped virtually every college in the country. Michigan State University had to set up veterans quarters in the field house. Colorado A&M begged the Army to send them 125 prefab housing units. Augustana College in Rock Island, Illinois, ordered students to bring their own eating utensils because of a silverware shortage.

The culture of college changed, too, almost overnight, once and for good. Veterans were older and eager to make up for lost time: starting families, finishing educations, and seizing this opportunity at a time when, unexpectedly, out of the crucible of war,

America emerged relatively unscathed and economically, militarily, and socially atop the world. The changes would endure long after the vets graduated and moved on. Marriage, once a cause for expulsion at many colleges where higher education and family life were thought to be mutually exclusive, was not only permitted, but welcomed, as hundreds of thousands of new apartments were constructed for married college students—and their newborn children—on and near campuses nationwide. And so the impact the G.I. Bill had on the social mores of college culture proved huge and lasting: Marriage and children would never again have to mean the end of full-time college education for men or women.

In the first full school years that followed the end of the war, many college administrators expected a healthy (and welcome) bump in enrollments. Most, familiar with the estimates out of Washington that only a few hundred thousand G.I.s would want to go to college than would have attended had there been no G.I. Bill, thought they were well prepared.

One look at the high number of applicants for the 1946 school year, and the abnormally high percentage of accepted students who went on to become admitted students, and the nation's colleges realized they had woefully underestimated the powerful desire of returning G.I.s to better themselves in ways previously unimagined, and the power of the G.I. Bill to let them do it. Schools on the brink of bankruptcy suddenly found their rosters overloaded, their classrooms overflowing. The flood of veterans to higher education that began gathering force in 1945 and peaked in 1947 exceeded even the most wildly inflated estimates by more than a million and a half students, straining the colleges' ability to keep pace. Enrollments shot up 75 percent higher than the prewar record high, and every enrollment record ever set was shattered by the college vets.

By 1947, half of all college students (and seven out of ten male students) were enrolled through the G.I. Bill. In a handful of years, college enrollments had expanded threefold. In all, nearly eight million World War II veterans—more than half of those who served and survived—would use the bill's education benefit. A third of those attended college, just under half enrolled in other types of trade and specialty schools (from culinary to acting, truck-driving to piloting), and the remainder split between farm training and subsidized on-the-job training. But it was the two and a half million college students on the G.I. Bill who turned higher education on its head.

As early as 1945, *The New York Times* reported that New York University's veterans (average age: twenty-two) were outperforming the recent high school graduates, in measurable grades and intangibles as well—from their seriousness in class to their willingness to challenge professors in intellectual argument. They also, reporter Edith Efron noted, tended to cuss more often than non-veteran students. Habits left over from the service die hard, one soldier explained, and they created a gulf between the veterans and the other students that went beyond age: "When you add war to the list of your experiences, then you're not only older, but you live in a different world."

Harvard's President Conant continued to predict doom, urging veterans to stay away from colleges and stick to trade schools. But within two years, he was forced to eat his words and admit he had been wrong: The veterans had not lowered academic standards at America's colleges as he and many of his colleagues had warned. They had raised them, earning admission to the top schools in the land in record numbers without the colleges extending any special considerations. "The G.I.s are hogging the honor rolls and the Dean's lists; they are walking away with the top marks in all of their courses," Benjamin Fine of *The New York Times* wrote in 1947. "Far from being an educational problem, the veteran has become an asset to higher education."

Two years later, Fine published the results of a follow-up study, in which the *Times* surveyed sixty colleges and universities around the country. College administrators unanimously agreed that the veterans had raised standards, democratized education, shattered myths about the academic abilities of low-income students and married students (veterans with spouses on average had higher grades, and those with children had the highest), and showed that older men and women adapted well to the rigors of college—better, as it turned out, than the seventeen- and eighteen-year-olds who supposedly fit in more easily. The colleges themselves found they had to improve their game and make classes more intellectually rigorous—high school methods would no longer suffice, Fine wrote. Even the Ivy League was impressed, as representatives of Cornell, Dartmouth, the University of Pennsylvania, and Yale all raved to the *Times* about their veteran-students. "The G.I. Bill has brought to Yale many students of excellent quality who might not have been able to come otherwise, and it has extended the economic and geographic range of our student body," Dean William C. DeVane of Yale told the *Times*. "All this is good for democracy in education, in our country, and good for Yale."

The G.I. Bill began the long, slow process of breaking down the system of ethnic quotas and legacy admissions at the nation's top universities, as well as shattering color barriers. Black veterans had more luck putting their education benefits to work than they had with the home loan benefit, although they were still severely underrepresented at most of the nation's colleges and universities, despite the G.I. Bill. The vast majority of college-bound black veterans found their only viable option was to attend traditionally black institutions of higher learning in the South, where enrollments rose 212 percent by 1947.

The University of Denver was particularly egalitarian in its admissions, with a school charter that mandated diversity and an administration that went out of its way to welcome students of color, including Japanese Americans and other Asian students who were being subjected to considerable prejudice elsewhere during and immediately after the war.

As veterans filled the campus, the scene in Denver, like so many other schools, was one of chaos—four-hour waits to sign up for courses, classes filled to overflowing, students with no place to sleep or eat. Old hotels were converted into dormitories. The law school tripled its enrollment and convened classes in hallways. Cigarette smoke hazed the jam-packed classrooms so that, from the back row, the professor appeared barely visible—leading to an early adoption of No Smoking signs in public places, not for health reasons, but because the teachers wanted to be able to see their students.

If there had been any doubt about the ability of the veterans to compete academically, the G.I.s of the University of Denver, mirroring the national trend, dispelled it in a hurry. The campus paper, rather abjectly, reported that the veterans had higher average grade point averages than nonveteran students.

This was not a carefree bunch, however; they had seen too much, suffered too much. Survivors of the Bataan Death March enrolled at DU, as did prison camp survivors, soldiers who had stormed the beaches at Normandy and climbed past the bodies of their fallen friends, sailors whose vessels had sunk beneath them. There was the war hero, Jimmy Braden, with a chest full of medals and a confession: He had been fourteen when he enlisted, served four years in the Air Corps, then came to Denver on the G.I. Bill at age eighteen. No one had the heart to raise questions about his eligibility or his paperwork.

For some, Bill Kingsley recalls, there were nightmares and night sweats, cries in the dark that everyone studiously ignored. There were even a few suicides. Winning a war does not banish its demons, nor are they papered over by education and opportunity.

But for most there was a sense of community that helped the healing, a watching out for one another, and it mattered, unlike wars that have followed, that there were no doubts about the righteousness of America's role in this conflict, no divisiveness at home, no shortage of pride in what had been achieved. There was a palpable sense that Americans, ordinary Americans, had done something extraordinary—had saved the world. The wonder of it colored the culture of the country for years. For if that were possible, when in 1941 all anyone really worried about was holding their own and surviving, what else might be possible? It was this sort of attitude, Bill and Vivian Kingsley and their fellow students suggest, that led so many of the G.I.s to work so hard, to take those extra courses, and to take it as a matter of course that their admittedly astonished professors would end up pronouncing them the best students the school had ever seen.

They also had little patience for the old rituals of freshman abuse and senior privilege. No ex-G.I. just returned from the Philippines or the occupation of Japan or from Patton's fearsome tank squadrons was going to wear some demeaning freshman beanie or be subjected to hazing by a fraternity. There would be no letting seniors pass through doors first or cut to the head of the line, as had been the tradition in years past. And most of the non-veteran students, years younger than their G.I. counterparts, were too intimidated to do more than mutter about it. Indeed, the tradition-minded dean of women at the University of Denver grew so concerned about the assertiveness of the G.I.s that she issued an order forbidding young women to go barefoot in summer on campus, lest the sight arouse uncontrollable passions in the returning warriors. The vets, far from being insulted, found this hilarious.

"They were in a hurry to get on with their lives," recalls law professor J.J. Johnston, who joined the faculty in 1946 and still taught there in 2005, a university record. "They wanted to cut to the chase and focus on what was important, and who could blame them? They worked hard, they played hard, and they were the best students I've ever taught."

By the time Bill and Vivian Kingsley arrived in 1947, the school was well on its way to its peak enrollment of just under 12,000 (7,500 of whom were vets attending on the G.I. Bill). Twelve thousand students at the University of Denver is a remarkable number considering that a mere twenty years earlier the number of degrees conferred by colleges, both two- and four-year schools, was only 48,000 nationwide. There are college sports stadiums that can hold that many people today. Instructors could not be hired fast enough to keep up with the influx of students—hundreds would be added to the Denver faculty each year after the war ended, yet the professors never could seem to catch up with the burgeoning enrollments.

Bill Kingsley started classes first, and Vivian entered the nursing program a year later, although it was discontinued before she could graduate (she finished her degree ten years later at Colorado State University).

Any nervousness Bill felt about returning to school disappeared after he aced his first test in biology. "I realized all I had to do was study hard, and I could get by. The eighteen-year-olds all figured, 'Ahh, these old guys can't keep up.' After the first test, that attitude disappeared. They started complaining we were raising the grading curve too high!"

By then, the Kingsleys had two children, a son and a daughter (with another boy soon to come), and they were living in one of the war-surplus Quonset huts that the college had erected to accommodate the influx of G.I. Bill students, row upon row of silver metal buildings. Later, the Kingsleys managed to get one of the coveted surplus prefabricated Butler units to live in, which had more space for changing diapers and for rambunctious toddlers. The G.I. Bill paid their tuition and a stipend for books, with $75 a month (it was later raised to $90, and it finally jumped to $120 for married couples with children) to pay for rent, food, clothing, and all other expenses. Most of the G.I.s, including Bill and Vivian, worked part-time jobs while attending classes full time to make ends meet.

The G.I. housing at the university, meanwhile, had turned into a virtual city within a city—which then became two cities. There was Pioneer Village, with 340 families (about a thousand men, women, and children) living in Quonset huts and Butler units that had previously done service as medical quarters at a Japanese internment camp. This is where the Kingsleys lived. A year later, with a waiting list for Pioneer of several hundred, the university built

Buchtel Village, eight rows of six long, prefabricated frame buildings, laid out barracks style—also war surplus—where 237 families lived.

Each village had its own elected mayor and council, weekly church services, a co-op store, an ambulance service run by a group of students, and its own weekly newspaper. The veteran students raised money for building materials and made playgrounds for their children, painted the old buildings, and landscaped the barren ground that had been hastily scraped by bulldozers in preparation for construction. The veterans even organized a day care and a babysitting cooperative, so that both fathers and mothers could go to class and work jobs off campus.

"None of us had any money, but we loved it, anyway," Bill says, recalling how the vets and their families gathered in the evenings to play bridge and poker, hold block parties, or to study and share dessert and coffee.

"We didn't have much, just enough to live. You look at what kids take to college with them now, computers and stereos and TVs. Kids are so spoiled now. They have no idea. But we considered ourselves lucky. We were alive, we had made it, and, it was just amazing, we were getting an education I could never have afforded on my own, at a world-class school."

Bill ended up accumulating all the credits he needed to graduate in two and a half years by attending classes in summer and cramming each semester with the maximum course load. He felt he had a family to care for and he had begun to feel panicked about not starting a career with a steady income. Already the notion of what it meant to have a good life in America was shifting in his mind.

The G.I. Bill would make it possible for the Kingsleys not just to get an education, but to buy a home as well, something they had never considered before the war, when a home loan and down payment seemed a distant hope at best. Even deeper than that, the G.I. Bill had shown people like Bill and Vivian Kingsley that college was not for a privileged few anymore; the grunts had stormed the campuses and proved themselves on the academic battlefield, just as they had in Europe and in the Pacific. The colleges were forced to reconsider what it meant to be "college material"—finding out that higher education was a potential gold mine they had not even come close to tapping. With student bodies, facilities, and faculties doubled and tripled in size to accommodate the veterans, few colleges wanted to turn the clock back to more modest days, and so the age of expanded enrollments, competition for students, and marketing of higher education began. The Kingsleys, meanwhile, like all the other veterans, began thinking they would need to be able to pay for their children to attend college as well. Surely they could not enjoy such an opportunity without providing at least as much for their own children. And in this way, college became not just a prize won at war, a one-time affair that would fade with the memories of war, but a rite of passage for America's new and burgeoning middle class.

But before the opportunity could become a legacy, Bill and Vivian knew they had to parlay his (and eventually her) degree into a job—a good job, a profession, a career. Bill's grades were good, all As and Bs, but not quite good enough for immediate admission to medical school. The demand for admission was so high, with so many veterans applying in record numbers to the med schools, that he was passed over.

He considered waiting and reapplying—he had made a few waiting lists, and he still could see himself as an MD—but then a recruiter for the Denver schools came to the campus right after graduation. There were openings, the recruiter said, immediate openings, classrooms ready to be led.

So Bill said okay. He'd take a one-year contract. The recruiter peeked at his transcripts and hired him on the spot, and Bill went to teach second graders how to add, subtract, and read. He figured it would be merely temporary, until he and Vivian figured out their next move.

"The next forty years went by pretty quickly," he says with a laugh. "Once I started, I never wanted to do anything else . . . I'm so glad that I did not become a doctor, that I found my true calling. Or rather, it found me."

Bill's first teaching contract in 1950 paid him $2,700 a year, and when he got a raise to $3,000 a year later, he and Vivian, who had lived so modestly for so long, thought they were making a fortune.

Both he and Vivian used their G.I. Bill benefits to get their masters degrees, and Vivian finally got the credentials she needed to become a school nurse. Meanwhile, Bill worked his way up through the grade levels, spending the bulk of his career, more than twenty years, with high school students, teaching biology, zoology, ecology, and photography, which has become his delight in later life.

Bill kept teaching until he reached seventy, then he and Vivian both retired and began traveling the world. They finally left Denver in the midnineties for a home in Sun City, Arizona. They say they stay young through regular exercise, and through something "terrible" that Vivian did to Bill: She gave him a set of golf clubs, which never remain idle for long.

Golf and photography are his passions now, while painting is Vivian's, along with computers—she's taken classes on image editing software to use with Bill's photos and her art, and finds herself still returning to school for more classes. She fusses and demurs when Bill mentions how brilliant and capable she is, turning the compliments back on her husband. "When we met, he had never had a long-term relationship. He had nothing to compare me to. But I did. So I knew just how special he was, right from the start. A lot of women dream of a great marriage, but it often doesn't come about. I got the dream."

Eight thousand students later and sixteen years into his retirement, Bill still remembers the girl in his biology class who was fascinated by the right-brain versus left-brain functions. Years later, she stopped by to visit his class, a grown woman by then with a family of her own, and she fondly remembered the tough-but-fair ex-G.I. teacher who loved being in the classroom, who got to school early every day, and who looked forward to the end of school vacations as much as he looked forward to their beginning. "I'm in the work now," she told him. "I became a biologist—because of your class."

Another student who shared his teacher's interest in photography dropped out, and Bill worried that he had been lost for good. But years later he came back, toting a portfolio. He was working for a professional photographer and learning the business, and his work was good, Bill saw, really good. And the young man thanked his old teacher for giving him something to aspire to in photography, something he loved.

"I came home and I said, 'Boy, that makes it all worth the effort.' I could go on all day with stories like that, but the thing is, none of it would have happened without the G.I. Bill. We just didn't have enough money otherwise. She was a private-duty nurse, I was a high school dropout. Where would we be without that G.I. Bill?"

There are dollar-and-cents calculations of the benefits of the G.I. Bill, how every dollar of the 15 billion spent returned seven dollars to the economy. This is all well and good, as Bill and Vivian see it. But these direct measurements do not begin to encompass the indirect yet undeniable contributions of even one retired married couple, the Kingsleys, who together influenced the lives of thousands of young people and sent their own three children through college, who, in turn, became teachers and influenced the next generation—a ripple effect beyond measurement. "Eight thousand students—that's a lot of minds," Bill says, "a lot of lives I got to be part of."

Bill says he wishes there was as far-reaching an equivalent today to the original G.I. Bill, something that could have just as much impact on more recent generations as the original legislation had on his; something not just limited to veterans, because they will never again make up such a high percentage of the population, but which could make full-time, rigorous, high-quality college education more attainable for all young people who want it.

"It was a magnificent program. It was the best program we've ever had from the government. It helped us realize so much potential. Without something like it now, we will throw away so much of our intellect, so much potential."

☆ 5 ☆

Out of the Blue: Medical Miracles

From Newton to Einstein, Mozart to Miles, that indefinable, elusive, essential thing we call inspiration most often seems to arrive as a bolt from the blue.

For Dr. Richard Koch, the reverse proved to be true. It was he who came hurtling out of an achingly blue sky toward his own unique source of inspiration—even as an angry mob of pitchfork-waving villagers waited for his parachute to deposit him in their grasp, the ruin of his B-24 Liberator bomber belching thick, black smoke nearby.

Not everyone could have survived that tense moment in the hamlet of Wintermoor, Germany, on Easter Sunday 1944, much less find one's calling in life along the way. But Dick Koch has always seen and done things differently. The son of immigrant farmers found the inspiration in his own wartime ordeal of parachutes and prison camps to return home, seize the opportunity afforded him by the G.I. Bill, and head to college and medical school—something he had never before imagined doing.

Then he began a lifetime of research, treatment, and advocacy for those least able to speak for themselves, saving thousands from needless disability and sorrow—and inspiring subsequent generations of physicians and researchers.

At age eighty-five he is still actively practicing medicine, researching, mentoring, publishing articles, speaking at international conferences, and regularly riding his bicycle, tie flapping, the two miles to work at Childrens Hospital Los Angeles. He is something of a legend at this premier pediatrics center—the pediatrician known throughout the world for pioneering treatments, and who has continued treating some of his former infant patients well into their fifties.

"I can't quit," he says, shaking his head and casting a wary eye at his wife, Jean, who playfully complains that it would be nice to take a vacation sometime that didn't include a medical conference. The doctor laughs, something he does often—he likes to punctuate his sentences with a chuckle, his shock of white Einstein hair moving back and forth with a life of its own. "There's too much to do before I can retire. And it's too much fun doing it. It's too . . . well, there's only one word for it: inspiring."

Dick Koch (pronounced "coke") started life on a frigid farm in rural North Dakota in 1921, the sixth of nine children born to immigrant sheep farmers of German and Russian descent. His main garments were his overalls, handed down from older brothers. His most vivid memory of his early childhood on the prairie was awakening one bitter cold morning after a particularly nasty blizzard to find all the sheep frozen to death.

Next thing he knew, the whole family had packed up and moved to Petaluma, California, to live near family friends who had long urged the Kochs to give up the ranch for a warmer clime. They moved into an old motel, all they could afford at the time, and Dick's father went to work on a poultry farm, a difficult, dirty job, but one he managed to hold on to even when the economy slid into the Depression.

Because of the move, Dick started first grade over again in Petaluma, which made him a year older than his fellow students, giving him a head start. "It worked out well for me—I was the top student because it was my second time around," he says. "Kind of nice, actually."

The good grades continued all the way through high school, but given the family's poverty and the relatively few opportunities to further his education, Dick's prospects seemed uncertain at best. Perhaps some sort of farm job, something with a bit of security, though he quietly harbored hopes of earning a scholarship to the University of California.

He had turned nineteen, about to finish his last year of high school and working part time at a service station, when the radio in the cramped office where he worked informed him that Japan had just attacked Pearl Harbor. World War II suddenly became an American war, and Dick's plans and hopes changed for good, along with those of all his friends and most other nineteen-year-olds in the country.

Dick signed up to join the Army Air Corps. After finishing his senior year and earning his diploma, he reported for training at the new Santa Ana Army Air Base in Southern California (now the Orange County Fairgrounds, cows and pigs and Ferris wheels replacing the troops and trainer aircraft). Nearly 60,000 pilots and crew members received their initial nine-week training and aircraft assignments at the base.

Dick drew bombardier duty aboard the B-24 Liberator, the workhorse bomber of World War II, with its familiar glass bubble gun turrets on the nose, tail, belly, and topside—the aircraft that dropped more tons of bombs on Europe and the Pacific than any other type of aircraft. For Dick, this meant specialized training in navigation, trajectories, targeting, map reading—and an officer's commission as a second lieutenant.

Before he shipped out to Roswell and Tonopah for his advanced bombardier training, he attended a USO dance, where a dark-haired young woman in the band caught his eye. She played the marimba, and very well. They spent the night dancing and talking, and by October 1943, Jean Holt and Richard Koch married. That same month, he was assigned to Crew 56 of the 458th Bombardment Group, and he departed for England before the year was out. He sent home his crew picture to Jean, with Koch in the front row, handsome and smiling as always into the camera, wearing his bomber jacket and fur-lined boots, his officer's cap cocked jauntily.

On April 9, 1944—Easter Sunday—the 458th launched its eighteenth mission over Germany. Koch's crew had flown on twelve of those missions, more bombing runs than any other crew in the group at that time. Crew 56 was assigned to the Easter mission at the last moment, barely leaving time for a briefing before the squadron departed.

At that time, crews had to complete thirty missions to be sent home, a total that seemed all but insurmountable. "I later learned just how hard that was," he recalls. "Of the sixty crews I went over with, only six made it through the war."

The target that day was an airfield at Tutow, Germany. Second Lieutenant Koch clambered onboard the battle-scarred, four-engine bomber, the nose section painted vividly with a huge Daisy Mae cartoon figure, the nubile hillbilly character from the Li'l Abner comic strip standing next to the plane's name, *Bomb Totin' Mama.* He carried his bombardier's gear—the slide rules, maps, and other tools of the trade—in a zippered leather pouch. His job would not only be to target and drop the 8,000 pounds of bombs stowed in *Mama*'s belly, but to walk through the bomb racks and pull the pins on each explosive before the bombing run began, arming them like gigantic grenades.

The weather grew increasingly stormy as the bombers approached the German border. Over Denmark, the clouds became so thick and the weather so rough that the lead pilot ordered the group to change course, looking for a seam in the cloud cover. When they finally burst into the open, the bombers ran directly into a waiting squadron of FW-190 fighters, the fastest and most heavily armed fighters Germany ever produced for its Luftwaffe, considered a deadly match for the Allies' best aircraft, even the vaunted Corsair flown by the U.S. Navy. With a top speed of more than 400 miles an hour, the FW-190s made the heavy, bomb-laden American planes appear to be standing still as they stalked the bombers from behind, then surged ahead, ripping into the planes with cannon fire.

Before the gunners aboard *Bomb Totin' Mama* could react, the German fighter planes had destroyed their number three engine, forcing the pilot to feather the blades—to shut them down. The number two engine also was hit before the attack ended, though it continued to work, albeit leaking oil, which meant it would likely begin to smoke and then fail, the only question being when. The fighter attack took out the cabin intercom system, too, making communications between the cockpit, the machine gunners and turrets, and the bombardier all but impossible—every message had to be delivered in person by a crew member traversing the cramped, deafeningly noisy fuselage. Miraculously, when the attack ended, none of Koch's crewmates had suffered even a scratch from the 30-millimeter shells that had hit the engines and ripped through the plane's metal skin as if through paper.

The bomber continued on toward its target, but lagged farther and farther behind the rest of the group. When the second damaged engine sputtered and failed, the crew realized they could never make it to the target. The pilot, Lieutenant Walter Raiter, decided he had no choice but to turn back, dumping the bombs in the Baltic Sea before heading the plane westward toward England, alone and defenseless.

After ninety tense minutes, it became clear that the crippled plane would not make it back to friendly territory, and the pilot sent word back to the crew to don their parachutes and prepare to bail out. The plane at the time was about fifty miles southeast of Hamburg, Germany.

The crew opened the hatch and the cabin immediately filled with the roar of engines and the rush of cold air as the men awaited the order to jump. But then someone shouted and pointed, and they saw a German fighter approaching. The turret gunners raced back to their positions, threw off their parachutes in order to squeeze into their cramped bubbles, and manned their guns. Koch took up one of the machines guns in the waist of the plane and began firing along with the turret gunners. The attacking plane exploded. But two more came boring in on the bomber, and their aim was deadly: a fuel tank on *Bomb Totin' Mama* ruptured. The attackers had won.

Suddenly the plane shuddered and the cabin immediately filled with flames. Through the waist gun port, Koch could see the right wing aflame as well, and he knew the plane was going down. The navigator and one of the turret gunners had been shot and killed, and Koch ordered the other men to jump immediately. He followed suit. One turret gunner remained behind, still firing at the fighters, and he was killed before he could make it out. No one saw the pilot leave the plane before it exploded above their heads and parachutes, the wreckage auguring into the ground below.

The six survivors of Crew 56 fell to earth outside the small town of Wintermoor, where they were captured immediately by waiting German soldiers, who had seen everything from the ground. Then a mob of townspeople began to rush toward the prisoners, waving clubs and pitchforks, hungry for blood, and the shell-shocked air crew thought that having survived the battle in the sky, they would be beaten and stabbed to death on the ground.

But the young bombardier stepped forward. Richard Koch, the child of immigrants, spoke German fluently. He understood from the mutterings and shouts why the villagers were so enraged—they had seen the picture of a woman and the word *Mama* on the plane's wreckage and had concluded that this was a special bomber intended to target women and children as some sort of terrible terrorist campaign.

The young flight officer with the easy smile and calm manner shook his head and explained that this was just a cartoon from America, that the bomber was off course and not targeting the civilians of Wintermoor or anywhere else, convincing first the German soldiers, who then helped him calm the mob.

After two weeks in solitary confinement in a German jail, where Koch spent the time counting the straws in his mat ("I got up to 100,000"), the survivors of the *Bomb Totin' Mama* shipped out to the notorious Stalag Luft 1 prison camp in Barth, Germany, where captured air crews were imprisoned. They were delighted to find that their pilot, Lieutenant Raiter, had survived after all, having been blown out of the plane by the explosion. He landed far enough away to elude capture for several days before being brought to Luft 1.

Life in the prison camp was hard, marked by boredom and constant hunger that was only momentarily relieved by the small rations of black bread and thin soup that tasted like dishwater—the cuisine served meal after meal. The camp had several thousand American and British fliers when Koch arrived; by the time the war ended thirteen months later, more than 10,000 air crew members jammed the camp, most of them American.

As an officer, Koch had a few extra privileges, the most important of which involved the letters and packages Jean sent him via the Red Cross, which for the most part made it through to his eager hands. Her letters were his lifeline, and his were hers, during the long months apart—the only time they would ever be parted for any significant period of time for the next sixty years. ("They seem to be attached at the hip," one friend says. "You can't really talk about Dick without talking about Jean.")

Koch traded the cigarettes in his packages for an old typewriter the guards obligingly liberated from a camp office, enabling him to start a POW newspaper. His foray into journalism not only helped him pass the time, but also allowed him to provide an alternative to the Nazi propaganda supplied by the guards.

The rest of the time he spent reading. One of the few books Koch could wrest from the camp's meager library was a medical biography: *The Doctors Mayo.* He read this story of a family of doctors cover to cover several times, fascinated by the intricacies of medicine and the human body, so much more complex than even the thousands of moving parts that made up his old bomber, or the calculations he had to make to plot a successful bomb run. The story of the Mayos inspired him—what higher calling could there be, he thought, than helping the sick, the dying, the damaged?

And he began to ponder his future, knowing based on the increasingly upbeat news from freshly arrived POWs, and the increasing number of American bombers streaking unchallenged across the sky above Stalag Luft 1, that the war would end soon and the next stage of his life would begin.

In May 1945, the pounding sound of artillery grew close, and the German guards fled the camp in the night, freeing a few senior American officers from the locked barracks and turning over control to them. The guards wished their former captives good luck and one even suggested, prophetically as it turned out, that they would soon all be allies against the Russians and Communism. No one else believed it for a minute.

The next day, a Russian Army detachment threw open the gates and liberated their American comrades to a hero's rousing welcome, toting schnapps and a small herd of cattle to be butchered and fed to the half-starved G.I.s.

By that night, as the Americans settled in to await an American airlift, Koch had decided what he wanted to do with his life. He would be a doctor.

He had never imagined such a career choice before his time in the camp, but somehow, surrounded by the suffering of war and imprisonment, the hunger and frequent illnesses, it seemed the right choice, the only choice. Reading the medical book seemed natural to him, as if it had been waiting there for him. Somehow, he'd find a way and the money to do it.

He was sure of it.

Dick Koch flew out of Barth aboard an American transport, one of thousands of former prisoners of war airlifted through a devastated, eerily silent landscape, the roads littered with charred tanks and wrecked vehicles, even as spring flowers bloomed at their sides.

The airfield from which Koch departed, only a few miles from the prison camp, held a hangar full of half-assembled experimental jet fighters, ultimate weapons that, had Germany not run out of time and resources, might have tipped the scales in the war.

Koch next spent several weeks at an evacuation center, Camp Lucky Strike in France, where plenty of solid food, medical treatment, debriefing, and processing for the trip home awaited him. Finally that summer, he and his wife, Jean, reunited. She had been living with her family in Garden Grove, California, where her family grew oranges and walnuts back in the days when Orange County actually grew its namesake fruit, before suburbia knocked down and absorbed the groves.

In the fall, they moved to northern California, where Dick attended his dream school, the University of California–Berkeley, while his wife finished her own war-interrupted education at San Jose State. The G.I. Bill covered his tuition and expenses, and the

Kochs received $90 a month in living expenses—there simply was no other way they could have managed, the couple says. "We owe everything to the G.I. Bill," Koch says matter-of-factly. "Four of my five brothers got out of the service and went to school on the G.I. Bill as well. My whole family owes it a very big debt of gratitude."

Even so, the money was barely enough to pay the rent and buy groceries, with nothing much left over. Jean cut her husband's hair to save a bit of cash, and she sold eggs for a few extra bucks. Dick coaxed the school into giving him credits for his bombardier training so he could graduate early, so eager were they to reach the next big thing.

They celebrated when Dick was accepted to the University of Rochester's medical school in upstate New York. Jean says she'll never forget that cross-country trip. Dick bought an Army surplus Jeep. It arrived brand-new—in a crate. He had to assemble it, put the wheels on, and then he built a hard top for it, because the Army issue canvas just would not cut it in the bitter Rochester winters. "Our first new car," Jean says, and they both laugh still at the old snapshot of it. "And it came in a box."

Once the Jeep was ready to roll, they packed everything they owned, which wasn't much, along with their five-month-old daughter—the first of five children—and took off for medical school.

And as soon as he completed his three years in Rochester, he, Jean, and their growing family immediately packed up and headed back to the warmth of California, jumping at the offer of a pediatric internship at Childrens Hospital of Los Angeles, where in 1951 the life's work of a newly minted doctor awaited.

Few eras have offered more excitement for a young doctor than the postwar years, when a hospital building boom swept across the nation, replacing antiquated, nineteenth-century hospitals with gleaming new facilities. New technology, from improved sutures to infant incubators, and new medicines and vaccines seemed to appear daily, as a nation that had amassed so much energy and capacity to wage war unleashed a portion of its newfound manufacturing and research capabilities in more productive directions. G.I. Bill–educated doctors, more than 60,000 of them, flooded these new hospitals and emergency rooms, delivering care to patients, conducting research, devising new treatments—from chemotheraphy regimens to heart pacemakers, neurosurgical breakthroughs to instruments for detecting osteoporosis. Baruch Blumberg, who commanded a landing ship during World War II, won a Nobel Prize for groundbreaking research on infectious disease that led to a vaccine for hepatitis B, a major cause of liver failure and liver cancer. Irwin Rose's medical research on protein sequences led to new treatments for numerous cancers and cystic fibrosis. Medical physicist John Cameron, an Army Signal Corpsman for the duration of World War II, perfected X-ray diagnostic techniques used the world over to detect a host of ailments and to measure and protect against excessive radiation exposure. The ripple effect of G.I. Bill–backed physicians' and medical researchers' educations has touched, cured and saved, literally, millions of lives.

Dick Koch had first thought he was most interested in a general practice. After completing his residency, the fledgling pediatrician turned down an offer from his hospital's chief of medicine to head a new child development unit for disabled patients. It was to be a one-of-a-kind program, focused on the developmentally disabled (then universally referred to as the mentally retarded). "It would be a chance," the chief urged, "to make your mark and do something for patients who really need you."

The young Dr. Koch said thanks but no thanks, and instead he joined a large and thriving private general pediatric practice: plenty of shots and sore throats and earaches and whooping coughs. He was busy, doing well, helping people, and finally earning a decent living—but something wasn't right. He felt he was missing something. He kept thinking about those Mayos who made life bearable for him at Stalag Luft 1, two generations of doctors often working on the cutting edge, and about his old hospital chief's offer and the possibilities it suggested—of breaking new ground and helping children whom most people, including most doctors, considered hopeless. Those kids, and their heartbroken parents, deserved better, he decided.

So he called his old boss at the children's hospital and asked, "Is that child development job offer still open?"

He says now it was the best decision he ever made, and there are many others who agree.

"Thousands of lives have been changed," one parent said at a testimonial for Koch to celebrate his eightieth birthday and his fiftieth year in medicine. "Many who would have been mentally retarded weren't—because of him."

In the fifties, when Koch started the child development center, developmentally disabled children routinely ended up warehoused in large state mental institutions, often in neglectful or abusive conditions, with little in the way of treatment, education, or simple kindness. They were simply hidden away, thrown away, stigmatized, and forgotten—more than 13,000 in California alone. And if parents didn't like it or wanted more or better for their child, they were on their own—at the time, public schools could legally refuse to educate the mentally retarded, and their parents had no standing to object or right to any other form of state assistance.

Medical insurance policies provided no coverage for therapy or other services. Now and again, an enterprising reporter or conscience-stricken legislator would visit one of the state facilities and be horrified, leading to a flurry of investigations and much lip service. But interest would soon fade, and nothing ever seemed to change. For the developmentally disabled, the Dark Ages hadn't yet ended—until Koch's efforts finally helped lead to the dismantling of the old institutions.

He began his campaign in 1955, ensconced as the first director of the newly established Clinic for the Study of Mental Retardation at Childrens Hospital of Los Angeles. Koch scrounged grant money to create a series of traveling clinics for small towns, rural areas, and neighborhoods with little or no medical services. He assembled teams of doctors, nurses, and therapists to provide counseling, treatment, and therapy programs for the developmentally disabled, correcting common misdiagnoses that added to their woes. Often Koch would provide families with their first contact with caregivers who saw their special-needs children as just that—children—rather than objects to be pitied and cast aside. There had never been anything like it, and parents who previously had nowhere to turn flocked to the clinics and the compassionate young doctor who really seemed to care. "There was such a need, such a hunger," Koch recalls. "You can never forget that."

The traveling clinics became a model for a new concept in the care of the developmentally disabled—dedicated regional centers that amassed counselors, doctors, therapists, and special education experts in one place, providing a suite of services to the developmentally disabled so that they could remain at home with their families or in noninstitutional or mainstream settings, living more happily and productively.

California created two such regional centers in 1966 as a pilot program, one in San Francisco and one in Los Angeles, with Koch as the LA center's first director. One of the key ingredients of success, Koch says, involved incorporating the parents of the developmentally disabled into the governance of the center as members of the board of directors—an unusual level of partnership between medical experts and laypeople, especially for the times.

Though they had very little money, the pilot centers were wildly successful, light years ahead of the old warehouse-style state hospitals. With Koch and a legion of parents pressing for action, the California legislature created a network of twenty-one regional centers spread throughout the state, an approach that rapidly became a model for the rest of the nation. The regional center concept eventually led to the deinstitutionalization of the developmentally disabled, as the archaic and woefully inadequate state asylums were shut down one by one, first in California, then nationwide.

Koch next set his sights beyond merely housing and treating the developmentally disabled—he also devoted much of his career to seeking ways to prevent the disability in the first place. The medical community had gradually come to realize that developmental disabilities did not always have a direct genetic (and therefore incurable) cause, but sometimes came about indirectly, because of metabolic disorders in newborns that could be treated if detected in time. Koch lobbied tirelessly for legislation mandating newborn screening tests that could detect these newly discovered disorders—tests that are now required by laws Koch and like-minded colleagues in other states sponsored.

As a researcher, he devoted much of his career to a particular disorder, phenylketonuria—commonly called PKU—which afflicts about one in 12,000 newborns and was once a common cause of mental retardation. He pushed hard for the adoption of a simple, quick blood test that could easily detect the disorder in newborns. Babies with PKU have a genetic flaw in their metabolism that allows the amino acid phenylalanine, which is a common substance in many foods, to build up in their systems to toxic levels, causing irreversible brain damage. For every week the disorder remains undiagnosed, a child's IQ will drop precipitously.

"For a person with PKU, most food is poison," Koch says. "It's a very terrible thing."

PKU babies must be placed on a no-protein diet, except for a special form of treated and predigested protein that contains no phenylalanine. It's a tough diet, tasteless and boring, and one that, it was initially believed, a child must stick with until their brain is sufficiently developed, usually to age ten, depending on the severity of their disorder. But compared to the alternative, the diet is a blessing.

Until the mid-sixties, PKU often remained undetected or doctors confused it with other ailments. The disorder typically would not be discovered until parents noticed that a previously normal infant had stopped developing properly—no longer able to sit up, or hold a bottle or cup. The brain damage by then would be severe and irreversible. Thousands nationwide ended up institutionalized and deemed unreachable and untreatable.

Once mandatory testing was put in place, however, treatment stopped the disease in its tracks, one of the great success stories of modern medicine. After 1966, Koch proudly says, there was not a single institutionalization for PKU in the entire state of California—virtually every case had been caught and treated.

But years later, Koch began to wonder about those infant patients of his, who, after age ten, had been allowed to sample the burgers and pizza and milk shakes they had so long been denied. As adults, how had they fared?

He was shocked to learn that the female PKU patients he had treated and saved from disability were, in a terrible irony, giving birth to disabled babies of their own—not PKU babies, because the disease requires both parents to have the defective gene, but microcephalic infants and babies born with other congenital defects. Koch and his colleagues, so overjoyed at detecting and saving PKU babies from the damaged lives that in the past had been inevitable, had not considered that once the children were off their special diets, the condition could have a deleterious effect on the next generation. The unmetabolized phenylalanine in the mothers' bodies during pregnancy, no longer so harmful to the mother, proved toxic to their unborn children.

When this problem became apparent by the mid-eighties, Koch applied for yet another grant to conduct a study and to track down these patients. He could not bear the thought that a small army of patients that had been saved from this condition was producing a new flock of disabled children.

He was turned down twice for a federal grant but, as Jean Koch says, "There's not really any point in telling my husband no, because if he feels he is right about something, he will not stop until he has what he needs—and what his patients need."

The dogged lobbying eventually paid off—Koch finally got his grant, and Childrens Hospital of Los Angeles became the center of a national effort that recruited nearly 200 other hospitals in tracking down those old PKU patients, urging them to resume their special diets, particularly before and during pregnancy. PKU patients on their special diets have the same odds of giving birth to a normal child as any other expectant mother.

So these days, Koch is treating his old patients, who first came to him as infants decades ago, and are in their thirties or forties now. He urges many of them, particularly those with the severest form of PKU, to stay on their special diets, because new evidence suggests that adults can still suffer mental disorders, brain degeneration, and even early onset of Alzheimers disease from the excessive phenylalanine in their systems. They call him at home and on weekends, grousing about the limited diet, or its price—the special food is expensive, up to $8,000 a year—and Koch is always looking for a supplier with a good price, or dunning insurers who are reluctant to cover the cost.

"It's enough to make me favor socialized medicine," Koch grumbles.

"I owe so much to Dr. Koch," one of his adult patients says. "All of us do. I am so much more clearheaded now that I'm back on the diet. I'm not so scattered. No one has looked out for us like he has."

His latest initiative is to track down and treat the children who were born with PKU just before the mandatory newborn screening was put in place. There are several hundred PKU patients still living in California, now in their late forties and fifties or older, most of them hospitalized with severe brain damage, mental disabilities, and often mental illness. Koch has found that an experimental drug, biopterin, can alleviate some of their symptoms and allow them to function better and to experience a moderately better quality of life. He has assembled a group of doctors interested in experimenting with the new treatment, and in 2005 helped dedicate a new residential home for five such patients who, under the new medicine, improved sufficiently to leave full-time hospital care.

Koch and his wife have remained active well into their eighties—hiking, biking, and fishing, often with their children and grandchildren swarming around them. They cross-country ski in the winter, and they travel often. Shortly after the opening of the new residential home for PKU patients, the Kochs prepared for a vacation to Paris—where, naturally, he was to speak at an international medical conference. Koch is now known around the world as "Dr. PKU," and that German prison guard sixty years ago was right—they are allies now, though not against the Russians, but against a terrible, preventable disease. Several German hospitals are part of Koch's research network.

"Had I not survived the war, had I not decided to be a doctor while a prisoner of war, and had it not been for the G.I. Bill . . . ," Koch says, then trails off, contemplating what might have been, had other opinions prevailed in the postwar planning, those who thought the G.I. Bill too far-reaching or too expensive or too wasteful. Then Dr. PKU lets loose his trademark chuckle. "Well, it was just meant to be. We came home from the war and had a great opportunity, and fortunately, quite a few of us had the sense to take it."

☆ 6 ☆

Nixon and Kennedy, *Bonnie and Clyde:* The G.I. Bill and the Arts

"Close-up," Arthur Penn murmured into the control-room microphone. "Nice and tight."

The junior senator's chiseled features filled the screen in response to Penn's command, a handsome face, eyes unwavering at the camera, the politician's words simple and direct, just as he had been coached. The senator finished his thought, then the television picture shifted to the other candidate in the debate: the far more seasoned and experienced of the two, probably smarter as well, but also pale, shifty-eyed, his clothes a poor fit, his five-o'clock shadow plainly visible. The contrast couldn't be plainer; it almost didn't matter what either man said, Penn knew.

Only one of them looked presidential.

Just as Penn had planned.

It was 1960, the golden era of live television, when giants of the stage, screen, and literature came together every night to invent and reinvent a new medium, never quite sure what would happen when they fired up those lumbering, balky video cameras, never quite sure what line would pop out of an actor's mouth, what glory or disaster would dance live across 20 million black-and-white screens, then disappear into the ether. In those days, the men in the control room, the directors and producers, most of them, like Penn, World War II vets with a G.I. Bill–financed degree behind them, had to have ice in their veins. There were no do-overs, there was no room for error, no filler material to populate the airwaves should disaster strike. The On the Air light came on and you were live, with the biggest audience in the world, in history, waiting to see what you were made of. Doing television in those days was exhilarating, adventurous, and merciless, and Penn was one of the pioneers and masters of that particular tightrope.

And now the men vying to be leader of the free world had arrived in his shop to stage the first-ever televised presidential debate. The advance man for the Democratic candidate had come to Penn and his producer, two rising stars in the business, and said, *We've never done this. No one's ever done this. We need you to tell us about television.*

So Penn told them—and thereby helped launch a new age of American politics, the modern era of image and sound bites and form over substance, though it seemed like so much more at the time. For the first time, a director of teleplays and theater and Hollywood films was called on to instruct a political candidate on the nature of television—how facial close-ups were critical and makeup a necessity; how short, punchy lines were far better than lengthy nuance; and how looking directly at the camera, rather than at the moderator or the panel of journalists who would be questioning the candidates, would create the illusion that you were staring every viewer in the eye and speaking directly to him or her. It was a trick, a bit of acting, this peering at the bulbous lens of a giant camera and pretending it was a person. But it was a great trick, Penn explained, not at all like mugging for the audience while onstage. It made you seem more real and less artificial, even as it went against a politician's most basic instinct to always look the person addressing him in the eye.

This proved to be good advice, good enough to convince seven out of ten viewers of the debate that a shifty-eyed man who had not been coached, who had no makeup, who rambled in his answers and who never seemed to look viewers in the eye—a fellow named Richard Nixon—had lost the debate by a wide margin (even as a majority of radio listeners, unaware of the carefully constructed imagery, decided he had won). And it was good enough advice to give just a bit of extra momentum to the other candidate, John F. Kennedy, who won the White House in one of the closest elections in history.

"It was TV more than anything else that turned the tide," Kennedy candidly admitted after the election. And if Kennedy was correct, if it was TV that did it, then much of the credit goes to director Arthur Penn, a television, stage, and film pioneer who brought such diverse classics as *The Miracle Worker* and *Bonnie and Clyde* to life, one of the thousands of G.I. Bill veterans who flooded the postwar world of the arts in America and, along the way, changed most everything they touched.

The crop of artists, novelists, poets, actors, and other creative talent who returned from wartime service to be educated and trained through the G.I. Bill is so vast as to be impossible to catalogue beyond a simple highlight reel: novelists and essayists Gore Vidal,

Norman Mailer, Joseph Heller, Frank McCourt, Art Buchwald, Pete Hamill, Edward Abbey, Elmore Leonard, Mario Puzo; poets James Dickey, James Wright, Lawrence Ferlinghetti, Randall Jarrell, Frank O'Hara, Anthony Hecht, Richard Wilbur, A.R. Ammons; stage and screen writers Paddy Chayefsky, Rod Serling, Aaron Spelling, Terry Southern; actors Walter Matthau, Robert Duvall, Tony Curtis, Harry Belafonte, Rod Steiger, Gene Hackman, Clint Eastwood, Paul Newman, Jason Robards, Charles Bronson, Ernest Borgnine; artists Robert Rauschenberg, Leo Krikorian, Dan Spiegle, Robert Miles Runyan, Kenneth Noland, LeRoy Nieman, Richard Collner, Ed Rossbach, Robert Perine. From coast to coast, schools for art, acting, photography, dance, and design were sustained by veterans returning from war, and by the G.I. Bill dollars they brought with them, in some cases rescuing the schools from imminent closures. The men and women who graduated from them after the war launched a twentieth-century renaissance in the arts in America, from new ways of using color on canvas, to the groundbreaking literary nonfiction of New Journalism, to Beat poetry, to entirely new and even shocking ways of telling a story on screens large and small. The fifties are often remembered for their bland conformity, but the postwar period in the arts heralded a time of enormous experimentation, advances, and daring.

Arthur Penn had not entered the war expecting to be part of any such moment or movement. His main hope at the outset had been typical and basic—to come home in one piece and not in a coffin—and, perhaps, to find something other than the family business to sustain him once the shooting stopped.

Born in 1922, Penn grew up a watchmaker's son with a watchmaker's destiny laid before him, an indifferent student whose one passion in school—theater—lay distinctly at odds with a future filled with springs and gears, jeweler's loupes, and the smell of machine oil.

The year of his birth had witnessed nearly unimaginable change and possibility: the Model T had revolutionized both travel and the art of mass production; radio and aircraft knit the world as never before; the discovery of King Tut's tomb had uncovered a new window on a glorious past; and Germany, driven by war debts and reparations, had begun its long march toward fascism and world war. Larger-than-life figures sprang daily from the news, from the inimitable humorist Will Rogers, to the extravagant exploits of a former spelling bee champion named Bonnie and her bank-robbing beau, Clyde. Penn grew up in a world that seemed propelled less by governments and corporations as by inventors, adventurers, and iconoclasts—a world in which the entire U.S. budget amounted to a mere third of the dollars spent by the Internal Revenue Service simply to collect taxes in the year 2000. How, Penn often thought, could he lock himself away in a watch shop when such a world awaited outside?

But once the Great Depression arrived, it seemed to Penn that with each passing year the realm of the possible became inexorably constricted, until basic survival, not upward mobility, weighed daily on the mind. The evidence of desperation lay everywhere, the most enduring images of Penn's youth: bread lines, soup lines, and, on the rail lines, an army of "tramps"—the homeless of the era, many of them veterans of World War I. He became a teenager when a ten-dollar bill in the pocket seemed a fortune, when a third of the adult population remained unemployed a decade after Black Friday, when college existed as a viable path for only eight out of a hundred young Americans. Half of all adults had only an eighth-grade education—or less.

Penn knew the business of repairing timepieces had sustained his fractured family, keeping things together through the Depression years, through his parents' divorce, through a childhood spent shuttling between a mother in New York and a father in Philadelphia, with the train becoming a de facto third home for two hours of the day as it swept through cities and farmland and the trackside haunts of the tramp army. He spent long hours in his father's cluttered shop in Philadelphia's old downtown jewelry district, where Harry Penn—a Lithuanian immigrant whose given name, Gregory, inexplicably was changed by the bored bureaucrats at Ellis Island—labored to teach his youngest son the surgical skills of his trade.

But the more he struggled to accomplish what his father did so effortlessly with those minute sprockets and flywheels, the more Arthur felt certain the little shop on Sansome Street was not for him. His only other option would be to try to follow the trail blazed by his older brother, Irving, who had moved in full time with his father so that he could attend a highly regarded Philadelphia high school. Irving had avoided his father's workbench by earning a scholarship to the Philadelphia Museum School of Industrial Art; he later took a job at *Vogue* magazine, the start of a long and admired career as a photographer. (Irving would go on to become one of America's most celebrated still photographers, his iconic portraits of Miles Davis, Anaïs Nin, Pablo Picasso, Spencer Tracy, hippies in San Francisco, and Hells Angels with their bikes instantly recognizable.) Given Irving's success, it was decided that Arthur, at age fourteen, should also ship out from New York and do the same.

Arthur idolized his big brother, but he did not share Irving's affinity for study, nor did he have any idea what he would like to do with his life, other than he desperately hoped it would not involve timepieces. He never had much patience for holding still—the watch shop was sheer torture for him, and he found the classroom only slightly more tolerable. "Irving's view of life is in the title of his book, *Moments Preserved,*" his younger brother would observe many years later. "Mine is the kineticism of life, the energy . . . School was not my strong suit. I was sent down to Philadelphia to do terribly well and earn a scholarship, just like Irving. So of course, I didn't."

In the end, the bombing of Pearl Harbor during Penn's senior year in high school and his enlistment in the Army after graduation saved him from the watch shop—and from having to say no to his father, who had fallen ill with cancer. Instead, he left for boot camp and infantry training at Fort Jackson, South Carolina, where the city boy who grew up with subways and skyscrapers battled the inevitable culture shock by forming a small theater troupe of enlisted men. He got help from a new friend, the director of a community theater in nearby Columbia, where Penn and a few other soldiers spent their leave time—and where he learned theater was not merely an art, but a business.

After six weeks, his brief venture into military entertainment ended and he left for Europe, part of the second great wave of soldiers sent to replenish the fallen of D-Day and its aftermath. At the time, the war news had been regularly horrifying: Allied victory seemed far from certain, and the casualty rate of U.S. dead, wounded, and missing in action had surpassed 12,000 a week. Slated as a replacement in a frontline combat unit that had suffered horrendous casualties, Penn boarded a troop ship, certain he was headed to the front—only to be reassigned after his arrival in

England to serve in a small and obscure administrative unit, the 15th Army Headquarters.

The 15th HQ, he soon found out, consisted of a curious command post based in a sprawling Belgian hunting lodge deep in the rugged, ancient folds of the Ardennes forest. Before the war, the lodge had long served as a royal retreat for the King of the Belgians. The peaceful, lush setting was the last thing Penn expected to find at the end of the long transatlantic voyage.

Penn, as one of the few infantry-trained soldiers among the officers and bean counters assigned to duty at the Château d'Ardennes, was charged with providing security—he worked as a guard, defending the command post. But exactly what, he often wondered, was he defending? The unit's role in the war effort seemed at once secretive and obscure to Penn and his fellow grunts—the troops never really knew what the forty or so enlisted men and officers were doing at this lovely, peaceful château in the forest. The 15th Army that the headquarters supposedly commanded never seemed to be in sight. Penn eventually came to believe that he had been attached to a hollow command without an army, a ruse designed to confound enemy intelligence-gathering. In any case, he had almost nothing to do for months.

Penn's isolation from the shooting war came to an abrupt end on December 16, 1944, when the German army, under cover of foul weather, began a final, fierce, and desperate offensive—a last-ditch attempt to push back the Allies and secure a badly needed open water port in Antwerp to replace bombed and blocked supply lines. Hitler chose the Ardennes for his surprise invasion, knowing the Allied command considered it an unlikely area of attack because of the frigid winter weather. A Nazi success could buy time to replenish supplies, aircraft, and troops, to sow doubt and bickering among the Allies, and to complete work on several secret weapons projects, including jet aircraft and a Nazi version of the Manhattan Project. The war's outcome would be decided in the snowy forests of Belgium, Hitler correctly deduced.

And the Château d'Ardennes stood near the crossroads Adolf Hitler personally chose for his army's last march to the sea.

When it became clear what the Germans were attempting, the 15th Army Headquarters received orders to quickly pack up and evacuate to France before they were overrun and killed. Dodging enemy forces, Penn's small, ragtag group reached relative safety near the French-Belgium border, only to discover that some of the command's most sensitive papers, as well as two Spanish housekeepers thought to be Nazi sympathizers, had been left behind. Penn and the handful of other infantry-trained soldiers had to sneak back to the lodge, by then deep behind enemy lines, to retrieve the papers and the servants. They did so without firing a shot. "That was the only hairy moment of the war for me, and to be honest, nothing happened," Penn recalls. "There were so few of us, the Germans couldn't be bothered. They were just racing up and down the roads, and we slipped in and out."

All around them, though, battle raged throughout the region. The German onslaught pushed the American and British lines back, but the attackers could never quite break through to complete the race to Antwerp. The lines merely "bulged," leading to the Ardennes offensive's memorable nickname: the Battle of the Bulge.

Hitler's gamble failed when the weather cleared the day before Christmas, and Allied aircraft began pounding German troops, forcing a slow, painful retreat as more than 100,000 German soldiers perished. The bloodiest battle American troops faced in the war—with more than 80,000 U.S. dead and wounded and 23,000 prisoners of war taken—had been won, hastening the end of the war and ensuring Allied victory.

At home, meanwhile, a small group of recently discharged veterans—about 28,000—launched a very different sort of battle as they became the first to enroll in college under the newly enacted G.I. Bill of Rights, their efforts seen as a risky but modest experiment in the democratization of higher education. "Veterans Storm the Academic Beachhead: They have taken the mental bunkers and are proving to be good college students," a headline in *The New York Times* reported after their first year in school. The accompanying article noted official astonishment at the G.I.s' collegiate success—and little hint that this surprising phenomenon would soon enough involve millions rather than just thousands of veterans-turned-students.

When the war ended in Europe five months later on May 8, 1945, Penn's unit moved into Germany as part of the occupation, a chaotic time in which many soldiers felt little in the way of relief. Penn, like hundreds of thousands of other troops amassed in Europe as the war continued in the Pacific, expected at any moment to be dispatched to an armada of ships to join an all-out ground invasion of Japan—a second, final, and terrible D-Day. Many who had hoped for discharge after Germany's surrender were kept in service. The Army began searching for ways to mollify increasingly restive citizen soldiers longing for home. Arthur Penn's life was about to take a dramatic change of course.

One day a soldier Penn knew from boot camp, Lester Shurr, appeared and asked if he'd be interested in joining the Soldier

Show Company, an Army entertainment project. Shurr worked in civilian life as a talent agent; his older brother, Louis "Doc" Shurr, was a Hollywood legend, representing Bob Hope, Betty Grable, Ginger Rogers, and a host of other top-tier stars of the era. The younger Shurr had been assigned to review Army personnel records, searching for soldiers with experience in theater, music, or film, and he had remembered Penn from basic training in South Carolina. Shurr had been among the soldiers who frequented the community theater in Columbia, along with Penn.

Penn had only one question: "When can I start?"

A few days later, orders arrived transferring Penn to Paris, where Captain Alan Campbell and an Army intelligence officer named Joshua Logan ran the Soldier Show Company to rave reviews and with little in the way of Army discipline. Campbell was an accomplished Hollywood screenwriter before the war, the husband of author and Algonquin Round Table doyenne Dorothy Parker. Logan, already a successful director and writer when he joined the service, would go on to even greater fame after the war, directing a string of hit plays and films, then receiving a Pulitzer Prize for cowriting the Oscar and Hammerstein World War II musical blockbuster *South Pacific,* which he also directed.

Given their connections and credentials, Logan and Campbell had attracted dozens of actors and writers from their original Army units to the program, along with one hundred actresses flown in from Broadway. Penn, who could hardly believe he was mixing with such characters, left his first meeting with Campbell as the new stage manager for a production of the Clifford Odets play *Golden Boy* that was touring Europe featuring the stage and film stars Constance Dowling and Billy Halop, one of the original Dead End Kids.

"I had no idea what I was doing," Penn would later say. "I just did it."

He soon learned that stage managing in the seat-of-the-pants world of the Soldier Show Company meant scrounging for equipment, staff, and just about everything else needed to keep the wheels on the new production, along with mollifying cast and crew, setting up the next stop on the tour, and cleaning up after the last. *Golden Boy*—the story of a man torn between a satisfying but financially insecure career as a musician and the lucrative but unfulfilling lifestyle of a prizefighter—opened to packed audiences of G.I.s in Paris, then began touring towns throughout occupied Europe. Penn was frantic and fascinated—and couldn't believe his good fortune.

The show had reached Heidelberg by August 6, still packing in the crowds three months after Germany's surrender, when a secret device was deployed from a B-29 Super Fortress flying 31,000 feet above Japan. The ten-foot-long, 9,000-pound device, inscribed with a hand-painted message—"Greetings to the Emperor from the men of the Indianapolis"—fell for a full minute before reaching an altitude of 1,840 feet, where it finally detonated. Until that moment, no one was sure what, if anything, the device code-named "Little Boy" would do, least of all the crew of the rapidly retreating B-29. Then the blinding light of an artificial sun drenched the cockpit, and the copilot, gazing back at a city laid waste with the push of a button, exulted aloud to his crew at their success, though he scribbled a more somber entry in his journal: *My God, what have we done?*

Seventy thousand residents of Hiroshima had just died. Eventually, the death toll from radiation and burns would double that number. Three days later, Nagasaki met a similar doom with a device code-named "Fat Man," and Japan soon surrendered. The threat of a massive deployment of troops from Europe to battle an intransigent enemy in the Pacific abruptly vanished. The world found itself unexpectedly at peace. "Boom, it was over, just like that," Penn recalls. "Regretfully now, a little, understanding as we do the true horror of what happened, but joyful then, without question. It was over. We had won. We could go home."

Once the celebration had abated and Penn had confronted the inevitable *Now what?* he realized "home" was, at best, a tenuous concept for him. He had precious little awaiting him stateside: no money, no job prospects, a meager education—even the watch shop was gone, his father having succumbed to cancer. Penn's postwar period in Europe, on the other hand, had been exhilarating. And he knew that, while a flood of veterans would head home immediately, a substantial occupation and reconstruction force would remain behind. So instead of returning home, Penn walked into a massive Army demobilization center in Heidelberg. He emerged a civilian with a new job: Penn would succeed Logan and Campbell as the new head of the entire Soldier Show Company, graduating from stage manager to CEO with the stroke of a pen and the luck of the draw.

The remaining forces scattered throughout the European theater still needed to be entertained. As head of the program, Penn received a $7,000 yearly salary, free hotel lodgings, a sumptuous office in the Wiesbaden Opera House, meals at the officers' club—and a chance to work in every aspect of the theater, including directing. His casts were an amalgam of amateurs and professionals and extras he recruited virtually from any military unit he could find. There were multiple shows going on throughout Europe and he oversaw them all, traveling from city to city, a watchmaker's son seeing the world, some of it shattered, some of it splendidly intact.

He even found time to sit in on the war crimes trials at Nuremberg, mesmerized by the combination of monumental evil, legal ritual, and the surprising mundanity of the proceedings. There were, to his surprise, plenty of seats available to watch a true trial of the century.

"I wanted to see those goddamn Nazis," he recalls sixty years later. "I saw them all. It was tedious but fascinating. You'd start to get bored, and then you'd say to yourself, 'Wait a minute. Remember what you're looking at.'"

After Penn spent a year running the Soldier Show Company, the military presence in Europe had contracted to the point that it was time to close up shop and head home. He had found the experience invaluable, leaving little doubt in his mind about his desire to pursue a career in theater, but his work for the Army also showed Penn how much he needed to learn. The holes in his education had been humbling at times—not merely in the theory and practice of bringing drama to the stage, but in the broader areas of literature and the arts, in how to analyze and understand the deeper meanings of the texts he had been trying to bring to life in grand old theaters and on makeshift plywood stages. He knew, now, what he wanted to do in life. He had heard by then about the G.I. Bill benefits that could be used to attend college. Veterans benefits had not been on his mind when he enlisted, but now he saw them as essential: full tuition, a stipend, money for books, the only limitation being his ability to convince a college to accept him—it sounded too good to be true. With so many possibilities suddenly before him, the only question was: Where to go?

When he returned to New York and happily exchanged his uniform for his civilian clothes (he did not share the separation anxiety some other vets felt), he told his brother he couldn't picture himself returning from the regimentation of the Army and the chaotic, seat-of-the-pants world of the Soldier Show Company only to march into some large university as a freshman, consigned to lecture halls and roll calls. "That just doesn't make any sense to me," he said. "I can't see myself doing that."

Irving suggested there was more than one sort of college to consider, some of them quite different from the stereotype Penn dreaded. He mentioned a tiny school in North Carolina called Black Mountain College, strong on the arts, full of interesting characters, resolutely nontraditional. "Why don't you take a bus down, have a look? It might suit you."

A week later, Penn took his brother's suggestion and bought a Greyhound ticket to Asheville, where he found a college nestled in the Blue Ridge Mountains unlike any he had imagined—unlike any other in the nation, for that matter. The campus held less than a hundred students (and considerably fewer during the war), an impressive array of faculty talent, and an atmosphere so informal it bordered on the anarchic.

Even Black Mountain's admissions process reflected the school's philosophy: In his first contact with the college, Penn was invited to stay the week and attend classes, which he soon found were loosely defined and frequently continued through lunch and into dinner when discussions grew intense. When Penn asked how these classes worked, he was told the process was simple: If someone here knows something you're interested in, go ask them to teach you. Others may or may not join in. The school, in other words, was an ongoing improvisation, and Penn instantly thought of the seat-of-the-pants Soldier Show Company he had run, a world of the last minute that forced you to swim or sink. He felt like his arrival at Black Mountain was a homecoming.

"What do you think of us?" one of the professors asked after a week had passed.

"I'm pretty taken with it," Penn said.

"Then why don't you stay?"

Penn shook his head sadly. "I don't have any money."

"You're a veteran. You've got the G.I. Bill. That's all you need."

And so he stayed. His classmates included ex-Marine and G.I. Bill student Robert Rauschenberg, destined to start an artistic revolution when he rebelled against his famous abstract expressionist mentors at Black Mountain by producing the first examples of pop art in his neo-Dadaist paintings and sculpture. Also in attendance was Army Air Corps veteran and abstract painter Kenneth Noland, whose two brothers attended Black Mountain as well after serving in the war—the Noland family was from a town near the campus. All used the G.I. Bill to pay their way. Army cryptologist-turned-painter Cy Twombly was also there, as was future sculptor Ruth Asawa, Black Mountain being one of the few campuses a Japanese American student fresh from the internment camps could not only feel welcome, but also meet her future husband. For ex-G.I.s—or ex-internees—who had experienced enough of war and regimentation and were ready for something completely different, Black Mountain became an academic magnet, a place to nurture one's talent in the arts along with one's taste for rebelliousness—long before such attitudes became commonplace on other college campuses in the sixties and seventies.

A collection of American educators disaffected with traditional universities had founded Black Mountain College in 1933 in the belief that learning was poorly served by rigid rosters, course requirements, and remote professors lecturing students by the hundred. They were soon joined by a group of German Bauhaus School artists fleeing Nazi oppression. Together they sought to fashion a more intimate, alternative school that immersed students in the arts, in invention, and in questioning conventional wisdom—an academic community in which students and teachers worked and governed their college together, hands-on, from creating courses to picking up the garbage to sharing (and cooking) the evening meals. Intellectual rigor and dressing well for Saturday evening dinner and dancing were the only rules imposed by the founders.

Built in a remote southern landscape of mountains, lakes, and strict segregation, Black Mountain existed as an island of liberalism in an area seldom considered hospitable to progressives, leftists, integrationists, and flouters of tradition. While Darwin's theories were banned by the surrounding public schools (the Scopes Trial had taken place less than two hundred miles away), evolutionary theory was the order of the day at Black Mountain. While other universities emphasized traditional technique in art instruction, Black Mountain's professors preached theory, experimentation, and defiance of tradition. While the rest of American academia rushed to embrace measurement as the new driving force of education—the grade curves, college boards, and standardized tests that dominate schools to this day—Black Mountain eschewed formal exams and grades, preferring to have students progress by completing substantive projects in their courses of study, with professors and outside experts judging the results.

The school lasted a mere quarter century—and it likely would have perished much sooner if not for the G.I. Bill and the postwar influx of veterans—yet its ideas and ideals, considered radical, even dangerous at the time, have had a lasting impact on American education and arts. Groundbreaking approaches to arts instruction and theory, interdisciplinary education, and project-based learning were passed on to other educators by the school's stellar faculty and students. The college became a center for the abstract expressionists, as well as for those who rebelled against that artistic school's somber nature by bringing on the new wave of pop art. And the Bauhaus influence on industrial design, pioneered by Walter Gropius and the other refugees who found safe harbor at Black Mountain (when other, more storied universities ignored the victims of Nazi persecution), continues to this day—from the ubiquitous tensor desk lamp to those tubular metal chairs used in virtually every public school in America.

Among the renowned teachers at Black Mountain with Penn were artists Jacob Lawrence and Josef and Anni Albers, composer John Cage, dancer and choreographer Merce Cunningham, architect and inventor Buckminster Fuller, artists Willem and Elaine de Kooning, and physicist Peter Bergmann, a collaborator of Albert Einstein's and a pioneer in studying modern gravity and field theory. Guest lecturers at Black Mountain included William Carlos Williams, Aldous Huxley, Anaïs Nin, Henry Miller, and Einstein. Farmers and hunters in the area would gawk when they saw a fuzzy haired stranger strolling past along a rural road, only to realize they had just brushed shoulders with the most famous physicist in the world.

Fuller built his first geodesic dome at Black Mountain; Cage staged his first "Happening" and helped forge a new form destined to be called performance art; Cunningham pioneered new methods of modern dance and composition and started his groundbreaking dance company; and Albers developed a breakthrough theory of color.

Celebrity lecturers and accolades aside, with such a tiny student body and a virtually nonexistent endowment, Black Mountain forever teetered on the verge of financial insolvency. Teachers worked for room and board during the Depression and for even less during World War II. School administrators used a mica mine on school property to support the college during the war, selling the vital mineral to the government for use in combat radios and electronics gear. Even so, the war years were perilously lean, as enrollment dropped precipitously at colleges nationwide, and Black Mountain's population dwindled to a couple dozen students. Closure seemed imminent.

But after the war, the G.I. Bill brought on the best of times for Black Mountain, as it did for so many other American colleges and universities, in ways both obvious and subtle. Schools on the brink of bankruptcy were soon overflowing, and Black Mountain, with a record enrollment approaching one hundred, found itself restored to a modest but stable financial footing by those $500-per-student payments from the Veterans Administration, an unimaginably kingly tuition in that place and time. Rescuing the likes of Black Mountain surely was never envisioned by the conservative American Legion, the Red-baiting John Rankin, or any of the other congressional champions of the G.I. Bill, who had in mind trade schools and correspondence courses, not wildly experimental colleges with few rules, a racially integrated faculty and student body, and an extraordinary (for the era) tolerance of eccentricity and alternative lifestyles. That such a radically different, academically subversive college could flourish in the increasingly conservative postwar era, right along with rural farm schools and traditional Ivy League campuses, is testament to just how flexible, democratic, and utterly nonjudgmental the G.I. Bill could be (intentionally or not).

Penn found an academic mentor in writer, sculptor, and philosopher Mary Caroline Richards, a literature professor who gave up a comfortable tenure at the University of Chicago to become the head of faculty at Black Mountain. While there, she authored, among a number of works, an enduringly influential underground classic, *Centering in Pottery, Poetry, and the Person.* In typical Black Mountain fashion, Penn approached her at lunch early in his first year and said, "I want to learn how to read. How to really *read.* Not the words, but the motives, the intentions, the themes."

Richards looked at the copy of *The Brothers Karamazov* he held in his hands, nodded, and said, "Let's get to work, then."

So began Penn's study of classical literature and poetry. Richards' lectures on seeing beneath the surface—whether focusing on the divine complexity within a simple leaf held aloft in the sunlight, or divining the murkiest undercurrents of Dostoevsky—connected with Penn in a way few teachings ever had. Aware of his background with the Soldier Show Company, Richards also urged him to put these ideas to the test by pursuing his interest in drama and even to teach some acting classes at Black Mountain. If you have to teach it, she told him, then you have to learn it.

"Well, I don't know beans about teaching acting," he replied. "But listen, I'll get a copy of Stanislavski and we'll see how we do."

He ended up directing French composer Erik Satie's surrealist lyric comedy, *The Ruse of Medusa,* a rousing production that is inevitably mentioned in histories and remembrances of Black Mountain. It boasted an all-star, offbeat cast and crew that had Richards translating the play from its original French, Cage composing and performing the music, Cunningham choreographing and dancing, Willem and Elaine de Kooning creating the sets, and an introverted Buckminster Fuller lured away from building his first geodesic dome to deliver an extravagant star turn as the title character, the elderly and perennially confused Baron Meduse. Penn's technique for loosening up his stiff and reluctant star was to order the cast to cavort about campus behaving like monkeys, and Fuller later credited Penn's production with enabling him to overcome his chronic shyness. Soon Fuller was lecturing throughout the world on his ideas about renewable energy and environmentally friendly policies, which became popularized in the seventies with his metaphor for the planet as Spaceship Earth.

Penn, too, came away with a sense of confidence and an embrace of improvisation as a critical element of education and creativity. "It's really something that I've taken with me, that I've embraced in my work, and in all my life," he later reflected.

After two years at Black Mountain, he used the G.I. Bill to finish college at the University of Florence, where he studied Italian and Renaissance poetry, part of his mission to "learn how to read," as he still describes it. Then he returned to New York to put his new education to work and to search for a job as a Broadway stage manager.

Finding the theater job market impossibly crowded despite his Army show experience, Penn instead took a job as one of NBC's floor managers at its new television operation, where the network hired him on the spot. Penn once again found himself surrounded by ex-G.I.s, now fresh out of school and busy building a new industry desperate for new talent. Most of the actors, directors, writers, producers, cameramen, and sound engineers he encountered had served in Europe or the Pacific or the Far East, and most had gone to college or technical school on the G.I. Bill.

America was transforming by this time, with new suburbs, new highways, new medical centers, new schools, and new industries springing up seemingly overnight to accommodate burgeoning postwar demand, and television rapidly claimed its place—still unrelinquished—as the cultural and media epicenter of the country. In 1945 few Americans had been exposed to television, much less owned a set. Within five years, it would become the most popular form of entertainment and information in the country, offering innumerable opportunities for young veterans back from the war and educated on the G.I. Bill.

As a floor manager at NBC, Penn served as a jack-of-all-trades, broken in on his first day with the less-than-glamorous task of holding cue cards for TV's first megastar, Milton Berle. Then he shipped out to the popular Colgate Comedy Hour, where he worked with the top TV celebrities of the era—Dean Martin, Jerry Lewis, Bob Hope, Eddie Cantor, Danny Thomas.

When newly laid coaxial cable joined East to West Coast in 1951—a video link made possible with a small army of newly minted, G.I. Bill–subsidized engineers and technicians—Penn, the perennial New Yorker, reluctantly moved to the new TV studios of Hollywood for his first opportunity to direct live television. He spent two miserable years there directing comedy shows he did not particularly like (staring comedians he liked even less), then jumped at the chance to return to New York at the invitation of an old friend from his boot camp days—Fred Coe. Coe had been the head of the little community theater in South Carolina where Penn had hung out during his basic training furloughs. Coe had come a long way since then: He had risen to be a producer and director of top-tier shows for NBC, to this day considered some of the finest ever broadcast. His specialty was giving work to a new generation of young writers, directors, and actors, including Gore Vidal, Sidney Lumet, Grace Kelly, and Steve McQueen. His shows became springboards for future stars of television, stage, and cinema—during his long career, he would produce more than 500 hours of original television dramas as well as numerous stage plays and feature films. Coe was working on the debut of an experimental Sunday night dramatic half-hour show called *First Person Singular,* in which the audience viewed everything through a single camera's point of view, and the actors addressed the camera as a character. He wanted Penn to direct. "Come out and if you're any good and can do it, I'll keep you on," Coe drawled.

Back in New York, Penn's first task was directing a teleplay written by Paddy Chayefsky, one of two ex-G.I.s busily setting the standard for television writing (he would later pen the screenplay for the biting and hilarious film about television news, *Network*). The other was Rod Serling, then of the respected anthology drama *Playhouse 90,* later of his own enduringly popular concoction, *The Twilight Zone.* The two young veterans and G.I. Bill college graduates were being hailed as the new Arthur Millers and Tennessee Williamses of the small screen. Anthology dominated the airwaves at that time—the age of series television would come later—and because these shows were based on original teleplays and filmed live on small indoor sets with the meager black-and-white, nine-inch screens of the day in mind, they had to rely on close-ups, strong character development, and psychological tension rather than action to generate interest. Coe's genius was in assembling writers, actors, and sophisticated storytelling to turn what today would be considered fatal shortcomings into dramatic advantages, creating entertainment by adults, for adults.

Penn had no idea he was joining what would later be revered as a high-water mark for the medium, the so-called golden age of television, when the best writers, directors, and actors in the country performed serious, challenging dramas on a regular basis.

Then he met his very first cast, which included the actresses Mildred Dunnock, who had starred in *Death of a Salesman* on Broadway and in the hit movie based on the play, and Kim Hunter, who played Stella opposite Marlon Brando in *A Streetcar Named Desire* on stage and in an Academy-Award-winning reprise of the role on film.

"My jaw just dropped," Penn recalls. "I was scared to death to even suggest the smallest thing to these great actors."

Out of necessity, Penn's timidity soon evaporated. The whirlwind environment of live television, stitched together with a minimum of rehearsals and vacuum tube powered cameras that blew out on an almost daily basis, was not for the timid, and Penn's improvisational skills from the Army and Black Mountain served him well. His colleagues considered him a natural. "Just about everyone in the control room, all the directors, had been in the war," Penn recalls. "You had to have cold blood to sit in that room, live, with those wonderful actors and those god-awful cameras, and you calling the shots."

Penn soon graduated to the top ranks of network television when he was invited to become one of three directors on the network's signature Sunday night drama hour, the Philco/Goodyear Playhouse combo of shows, where Coe also presided. These were showcase series that drew top performers of the era every week. Broadway was dark on Sundays in those days, and the chance to perform fresh material before a live audience of millions was a potent inducement to stage performers eager to try something different. Penn had hit the big time, and his skills and reputation began to mount.

His achievements on television finally led to the opportunities he had long coveted to direct on Broadway with the 1957 hit, *Two*

For the Seesaw, starring Henry Fonda and Anne Bancroft. A few months later, Penn turned a teleplay about Billy the Kid written by Gore Vidal into his first big-screen project, *The Left-Handed Gun,* with Paul Newman as the Kid and Penn directing. Next, with Coe as his producer, he brought a *Playhouse 90* television episode to the Broadway stage—*The Miracle Worker,* the award-winning play about Helen Keller and her indomitable teacher, Anne Sullivan.

Penn won a Tony Award for his direction, and he and Coe next brought the same play to the big screen, fighting the studio brass—who had horrified Penn with their heavy-handed editing of *The Left-Handed Gun*—to cast Bancroft, who originated the role of Anne Sullivan on stage, rather than Elizabeth Taylor, whom United Artists wanted.

"The film would have been a disaster," Penn says now. "We wouldn't budge." United Artists relented, then retaliated by slashing the production budget 75 percent, although Penn would be vindicated in the end: *The Miracle Worker* became a hit and has long been recognized as a masterpiece of filmmaking. Bancroft and Patty Duke, as the young Helen Keller, each won Academy Awards, and Penn found himself propelled to the top ranks of American film directors.

It was no surprise then that the Kennedy campaign would approach Penn and Coe for help with the historic 1960 presidential debate. The choice of Penn proved to be fortuitous for Kennedy, and not just because of the director's skill at bringing drama to life in the flickering of a nine-inch black-and-white screen. The stories to which Penn gravitated invariably involved outsiders and outcasts, archetypal figures whose stories resonated—Billy the Kid, the illiterate, lonely antihero; and Helen Keller, the ultimate outsider who, angry, frustrated, and cut off from the world, ended up reconnecting to her own humanity, forever changing the way society viewed the disabled. Now he had a man before him who would be the first Catholic president, about whom there already were mutterings about allegiance to the pope above the Constitution, taking on the seasoned political insider, Nixon. Penn sensed those same archetypal themes could be evoked in the presidential debates, shaping how viewers would see and remember the candidates and filter their words. The director knew the optimism and vigor of the postwar period could be epitomized far more readily by the youthful Kennedy than through his opponent. No one, Penn knew, would ever imagine Richard Nixon presiding over a new Camelot.

Penn also realized the rules of engagement the campaigns had hammered out for the debate unintentionally elevated style over substance. It had been decided by the campaigns that in the interest of fairness every shot and camera angle used for one candidate would be exactly duplicated for the opponent. Ruthlessly, Penn used as many close-ups as possible for his man during the broadcast, knowing that the opposition would have to do the same—and that there would be no contest. It would be Beauty versus the Beast, Penn said, confident that the camera would be far kinder to the classically handsome Kennedy than it would to the carelessly coiffed Nixon, with his legendary, incessant five-o'clock shadow and sharp, pallid features.

Penn's approach and director's eye for detail and performance paid off. Kennedy looked decisive, dynamic, and credible, a steely resolve looking out into the living rooms of America. Nixon, just released from a hospital stay for a knee injury, appeared pale, gaunt, and shifty-eyed, and less consistently looked at the camera, appearing to avoid eye contact even though at times he was staring directly at his journalistic questioners. He had refused makeup, and his clothes fit badly because of the weight he had lost in the hospital. The close-ups were merciless.

The result: Polls showed that a large majority of the 70 million viewers thought Kennedy had beaten Nixon roundly, while those who only heard the debate on radio thought Nixon edged Kennedy. For better or worse, Penn not only played a significant part in the fashioning of television as the dominant modern entertainment form, he also played a key role in its rise as the dominant medium of political communication and campaigning—and in the elevation of form over substance that has since shaped modern American politics, from the thirty-second attack commercial to the sound-bite mode of political discourse. In an election decided by a fraction of 1 percent of the vote, no politician since has forgotten the lessons of the first televised presidential debate.

Eight years later, Penn met Robert F. Kennedy as he prepared to take on a resurgent Nixon in his own run for the presidency—a candidacy Penn very much wished to support. He directed one commercial for RFK, who told Penn when they were through, "I'm going to California, but when I get back, let's talk about what's next."

But there was no next. Sirhan Sirhan's gun found Bobby Kennedy in the kitchen of the Ambassador Hotel in Los Angeles, a promising political star's career extinguished even as he won the California primary and seemed destined for the White House. Penn walked away from political campaigns for good.

Even as he left politics, Penn's work became more politically charged, as did much of theater and cinema in the sixties and seventies. The Kennedy brothers' violent ends and the national trauma they caused mirrored the themes Penn sought to explore in his work. His love of stories about outsiders and outcasts perfectly suited the sensibilities of sixties America and its struggles with Vietnam, civil unrest, the hippie movement, and the seemingly endless series of assassinations—Kennedy, King, Kennedy.

Penn struck cinematic gold with what would be his most praised and famous feature film, *Bonnie and Clyde,* his story of outcasts rebelling in Depression-era America, with its hard life and meager dreams—the times in which Penn came of age. But unlike Penn, who found his way out through the service and the G.I. Bill, the Clyde Barrow and Bonnie Parker he brought to the screen saw little hope for themselves and little reason to respect authority or to restrain their anger.

The film was revolutionary, humor and graphic violence constantly juxtaposed, the realism shocking and, at the time, utterly unlike anything Hollywood had ever produced. Bonnie and Clyde, portrayed as vicious outlaws in the news reports at the time of their crimes, were depicted as brutal in Penn's film, too—but they were also the beautiful and doomed heroes, left behind by a financially crushed country and a corrupt justice system, with Bonnie the former spelling bee champ writing poetry between bank jobs, and Clyde warm and funny between murders. They had family values of a sort, at once loyal and brave and twisted and sadistic. They were the evil heroes, the sympathetic villains—Penn's film defied Hollywood's traditions of filmmaking and storytelling and moral clarity.

When he filmed the brutal climax, in which the stars, Warren Beatty and Faye Dunaway as the title characters, were riddled with bullets, a piece of Beatty's skull seemed to fly into the air. Penn had deliberately evoked the dreadful film footage of the assassination of John F. Kennedy. Every modern depiction of violence in film—from slow-motion carnage to the replacement of the typical "bloodless" death of earlier gangster movies with vivid realism—owes its origin, for better or worse, to *Bonnie and Clyde,* the first film to break all the old conventions.

Penn broke so many of the unwritten rules of Hollywood that the film almost was shelved by Warner Brothers studio, where one of the last of the old-time studio chiefs, Jack Warner, still ruled. When Penn and Beatty, who had produced the film in addition to starring in the title role, brought a rough cut to the mogul's mansion, Warner plopped down in the screening room and delivered a gruff warning: "Listen, if I have to go to the bathroom in the first ten minutes of the film, it stinks."

Seven minutes in, Warner disappeared to use the bathroom. He got up a second time within fifteen minutes. Pretty soon, he was spending more time in the toilet than in the screening room. He clearly just didn't get it. In the end, when it seemed Warner might kill the whole project, Beatty resorted to abject flattery. "Don't you realize, Jack, this is an homage to the Warner Brothers gangster movies from the thirties?"

Warner just stared at him for a second, then asked, "And what the fuck is an homage?"

But the notion that the filmmakers were honoring some classic Warner films dear to the old man's heart appealed to his vanity, and he provided the necessary, if lukewarm, thumbs-up to proceed, although the studio's support for marketing the film barely had a pulse. Beatty, certain they were on to something big, all but stood on street corners hawking the film, even penning personally addressed notes to projectionists at theaters around the country, slipping them one by one into film cans. The notes asked the projectionists to set the volume higher than usual to make certain scenes more vivid and shocking.

The initial wave of reviews was almost exclusively horrible, led by not one, but three separate denunciations from *The New York Times'* feared and influential reviewer, Bosley Crowther, who had been making and breaking new movies since the end of World War II. Crowther likened the Barrow gang to a big-screen, hair-trigger, nose-picking version of the Beverly Hillbillies, and the film's theme "a cheap piece of bald-faced slapstick comedy that treats the hideous depredations of that sleazy, moronic pair as though they were as full of fun and frolic as the jazz-age cut-ups in *Thoroughly Modern Millie.*"

Only one critic who reviewed the film on opening day, a neophyte just six months in the business in Chicago, perceived something of value, stating (presciently, it turned out), "Years from now it is quite possible that 'Bonnie and Clyde' will be seen as the definitive film of the 1960s." The young reviewer—Roger Ebert, who would later rise to national prominence through his televised movie reviews—found the film disturbing, exciting, and groundbreaking, "a milestone in the history of American movies, a work of truth and brilliance."

One good review was not enough, however, and to Penn's great disappointment, *Bonnie and Clyde* opened and closed quickly in the autumn of 1967. His film career, so full of promise in the wake of *The Miracle Worker,* and the critical praise heaped on his other efforts, seemed to be over, and he prepared to return to his first love, the stage.

"I thought that was it," Penn would later muse.

Yet a film set in the Depression, mythologizing a doomed couple's violent crime spree while also embodying the rebellious, disaffected, antiestablishment tone of the sixties, told in a thoroughly fresh, uncensored, and unpredictable way, could not so easily be killed. Fans, first in Europe, then in America, made their opinions known. Letters flooded *The New York Times,* the flow increasing every time Crowther penned yet another pan. Faye Dunaway's costumes—French berets and maxiskirts—became a worldwide fashion craze. The infectious Flatt and Scruggs bluegrass sound track topped the charts.

Then critics, too, began to see the film differently, with a belated series of raves appearing in national magazines, including a stunning reversal by Joe Morgenstern, then movie critic at *Newsweek,* in which he retracted his initial pan of the film with an apology and praise. Morgenstern would later recall going to see the movie a second time with his wife after his first review had been published and watching, first in amazement, then in horror, as the audience went wild: "The cold sweat started to form on my neck. I knew I'd blown it."

Soon *Bonnie and Clyde* reopened, and this time Warner spared no expense promoting the film with a catchy, sardonic tagline emblazoned across the ads: "They're young . . . they're in love . . . and they kill people."

Bonnie and Clyde went on to become a smash hit, launching an entirely new type of filmmaking, of independent, auteur-driven cinema—what would be called yet another golden age, launched in part by Penn's work, this time in film instead of television. In retrospect, long after *Bonnie and Clyde*'s 1967 debut, long after graphic violence in film has grown numbingly commonplace, and the slow-motion duel a cliché rather than clever, it can be difficult to comprehend just how different Penn's movie seemed at the time of its premiere, with its daring sensibilities, its attention to details that made a visceral, physical connection with the audience. And though it was criticized for its intense and graphic violence, none of Penn's characters ever avoided moral responsibility for their actions, and all of them (most of all the title characters) paid a heavy price for resorting to violence—unlike the flood of subsequent and lesser films that have glorified carnage for its own sake and made unalloyed heroes of its perpetrators.

The film assured that Penn would be remembered as one of the great American filmmakers, but it also had a sweeping impact on the careers of others. Actors Faye Dunaway and Gene Hackman, little known before *Bonnie and Clyde,* achieved stardom. Beatty, whose career had been previously perceived as in decline, would from then on enjoy a freedom to star in and create films as he saw fit. Other members of the cast and crew saw their stars rise dramatically as well—editors, cinematographers, writers, and actors moved on to help create many of the signature films of the next decade. Penn went on to direct several other highly praised films, and to continue his career directing and producing television well past his eightieth birthday, still living in New York and most recently working with his son, also a television director.

And so the multifaceted career of the film director, affecting the lives and the course of events in so many instances—in politics, in television, in film—ends up as a metaphor for the G.I. Bill itself, the ripples caused by one life, or one piece of legislation, spreading far and with unforeseeable consequences.

"I have a deep and abiding affection for the G.I. Bill," Penn says. "I can't imagine what my life would have been without it, the opportunities I would probably have missed. It seemed so fantastic at the time, that you could study anywhere—anywhere, even in Europe—and it would all be paid for. We came home from war and used it to build a new world. There's never been anything else like it. . . . There's nothing quite like it now. More's the pity."

☆ 7 ☆

Gunnery Mates and Other Invisible Veterans:

Women and the G.I. Bill that Wasn't

Josette Dermody strung the red, white, and blue streamers for her going-away party that night, then rushed off to Sunday morning Mass, bursting with pride and impatience over what she was about to do: defend her Constitution and country as the newest member of the United States Navy Women's Reserve. She had aced the tests, passed the physical, and her father, however reluctantly, had signed the permission slip for his twenty-year-old daughter to join (a bit of paternalistic fine print that had vexed Josette, given that no permission had been sought or given when her eighteen-year-old brother volunteered after Pearl Harbor).

But she would not let anything spoil the moment or her heady excitement at joining the most important conflict the world had ever seen—not to mention her giddiness at the prospect of finally getting out of Detroit. Visions of boarding a ship to Europe or the South Pacific had kept her awake more than one night, at least until she realized the Navy WAVES were not allowed to serve overseas.

At church, the parish priest delivered his usual exhortations for his congregation to pray for the boys "over there." The war news in the spring of 1944 was not so good: Just that morning the papers had reported on some new and terrible buzz bomb the Germans had unleashed, and it seemed clear the G.I.s needed all the help they could get.

"This morning we want to ask God's special blessing on Keith Applegate and Josette Dermody, who have answered their country's call to arms and will be leaving soon," the priest intoned, and Josette sat up extra straight, her expression serene—until she heard the pastor's next words. Then her stomach flopped and her face turned a hot, angry crimson as she listened, fists clenched in her lap. "To be sure, I don't know what our beloved country is coming to when we send our young ladies off to war. Let us pray."

Years later, she would recall the moment—and the thoughts she kept to herself—in her autobiography, *Mother Was a Gunner's Mate*: "Doesn't he know it's 1944? And hasn't he ever heard of Joan of Arc?"

Dermody's complaint would turn out to be a common one of the era, when women veterans and defense workers found that, despite their immense contributions to winning the war, their efforts were often minimized, dismissed, or derided. Women were, in many respects, invisible veterans, Dermody says. And despite the G.I. Bill's theoretical blindness to race and gender, the same sort of veiled resentment Josette's parish priest had voiced during the war created a host of barriers in peacetime for women veterans eager to use their G.I. Bill's benefits at home and in school.

For American women, the G.I. Bill proved a much more mixed blessing that it was for men, even for those who loved their time in the service. "We wanted to fight for our country," Dermody says. "But we had to fight the woman haters while we were in. And then when we got home, we had to fight again for what was ours."

Given the raw numbers—16 million men in uniform during World War II versus 350,000 women—it seems obvious that the G.I. Bill by definition had to benefit men disproportionately. If America fights and helps win an epochal war against tyranny and terror, and that war is fought by men, and the country's leaders wish to reward those millions of veterans while simultaneously cushioning the economy from the shock of their sudden return to the labor force, what choice is there but to create a benefits buffet that favors the half of Americans who happen to be male?

In all the many celebrations of the G.I. Bill's success across the years, this deliberate lack of gender neutrality is barely noted and rarely questioned. It has been assumed, when considered at all, to have been the only approach possible, as if no other choices existed.

But, in fact, this was a choice, not an inevitability. And there were other options on the table, other paths that could have been taken to America's future.

The Roosevelt administration, in keeping with the president's desire to pursue a wider economic bill of rights for all citizens, had advocated a different approach early in the national debate on how best to avoid postwar unrest, depression, and economic free fall. Until Congress killed it for its effrontery, the president's National Resources Planning Board—chaired by Roosevelt's uncle, Frederic Delano—had suggested that postwar training, job placement, unemployment, medical, housing, and education benefits ought not be limited to veterans. Civilian military and defense workers, many of whose jobs also would vanish with the advent of peace, deserved consideration as well, the board argued. The logic of this proposition seemed inescapable: Civilian defense efforts were no less critical to the war effort than the military's, and many war workers' tasks and sacrifices differed little from the duties of the millions of servicemen working noncombat duties stateside and overseas. In some instances, such as working in explosives and chemical weapons plants, the civilian work was as hazardous—and sometimes as deadly—as the duties of many soldiers, airmen, sailors, and Marines in the combat zone.

The G.I. Bill, after all, drew no distinction between combat and noncombat duty; so long as they served for ninety days, any member of the military, from battlefield heroes to War Department file clerks, could qualify for the richest treasure trove of benefits any nation has ever offered its veterans. Why, then, shouldn't civilians who performed vital defense-related work, often for years at a time, working long hours with few days off, receive similar consideration?

Answering that question represented a monumental turning point in planning for peacetime and guiding the nation's future course, for on one side lay a narrower but beneficial boon to veterans, and on the other lay Roosevelt's democratic Holy Grail, his proposal for a second bill of rights. One prominent editorialist of the era summed up the crossroads this way: "Posterity may look back and see the Roosevelt plan as a mirage, but if it does, the fault will also be ours . . . The President has launched out on the greatest battle of our time."

And no one had more at stake in that battle than American women.

Record legions of men may have been drafted or volunteered to join the military after the attack on Pearl Harbor, but an even greater legion of women—19 million—marched to work on the home front, a 50 percent increase over peacetime. During four years of war, the proportion of women in the work force rose, from 24 to 37 percent—a level of female employment that would not be matched again in the United States for another quarter century.

This was not merely a matter of numbers: With men gone to war, the jobs women took often defied traditional roles as well, taking them beyond teaching, nursing, secretarial, and domestic work and putting them in direct competition with men for the first time. During the war, the number of women working as maids fell by half, while the female ranks in the defense industry soared 460 percent. In very tangible ways, desperation trumped discrimination, and manpower needs trumped traditional mores as the nation early in the war faced the very real possibility of defeat. American freighters were being sunk by U-boats spewing torpedoes with impunity, the proudest ships in the Navy had been decimated at Pearl Harbor, the Army's tanks in 1941 were pitiful remnants of World War I technology, and the Japanese and German pilots and aircraft flew rings around the Americans' older planes and inexperienced aviators. Throwing women into a war effort the United States had long sought to avoid was not just a nice extra; it was an absolute necessity. When Roosevelt warned the nation in one of his fireside chats that America was engaged in total war, it was not hyperbole.

As a result, for the first time significant numbers of American women took on high-paying industrial jobs, spurred by a government campaign designed to overcome traditional notions of "a woman's place," while appealing to patriotic fervor in a national crisis. Immortalized by the iconic war poster of a cover-all-clad Rosie the Riveter—flexing her right bicep while announcing, "We can do it!"—women shouldered the burden of building ships, bombs, aircraft parts, mess kits, grenades, helmets, and carbines (while being paid considerably less than their male counterparts for the same work, despite unprecedented federal equal-pay regulations imposed during the war). The Greatest Generation fought the Axis powers not only through the justly celebrated efforts of men in combat, but through the far less heralded army of women who built the weapons of war, without which Germany and Japan could not have been defeated. This ramped-up, women-powered industrial mobilization—planned for in secret by the Roosevelt administration since 1939—enabled America to outproduce its enemies by orders of magnitude, building one hundred aircraft carriers during the war compared to Japan's nine.

Recognition that women played significant roles in this war effort is not a matter of revisionist history, belated hindsight, or contemporary political correctness. Their contributions created a sensation at the time, celebrated, embraced, and occasionally condemned as an assault on family values. Nor is there any doubt that women tackled tough and dangerous wartime jobs as they helped build a superpower out of a nation that, until 1941, had a weak military with few modern ships, tanks, cannons, jeeps, or planes. The Redstone and Huntsville Arsenals in Alabama, crucial links in the military ordnance chain, had all-male factory crews in 1940; those crews were 63 percent female before the war ended, with many crews made up entirely of women, more than 4,000 in all. They produced a vital stream of bombs, grenades, napalm, and chemical weapons that included deadly and difficult-to-handle mustard and phosgene gases—27 million chemical munitions and

45 million rounds of ammunition and bombs in all. Press accounts referred to Redstone women as "production soldiers" and "modern-day Amazons." Several of the all-women crews proved to be the most productive the arsenal had ever seen, and a senior male foreman, who had been opposed to employing women on weapons crews, said at the end of the war that he stood in awe of his female workers, the best he had ever managed. The women weapons workers wore military-style uniforms and jumpsuits, worked forty-eight-hour days, six-day weeks, and braved noisy, tense, hazardous workplaces daily, where the slightest mistake handling explosives or volatile chemicals could maim or kill. Five of the Woman Ordnance Workers—they went by the acronym WOW—were killed on the job, and dozens more were injured during the manufacture of these weapons of war.

In a very different but equally vital role, the Women Airforce Service Pilots (the WASP—apparently great acronyms were a specialty of World War II women warriors) took over the task of testing new production aircraft and piloting them from factories to Army and Navy airfields, as well as towing targets for antiaircraft practice. More than a thousand female pilots completed the same basic and advanced training as male military pilots, flying every aircraft in the inventory and, during a critical pilot shortage, freeing up male pilots for combat duty. The WASP's founder and leader was a swashbuckling adventurer, Jacqueline Cochran, a renowned aviator, holder (to this day) of more air distance and speed records than any flier (male or female), friend of Amelia Earhart, Chuck Yeager, and Dwight Eisenhower (she helped convince him to run for president), and founder of a cosmetics empire whose signature fragrance was called, naturally, Wings. She received the Distinguished Service Medal at the end of the war and lobbied hard, but unsuccessfully, for a permanent role for women pilots in the peacetime U.S. Air Force. Thirty-eight of her WASP pilots were killed in the line of duty flying high-performance and sometimes unreliable new warplanes.

Hungry for more manpower—or in this case, womanpower—and buoyed by the success of the WASP program, the Army launched a secret experiment in 1943 to place servicewomen on antiaircraft battery crews. To the lasting surprise of the Army's general staff, mixed male-female crews consistently outperformed all-male crews at shooting down enemy planes, with women on average proving more adept at identifying the range and height of approaching aircraft, at exercising care and patience in targeting, and at using the early radar and sighting devices of the era. Conventional wisdom (that women couldn't handle such high-pressure combat duties) once again was shattered. Tradition, however, was another matter: Despite the pleas of the commanding general who oversaw the experiment and promptly requested 4,000 more women for anti-aircraft duty, the Army killed the program and kept it secret for decades—a bow not to sound military policy, but to concerns over likely public and congressional outcries at placing women in combat roles.

Two years later, however, the military manpower shortage had become so acute that President Roosevelt called for a new military draft for women. The proposal specifically limited the military to conscripting women to serve as nurses at home and in war zones, but it still represented an enormous shift in policy and, apparently, public opinion. For there was no outcry, congressional or public, over the new draft proposal; the bill passed the House easily and was about to be voted on in the Senate (with more than enough votes in its favor lined up) when Germany surrendered, the only development that could have headed off an unprecedented women's draft.

The great need for women to take on critical and often dangerous military and defense jobs overcame many longstanding prejudices and social taboos: Even pregnant women were recruited explicitly in defense department advertisements for jobs producing knitted goods and other textiles, so that other women could be freed up for heavier work. The percentage of women with young children who took jobs outside the home doubled from prewar levels. And industry and the government accommodated these young mothers in ways the country has never done before or since, constructing more than three thousand subsidized jobsite day care centers. From office buildings to shipyards, these centers cared for more than one and a half million children of working women.

Roosevelt's New Deal planners knew an opportunity to change the world when they saw one. Their postwar goal was to create a new economy with "full employment" as its cornerstone, a catchphrase then popular with progressives and conservatives alike, although the political factions differed predictably on methods of achieving that goal. Had Congress chosen to enact a New Deal–style War Service Bill of Rights instead of the G.I. Bill of Rights, conferring benefits on sixteen million veterans and the millions of women and men working in war-related industries, America would have been transformed in different ways from the path actually taken after the war. And the principal beneficiaries of the choice not taken—in terms of earning power, expectations, equality, and opportunities—would have been the nation's women.

How that would have played out in postwar America is a matter of sheer speculation. The societal impact of a broader benefits bill could have been double that of the actual G.I. Bill (at double the cost), but it also could have led Congress to make the benefits far less generous to keep costs down, in which case the overall impact on the country would have been diminished. The New Dealers also wanted a larger role for government planners than the actual G.I. Bill allowed, so that students and workers could be channeled into fields where the need was thought to be greatest, rather than leaving everything to the individual veteran's tastes and the market forces. As such, "the greatest legislation" might have become just another mediocre bit of social engineering, and the grand achievements that followed the G.I. Bill could have been lost if the target population of beneficiaries grew too large and the benefits too miserly and regimented.

However, if benefits as generous and flexible as the G.I. Bill had been extended to war workers as well as veterans, the America that followed could well have surpassed our own in prosperity and opportunity, with far fewer of the social ills that currently plague the country and its shrinking middle class. Extending training and other benefits to war workers, men and women alike, would have required preserving and expanding the national network of day care centers created in wartime, which not only would have empowered mothers to work or go back to school in far greater numbers, but could have provided a (still elusive) vehicle for improving children's academic readiness and the overall quality of public schools. National health insurance largely would have been realized, and relatively painlessly, if medical coverage had been provided to veterans and war workers (and their dependents), easing if not preventing the twenty-first century's health care crisis. Housing benefits conferred on such a large population would have had to be balanced between the suburban explosion America actually experienced and the urban renewal and housing programs that Roosevelt wanted but never achieved on a large scale. America could have experienced the same creation of suburbia and increase in home ownership, but without the hollowing out and decay of the inner cities.

Roosevelt's second bill of rights, in short, would have become a reality, because the population of war workers was not limited to those who only labored in defense plants and airplane factories. War workers were defined as virtually any worker who filled any job that freed an able-bodied man to join the military. Women who took on the tasks of bus drivers, stevedores, truckers, auto mechanics, and other traditionally male jobs could have qualified for G.I. Bill–like benefits, which would have meant a majority of Americans would have been covered one way or another. And the next logical step—to make the program all-inclusive—would have appeared doable, beneficial, even inevitable. The record of the actual G.I. Bill shows that spending for the program was paid back many times over in the form of increased tax revenues, income, consumer spending, and productivity; an even more inclusive benefits package likely would have paid even greater societal dividends.

Was this alternative universe even remotely possible? Alone among American politicians, the four-term Roosevelt, routinely ranked by historians as one of the greatest three presidents (and considered the only truly great president since Lincoln), might have pulled it off, turning, as the commentator Walter Lippmann observed, a recipe for political suicide for any other politician into a sensible-sounding and inspiring call to arms. Roosevelt and his New Deal may not have cured the Depression, but they had stabilized the nation at a time when other democratic countries had fallen to revolution and fascism. His policies set the stage for victory in war and for the boom that followed. Just as importantly,

Roosevelt inspired Americans to rediscover their values, tarnished during the long decades of Gilded Age and Depression: that America should be about leaving no one behind, about offering opportunity and hope for a better life to all, and about embracing freedom and democracy, not totalitarianism, as solutions to social ills. When he died, America came to a standstill, bereft. Soldiers stood and wept. Airfields ground to a halt. Army cryptographers gaped in teary astonishment at their teletypes as they read the only message to come across the wires during the entire war that was not in code: *The President of the United States has died.* He had strengthened the resolve of a nation with his condemnation of a day of infamy, he had convinced Americans they were the arsenal of democracy. For those who went to war, Roosevelt had been their president for most of their lifetimes, the one man they believed when he said they would prevail. If anyone could have convinced the country to embrace the notion of an economic bill of rights for all Americans as the ultimate legacy of World War II, it would have been FDR.

History took a different course, however, though the reasons, like the unintentional greatness of the G.I. Bill itself, had less to do with lofty goals and careful debate and more to do with petty politics, special interest clout, and plain, old-fashioned sexism. Roosevelt died before the war ended, and his successor did not have the same political capital and enormous popularity to see such a program through, though he tried. Cost concerns were an important issue, too, and the mostly male veterans' vote was considered a far more formidable force than the votes of women. The American Legion and other servicemen's lobbies, weaned on the Bonus March and the Depression-era bonus cuts, relentlessly pushed Congress to keep benefits limited to veterans, going so far as to help kill a modest and humane proposal that would have trained disabled civilians alongside disabled veterans to fill key defense jobs. The Legion opposed even the slightest dilution of veterans' benefits. They flatly rejected the idea of sharing their slice of the pie with war workers, and this view carried the day in Congress.

The results of this political admixture were sometimes cruelly dismissive of women's contributions and accomplishments. The WOW crews at the Army arsenals and the WASP pilots—just two of many examples in which women risked and sometimes gave their lives for their country—were never recognized as members of the military, and therefore received no benefits as veterans, not even burial honors or Purple Heart commendations, much less free college educations and home loans. Cochran had been promised that her WASP pilots would be militarized, but male pilots who wanted the "safe" WASP jobs at the end of the war lobbied Congress, which killed the program without honoring the War Department's promise. (It was not until 1977 that Congress corrected that old wrong, when WASP pilots were finally recognized and honored as veterans, though even then the surviving members received far more modest and belated benefits.)

Finally, public uneasiness over the changing role of women—at home and in the workplace—worked against the logic of expanding benefits to include war workers. While polls showed that anywhere from a third to a half of all working women wanted to keep their jobs and newfound economic clout after the war, other polls showed most returning servicemen did not want to compete with their wives and their sisters and girlfriends for jobs, nor did they wish to assume any homemaking duties traditionally left to women so that their wives could go to work or school. There was a deep longing to return to the way things were before the war—even if that return was aimed at an idealized version of a past America that never really existed, with the trials of the Depression, hunger, and social insecurity conveniently minimized. This public sentiment had political as well as cultural repercussions: Congressional policy makers, already tired of the New Deal and Roosevelt's utopian proposals, knew it would be far easier and quite a bit cheaper to achieve something close to full employment if women went home, had babies, and removed themselves from the labor pool, leaving the postwar jobs to men.

This attitude was summed up in a War Department pamphlet that quoted a serviceman stationed in the South Pacific: "There are two things I want to be sure of after the war: I want my wife waiting for me and I want my job waiting for me. I don't want to find my wife busy with a job that some returning soldier needs, and I don't want to find that some other man's wife has my job."

The G.I. Bill's provisions favored these traditional attitudes about "a woman's place": By subsidizing veterans' home purchases in a new suburbia, with its housing tracts far from city centers and most places of employment, the G.I. Bill left a generation of married women homebound. Most families had but one car in that era, public transportation serving suburbia was in its infancy where it existed at all, and with the dismantling of wartime day care programs coming during the baby boom, many women were bound to child care responsibilities. The archetypal nuclear family of working father and stay-at-home mother, later held up as the defining icon of the golden age of 1950s America and as a pure expression of "family values," in truth was neither the "natural order of things," as it is often remembered, nor was it even a traditional American virtue. Working-wife households, after all, were the rule, not the exception, in America's agrarian past (when the whole family worked the farm). Married women rushed to take jobs during the Great Depression whenever and wherever they could find them—indeed, there were often more opportunities available to women during the hard times because they traditionally were paid less than men for the same work. And that women worked outside the home during both world wars was considered a fulfillment, not a betrayal, of the values Americans professed to hold dear. That attitude changed, however, when World War II ended and veterans' subsidized education, business loans, and home purchases made it easy for families to prosper with only one income—the man's. The iconic fifties family, then, far from a natural evolution, was the product of social engineering and government assistance on a massive scale, courtesy of a G.I. Bill that, despite its many beneficial effects, left women as second-class citizens after the wartime economy had lifted them up, if briefly, to near equality.

Sometimes people would stare at Josette Dermody and ask why in the world would she join the Navy. It was the question that WAVES and WACs and woman Marines (no jaunty acronyms for them) always faced. Josette had no patience for these inquisitors. She'd shoot them a look of disbelief and say, "Because there's a war on, you twit."

The elfin granddaughter of Irish immigrants, Josette was a bookworm valedictorian with an overwhelming case of wanderlust, convinced that joining the military would be as much a romantic adventure as a fulfillment of duty.

She is the first to admit how naïve and unrealistic she was at the time she signed up—like most of her fellow G.I.s, male and female. The Greatest Generation is revered today for its commitment, sense of duty, accomplishments, and sacrifice in fighting the last world war. But Josette can close her eyes and return to 1944 in an instant, when that Greatest Generation was little more than a group of painfully young, confused, terrified, reckless, thoughtless, and foolish kids—worried about dying, worried about the future, worried that life would pass them by while friends stayed at home, got married, and started lives. Josette saw herself as working to defeat Hitler, so proud the day she first learned how to break down and reassemble a twenty-millimeter antiaircraft cannon—blindfolded—while the master chief's stopwatch ticked away. Then her triumph faded as she slowly learned the hard way that the Navy had no real idea what to do with the women it recruited, that its officers and gentlemen and instructors hated having women around, and that it would never, ever let her really use the weapon it had trained her to master. She would leave that base and draw sneers from the guards, while the shore patrol would scrutinize her and her friends for any slight infraction or dress code violation. Sailors on leave would get drunk and expect her to be their comfort woman in some sort of twisted act of patriotism, getting furious when she told them to shove off.

Josette's generation did something great, something monumental, but it's easy to forget, more than a half century later, that they were eighteen and nineteen and twenty when they did it, making it up as they went along and getting plenty wrong in the process. We fight our wars with children, Josette reminds those who would romanticize the worst cataclysm man has ever inflicted on itself—and she is not just talking about childish misbehavior. That the war was anything but romantic hammered its way into her heart sixty years ago during her first home leave, when she walked up to her house in Detroit and saw with satisfaction the flag with the two blue stars in her window, one star for her, one for her brother. Then she gazed across the street to see the gold star in her neighbor's window, where the boy she had grown up with, gone to school with, joked every day with, was now being mourned. Up and down the street, the gold stars could be seen, an entire constellation, each one representing a young man barely old enough to shave, who had gone off to war, never to return. Just on one block.

"We were so darn young," Josette says. "We had no idea what we were getting into."

Once the decision was made to exclude war workers from veterans' benefits, the pool of women eligible for G.I. Bill benefits, while substantial, represented only a tiny fraction of the recipients of all that largesse.

Sixty thousand women served as Army nurses during the war, and another 150,000 joined the Women's Army Corps (WAC). In the Navy, there were 14,000 military nurses and 86,000 WAVES (Women Accepted for Volunteer Emergency Service). Twenty thousand women joined the Marine Corps Women's Reserve, and another 10,000 formed the women's auxiliary of the Coast Guard. They worked in intelligence, in clerical duties, and as drivers, mechanics, pharmacists' mates, communications technicians, and air traffic controllers.

Servicewomen were stationed in the U.S., Europe, and throughout the Pacific. Though none were involved in combat and all were supposed to stay far from battle, thousands of women were killed or wounded. More than 200 Army nurses died during the war as they staffed field hospitals close to the frontlines. More than a hundred were taken as prisoners of war. During the Battle of Anzio, six Army nurses were killed in a matter of days, while another four received Silver Stars for courage under fire.

The women who served in these special military divisions were considered veterans entitled to the same G.I. Bill benefits as any male veteran—the law, on paper at least, drew no distinction.

The reality of the G.I. Bill turned out to be another matter. Many servicewomen received little or no information about the benefits before they were discharged. Surveys after the war revealed that more than a third of military women had no idea they were eligible for the G.I. Bill's benefits.

G.I. Bill regulations—the fine print developed by federal agencies to put into practice the broad outlines provided by the legislation—also discriminated against women. Servicemen knew their benefits would be passed on to their widows if they died; servicewomen enjoyed no such security—widowers got nothing. Thousands of women who served in the first two years of the Women's Army Corps, in its original nonmilitary incarnation as the Women's Auxiliary Army Corps, also received no benefits—a technicality that was not corrected until the early 1980s, long after most benefits, other than burial services, had expired.

Of the women who knew they were eligible for the G.I. Bill, many faced an uphill battle in securing their benefits, particularly from banks and institutions of higher education, in which longstanding codes and traditions had explicitly discriminated against women. The home loan benefit was particularly striking in its discrimination, given that women in general, and married women in particular, were routinely denied access to credit in the postwar era strictly on the basis of gender. The Veterans Administration saw no reason to alter those practices in its G.I. Bill home loan policies: When working women sought veterans' home loans, they were forced to submit demeaning testimonials, such as letters and doctors' notes attesting to the fact that they could not or would not have children either because of sterility or the use of birth control. Needless to say, male veterans were not required to make any such assurances.

Colleges often gave preference to male veterans as well, both in making admissions decisions and in allotting coveted spots in crowded classes. The combination of preferences and the overall tilt of the G.I. Bill toward men had a predictable effect on college graduation rates: During the course of the World War II G.I. Bill's run, the percentage of American men with four-year college degrees went from 6 percent to more than 10 percent. But women increased their degree-earning potential far less during the same time frame, moving from 5 percent to just 6 percent of American women—with the college gap between men and women widened because of the G.I. Bill. Of the veterans who attended college on the G.I. Bill, fewer than 3 percent were women. Yet even with all these disadvantages, and despite the tiny number, that 3 percent represented a victory of sorts for women—it meant 64,000, or one out of five G.I. Janes went to college on the G I. Bill. Only one in seven male veterans opted for college.

In considering all G.I. Bill benefits, however, the picture tilted much more toward men: three out of four eligible male World War II veterans used at least one benefit derived from the G.I. Bill—they drew support from the Fifty-two/Twenty Club, got vocational training, home loans, employment counseling, or college aid. But only one in three eligible women did.

Women veterans were saddled with additional stigma that discouraged them from enjoying their G.I. Bill benefits fully—that they, somehow, had done something improper by joining the military. This was a kind of social conservative pushback against the government campaign urging women to join the service during the war for the greater good, a vague, ill-defined, and far-from-unanimous societal label, but one that civilian women war workers did not have to contend with at all. Certain factions in Congress—notably the same forces that opposed soldier-vote legislation and color-blind G.I. Bill benefits because they might undermine segregation—were deeply unhappy with women serving in the military in any capacity, and adamantly opposed assigning them any duties remotely related to combat. Secretaries, nurses, orderlies—those "feminine" roles were grudgingly accepted in a time of great need. But assigning women to "men's work" created a host of controversies, ranging from committee chairmen who held up appropriations bills to a threat to kill the WAC program outright if the Army went ahead with assigning women to antiaircraft batteries. Congress specifically barred Navy WAVES from ever serving overseas, severely handicapping the Navy's efforts to use them in support jobs. Then, in 1943, as the Army began a drive to recruit one million women, a campaign of rumor and innuendo began among enlisted men and, soon, the public at large, in which it was said women were joining the service either because they were lesbians, or because they were promiscuous and could thus be cast as camp followers or camp wives.

The rumors quickly became pervasive, as attested to in a series of oral histories collected by the University of North Carolina: When Elizabeth Baker signed up for the Army, her friends and classmates in Virginia crushed her by opining, "You're going to throw your life away." The man who inducted nurse Alice Boehret into the Army in Philadelphia looked at her in disbelief and asked, "What's a nice girl like you doing joining the WACs?" Boehret, who would go on to use the G.I. Bill to earn masters and PhD degrees, then design a new nursing program at Rutgers University, recalls that the man, like many members of the public, believed the widespread rumor that WACs would serve as "what the Japanese called 'comfort girls.'"

And Sarah Greenlee, who served in the Army and used her G.I. Bill benefits to buy a house and become a teacher of disabled children, had an even stronger negative reaction from her relatives in South Florida when she decided to sign up. "Oh, they wanted to kick me out of the family," she later observed in one of the University of North Carolina oral histories. "Some of my uncles did say that they would just disown me because they heard so many dirty things. None of the stuff that they heard, that they tried to tell me was happening—that didn't happen to me, and I didn't see it happening, either."

None of these anti-women-in-the-military attitudes or policies was based on actual experience or research, mainly because actual experience and research supported the use of women in virtually every military job they were allowed to attempt. The rumors of rampant promiscuity and lesbianism have been debunked by both academic studies and the memoirs of the servicewomen themselves. If anything, military women were less sexually active than their civilian counterparts and certainly less so than men in the service, for whom the military provided thousands of "prophylactic stations" (bowls of government-issue condoms free for the taking for furloughs and shore leave) and "orientation lectures" for troops overseas, in which soldiers were urged to maintain morale by having sex with foreign women at every opportunity. The rumors likely arose because of a mixture of offended traditional sensibilities, disdain for women invading the all-male bastion of the military, and fear by some male members of the military that they would be sent to the front if they lost safe stateside billets to women. The War Department did, in fact, recruit women with posters that explicitly promised that every volunteer who joined the WAVES or the WACs would "free a soldier [or Marine or sailor] to fight." Perhaps it's not so surprising that the ugly rumors began shortly after the million-woman recruitment goal was announced, and a sizable contingent of servicemen who had not seen any action suddenly realized they might have to fill the boots of fallen soldiers on the front if women were available to take their stateside jobs.

The rumors had their desired effect: The military's ability to recruit women flagged precipitously. For every Sarah Greenlee, who ignored her relatives' jeers at serving her country, there were ten others who succumbed to the pressure and stigma. In the end, the Army fell far short of its recruitment goal—lowering the number of women who otherwise would have signed up for service, and therefore lowering the number of women who would have become eligible for G.I. Bill benefits by many hundreds of thousands.

Josette Dermody received her basic training at Hunter College in the Bronx—a military-occupied urban campus where naval and Marine trainees had to pretend they were aboard ship, even dispensing directions to class in terms of starboard and aft under the watchful eyes of reluctant drill instructors transferred from duty training men. During marching drills, neighborhood children would post themselves nearby and mimic the uniformed young women's cadences, stomping their feet, tossing them mock salutes, and giggling madly until their mothers finally dragged them off.

The rumors and stereotyping had an impact on Josette, though it served only to heighten, not deter, her desire to serve with distinction and break the traditional molds: She deliberately bombed on her clerical aptitude tests, typing poorly and misfiling everything. She told her new friends in the barracks—a commandeered dormitory—that there was no way she was going to a secretarial pool or some other boring Defense Department office. "One way or another, I'm going to see the world."

Her gamble paid off: The Navy sent Josette to gunnery school, where her skills with the big naval antiaircraft guns landed her a job at San Francisco's Treasure Island military base. She wouldn't be taking out enemy aircraft, but she would be teaching men how to shoot them down. She joined a crew of female gunnery instructors at Treasure Island, working with the venerable Oerlikon twenty-millimeter antiaircraft cannon—a gun that, ironically, was designed by Germany for World War I, variations of which were in use by all sides in World War II, and which can be found to this day aboard modern U.S. Navy vessels. These sorts of connections between the people trying to kill one another were crazy, and everywhere—in factories and tool boxes and the ethnic blenders of American cities. On Christmas Eve, the angel-voiced tenor who sang hymns at the Treasure Island chapel was a German prisoner of war. Try and make sense of that, Josette says. It can't be done.

Her time in the Navy was, like the war itself, exciting and boring, challenging and ridiculous, wonderful and terrible. Some of the Navy men welcomed the WAVES' arrival—it meant they could stop being instructors, that they had been set free to get into "the real war." Others were dismayed by the arrival of the women instructors, because it meant they had to stop teaching and face getting into the real war. Josette's father, an old Irish cop, expressed his own brand of dismay, regretful at having signed his permission for her to join; he gave her the cold shoulder for much of her time in the service, though they eventually made up. It turned out he didn't disapprove—he had just missed her terribly.

Most nights, Josette and her friends would get passes to go into San Francisco. During the war, the city teemed with sailors, Marines, and soldiers from every allied country, and the young women would be toasted alternately with Russian vodka, gin and bitters, or American whiskey, depending on the nationality of their companions. The wide-eyed WAVES would get unadulterated war news during these outings—not the propagandized happy news from the military, but a much seamier, darker series of reports about massacres, setbacks, and harrowing battles, from the men who had witnessed them firsthand. Long before news reports relayed the information, Josette and her friends heard the horrifying tale of the Malmédy Massacre, when German SS troops in the Ardennes machine-gunned eighty captured G.I.s during the Battle of the Bulge, the worst atrocity committed against American forces during the war. That same night on the radio, she heard nothing but tales of victory. "It was kind of schizy," she recalls. "They wanted us to be gung ho, but sometimes it was hard to feel that way." Later she had the chance to attend a meeting of the United Nations Organizing Conference in San Francisco, more history happening around her, and she was able, briefly at least, to feel a surge of optimism, as if the end of war, not just this war but all wars, might somehow be possible.

Twenty, naïve, and unattached—she had said no to marrying her high school sweetheart just before he shipped out, and he had promptly married an English girl—the vivacious Josette fell in love during her wartime service. A darkly handsome sailor named Blackie wooed her between cruises, an exciting rogue, yet a perfect gentleman, or so she thought. As the war ended, however, she turned down his marriage proposal when he blithely explained that after each of their dates, he had left her to patronize the prostitutes downtown—his method of protecting Josette's virtue while denying himself nothing. Everyone does it, he said of his shipmates, and Josette couldn't help but think of those prophylactic stations at the base guard booth, the ones the guards clumsily tried to screen from view when the WAVES walked past, and which the women obligingly pretended they didn't see. Blackie explained how there were two kinds of women, the sort you married, and the other sort, but Josette, heartbroken, told him he had it wrong. There were two kinds of women all right, and she was the kind who said good-bye.

That was the night the war ended, accompanied by a massive, delirious celebration in San Francisco that turned into a drunken, ugly riot of window-smashing and mindless stampeding. She remembers less the joyous imagery captured in those timeless news photos of confetti flying and couples kissing, and more of running in breathless panic down side alleys, trying simply to survive the mad crush of men suddenly given back their lives and their countries and their futures, and not quite knowing what to do with them.

Back at Treasure Island, the old Oerkilon trainers soon were shut down, the models of enemy Zeros and Fokkers and other Axis aircraft shoved into a box like discarded toys, and Josette finally got stuck with typing duty—typing separation papers. The lieutenant who supervised this winding down of the office helped her type up some papers of her own—an application to the University of Chicago. Josette had been certain to find out everything she could about the G.I. Bill well in advance. If she was going to see the world, she told her friends, college was going to be the next stop and her springboard to more adventure.

When her discharge came, she took the brass Navy buttons off of her uniform and replaced them with plain civilian buttons, removed the insignia carefully from her jacket, and she had a new suit for civilian life, a start at least. It was good wool, wore like iron, and Josette would carefully wash it, then stick it under her mattress for a home-style pressing. The seventy-five dollars a month in living expenses she was going to get from the G.I. Bill once she started college would not leave much room for clothing purchases.

The University of Chicago, where the president of the school had previously derided the G.I. Bill as a recipe for ruining higher education, overflowed with veterans by the time Josette arrived. Many of the veterans congregated in the married students housing: Quonset huts filled with men and women and babies and adult conversation. For single students like Josette, the regular dormitories, with their curfews and rules designed for kids, were unbearable, especially when she discovered there were cramped apartments filled with thrift-shop furniture available near campus.

School was a healing place for everyone, she would later reflect, not just for broken hearts, but for broken bodies and minds—men who had seen too much war, who screamed in their sleep, who had stories to tell, except they never did. For them, Plato and Thucydides and Shakespeare and political debates over beer were all the comfort they needed, and mostly found.

Josette graduated and became a teacher, fell in love again, married a college professor, became Josette Dermody Wingo, and went on to get a masters degree in education while raising two sons. The G.I. Bill sustained her throughout. She taught elementary school for years and, in retirement, wrote her memoirs at the behest of her kids.

She says she was no feminist and no pioneer—just a woman who wanted to do her part during the greatest crisis in generations, and who then used the opportunities afforded her. Nothing more, nothing less, she says. When it was all over, women were still slighted by the military, despite their many accomplishments, and the gains in college attendance were mostly experienced by the men. The G.I. Bill did a lot for Josette, she says, but it was still, for the most part, a men's club.

And yet, across generations, the G.I. Bill had a far more lasting impact on women in and out of the service. Just as the record of black soldiers during the war would help convince the military to abandon segregation in peacetime, so did the experience of WACs and WAVES and woman Marines eventually prod the military into opening up new opportunities for women. Pay and benefits were equalized, putting the military ahead of the private sector on this score. And though the number of women who went to college on the G.I. bill was relatively small compared to the men, 122,000 out of the 350,000 of those eligible, their children went to college in droves, boys and girls in equal measure.

However imperfect and discriminatory it could be, the G.I. Bill ultimately opened up college to the majority of Americans, regardless of class or income, men and women alike. Once the G.I. Bill broke the barrier of collegiate elitism, the simple rule of postwar, twentieth century America—that the children, on average, always exceed the educational attainment of the parents—took over. The veterans' children, regardless of gender, simply assumed they would get to go to college if they so chose—an assumption most of their parents never would have dreamed of making in their youth. But now, with their G.I. Bill–financed homes and prosperity well in place, many veterans could afford to send their kids off to college without the government assistance they had needed to finance their own educations. And the colleges, initially resistant to the G.I. Bill, very much liked the increased income all those extra students brought in. They did not want to turn the enrollment clock back. College was no longer a niche; it was big business, the more the merrier.

It took a generation for the G.I. Bill to benefit women on a large scale, but it eventually did so, if indirectly—a breaking of the ice rather than an out-and-out breakthrough.

"It was a great law that did good things for the country," Josette says, in her simple way of cutting to the heart of the matter. "But like a lot of things, it could have been better."

☆ 8 ☆

MONTE POSEY'S WAR:
Race and the G.I. Bill

Monte Posey sat before the Veterans Administration counselor, his initial disbelief at the words he was hearing slowly turning to comprehension, then a cool, calm rage.

He had walked in ready to go to school, to earn his degree, to start a new life, a better life. That's why he had waited patiently for hours in this crowded VA office in midtown Chicago. That's why he had put up with the disappointment of his military career—snatched from elite training as a fighter pilot after Hiroshima and Nagasaki and war's abrupt end made new aviators superfluous. As the massive, war-bloated Army quickly folded up, a parachute collapsing as its passenger's feet hit the ground, Posey had been offered two options: a spot in the infantry he certainly didn't want, or an early discharge if he could produce a college acceptance letter—something he very much *did* want.

Now he held that letter in his hands: He had been accepted at the University of Illinois' new Chicago campus, opened on the famous expanse of Navy Pier to accommodate the influx of veterans enrolling under the G.I. Bill. All he needed now was VA approval to cover his tuition and living expenses, and his education could begin. Something he had never expected to afford or attain was just one bureaucratic nod away.

"Well, let me tell you," the VA counselor said slowly, looking up from the letter, his pale face impassive behind a battered gray desk. "I recommend against this."

Posey took a moment for this to register. Then he asked, "Why?"

"Well, I think you should sign up for a trade. You'll be happier."

Posey knew what the man meant, but he wasn't going to make it easy for him. Again, he asked, "Why?"

Now the counselor appeared to be getting exasperated. "Look around. There are no opportunities out there for college-educated Negroes. You'll be wasting your time."

And there it was: The same white-versus-black calculus that had left Posey in a segregated Army unit in a segregated country, like every other black man in the military during the war. It was the same bitter pill that had led his father to pass as white during the Depression to keep his factory job, swallowing his anger and pain in silence every day at the racist jokes and comments his co-workers casually tossed about. And it was the same bruising discrimination that had ruined his years at the affluent, white high school his parents had chosen, where the other kids had befriended and accepted him but their parents and teachers had not. "We're having a party and we sure wish you could come, Monte," his friends would say, their words, intended to be kind, cutting like a knife. "But you know how it is: Our parents won't let you in the house."

Now here was this VA man saying, in essence, the same thing, minus the kindly intent: The white veterans were having a party, and Monte Posey, once again, wasn't invited. Except this time, things were different. This time it was not about the prejudice of white teachers and parents ruling the day, it was about the rule of law and the G.I. Bill of Rights, for nowhere in that legislation, not in its large print or fine, did it draw a distinction on the basis of race. The president had made a point of this when he signed the bill. The black press had celebrated it as history in the making, a national first: a color-blind law in a segregated society, offering the thrilling prospect that finally, through the black veterans, Jim Crow might be throttled into submission for the first time since Reconstruction. Posey had the law on his side, and he knew it. So did the VA man.

"I want a college education, not a trade," Posey insisted. "A four-year college education. With a degree."

They argued on for a time, the counselor pretending to be helpful, but Posey saw through him. The counselor wouldn't have hesitated a moment with a white veteran in an identical situation, he knew. If a college was accredited and a veteran had been accepted, the VA had no choice but to approve. Posey realized his counselor was not well intentioned—just the opposite: A helpful counselor would have said, *Yes, this will be hard, you'll be knocking against barriers, but if anything can change things, the G.I. Bill can. Things will get better down the line, and this is the way to start.* This is, in fact, what Posey fervently believed. He had caught glimpses of the possible while in the Army, moments when the question of race had vanished in an environment of respect and camaraderie, and for all the insults and discrimination he had endured at other times, he remained optimistic. To Posey, the G.I. Bill had the potential to jump-start the country's embryonic civil rights movement then and there, a decade before Rosa Parks said no to a white bus driver, if only the VA—which in 1946 still segregated its veterans' hospitals—would use its counselors and clout to empower black veterans rather than become their obstacles. How many black men in Posey's place would have doubted themselves and their country enough to take the counselor's advice that day? Posey had seen it a thousand times in the Army, the constant pressure to defer to white authority, even when you were in the right—especially when you were in the right. All this flashed through Posey's mind as he sat there, unyielding, silent.

Finally, the counselor considered the line of veterans still waiting to see him, then grudgingly nodded. "Fine. You're wasting your time, but since it's what you want to do, I'll approve it." A shuffle of papers and it was done.

Posey left that office with what he had come to get, approval to go to college on Uncle Sam's dime. His future, one year's worth of it at least, had been secured, to be spent in classrooms filled with other ex-G.I.s rebuilding their lives. But as he walked to the L station, he could not leave behind the anger—the sort of slow, rational fury that does not paralyze, but motivates. Monte Posey decided he wasn't just going off to college. He was going to find a career that would allow him to do something about the roots of that anger. The counselor, in spite of himself, had done more for Monte Posey—and, ultimately, the cause of equal rights—than he could ever have known or imagined.

There is no question that the G.I. Bill offered unprecedented opportunities for African Americans and other ethnic minorities in an era in which the government and society still practiced a racial discrimination so breathtakingly blatant that those who did not live through the times have trouble comprehending just how awful they truly were—or how hard it could be to turn even genuine opportunity into meaningful gains. In celebrating the G.I. Bill as the first explicitly race-neutral piece of social legislation, it is often forgotten that this was the *only* race-neutral social program at the time. It operated, literally, in a vacuum.

The military itself remained a bastion of racism throughout the war and for nearly a decade afterward. Consider that a young, black Army lieutenant named John Roosevelt Robinson faced court-martial and a long wartime prison sentence in Texas for simply refusing to give up his seat on a military bus to a white soldier—just two weeks after President Roosevelt signed the G.I. Bill into law in 1944. Robinson belonged to the Army's lone, all-black tank battalion—"Mrs. Roosevelt's Niggers," they were commonly called, in reference to First Lady Eleanor Roosevelt's strong advocacy on behalf of black servicemen. Despite inferior training and equipment and constant abuse, the 761st Tank Battalion went on to achieve a heroic combat record in Europe, nominated six separate times for presidential unit citations—honors that were somehow lost, forgotten, or ignored by the Pentagon until the scandalous slight finally came to light in 1978. As for Lieutenant Robinson, a military trial court acquitted him of all charges. Discrimination on military transport and recreation facilities had been outlawed early in the war, making his arrest and court-martial illegal from the start. He then moved on to an even more difficult battle against racism: He became the first black major league baseball player in America, his name by then shortened to the more familiar Jackie Robinson.

That the G.I. Bill began to alter America's racial equation seems clear, a conclusion based not on rosy nostalgia and anecdote, but on hard statistical evidence. A long-forgotten 1950 VA survey—unearthed from the National Archives by author and University of California–Santa Cruz politics professor Michael G. Brown—found that when it came to taking advantage of G.I. Bill benefits, a greater proportion of America's 1.3 million black veterans participated in at least one aspect of the bill's provisions compared to their white counterparts. In particular, black veterans avidly pursued educational benefits, especially to finance vocational training: By 1950, 43 percent of white veterans had used the G.I. Bill for education or training of some sort, while for black veterans, that figure had reached 49 percent. This would seem on its face solid evidence of the egalitarian and color-blind nature of the G.I. Bill—a quality routinely touted in every official paean to the bill since the fifties. Unfortunately, participation in the G.I. Bill program is not the whole story, as it says nothing about whether black (or Asian American, Native American, or Hispanic) veterans received the same quality of benefits with the same life-altering power as the largesse enjoyed by white G.I.s.

Monte Posey was correct that day at the Veterans Administration office in Chicago: The G.I. Bill had the potential to launch a civil rights revolution. How much of that potential was realized, and how much defeated by the larger societal forces of prejudice and discrimination, remains a matter of research and debate more than sixty years after the war. There is scorching criticism from one school of thought, represented by Columbia University's Ira

Katznelson, whose grim findings led him to conclude in *When Affirmative Action Was White,* "There was no greater instrument for widening an already huge racial gap in postwar America than the G.I. Bill." Others, however, see a far more positive picture in largely the same data, among them Syracuse University's Suzanne Mettler, who found evidence that the bill provided a "turning point" in large numbers of black veterans' lives, and was "relatively inclusive in terms of its reach among African-American veterans" at a time when no other law or program could make such a claim.

Which view is correct? Both, and neither: Once again, the reach and impact of the G.I. Bill, with all its many unintended consequences, is far too complex for absolutist views. The reality, it seems, lies somewhere between the poles, with the added complication that it is almost impossible to separate the pure effects of the G.I. Bill from the fact that its benefits were dispensed and used inside a society expressly designed to cheat, belittle, and oppress black Americans. The rose itself might have been hearty and bountiful, but its roots were planted in poisoned soil.

Because of this poisoned soil, when it came to the key benefits of home loans and college education—where the power to change the world was the greatest, as evidenced by the rapid creation of a new white middle class after the war—black veterans clearly fell behind, a squandering of potential on a grand scale that continues to have ripple effects on contemporary America. Many black veterans, like Monte Posey, demanded and received their full due of these benefits, and these veterans formed the backbone not only of an emerging black middle class, but of a far more politically active African American community, providing one of the driving forces behind the civil rights battles of the fifties and sixties. But those full benefits were enjoyed by proportionately fewer numbers of black veterans than a truly color-blind law should have delivered. And that meant black veterans and their families were denied their fair share of the multigenerational, enriching impact of home ownership and economic security that the G.I. Bill conferred on a majority of white veterans, their children, and their grandchildren.

Shamefully, this lost opportunity was both deliberate and well planned, an example of the power of the Southern Democratic voting bloc during and after the war, with its continual threat (eventually carried out) to fracture the then-ruling Democratic Party if segregation was attacked. Even such progressive legislation as the G.I. Bill ended up twisted to serve, or at the very least leave undisturbed, the government-enforced segregation and poor working conditions many African Americans had to endure upon their triumphant return from war.

Representative John Elliott Rankin and his segregationist allies in Congress had been devious and clever in constructing a G.I. Bill that, on its face, was free of discrimination, promising equality of benefits and opportunity to all. Their genius, however, was in making certain the practical administration of those benefits and opportunities remained in "safe" hands—hands that wouldn't rock the boat of Jim Crow. Rankin worked feverishly in the House, as did his allies in the Senate, to defeat alternative versions of the bill that would have provided far more federal controls and monitoring of the dispensation of benefits. Rankin insisted that distribution of college aid, employment counseling, home loan approvals, and all the other benefits of the G.I. Bill should be a matter of local control and states' rights—the age-old argument, which continues to this day, suggesting that local communities know better than the big and distant federal government when it comes to passing out grants and benefits.

The states' rights argument, at least in the case of the G.I. Bill, was a sham: It was this very local control that allowed a VA counselor in Chicago to do his best to discourage a black man named Monte Posey from going to a major university. In other parts of the country, particularly the Deep South in the years immediately after the war, the counselors didn't merely discourage black veterans. They just said no. No to home loans. No to job placement, except for the most menial positions. And no to college, except for historically black colleges, maintaining the sham of "separate but equal" that was in no way remotely equal except in the Supreme Court's cruel fantasy world of *Plessy v. Ferguson.*

For years, Rankin and his allies used the same arguments to defeat all sorts of legislation that would have benefited minorities, most dramatically an antilynching law in 1948 that President Truman sought after a series of brutal murders of black men in Mississippi and Georgia. The lynching victims had been jailed for such petty crimes as disturbing the peace (by simply walking through a white neighborhood) and "hogging the road," after which mobs removed them from jail and hung them from trees while other white citizens watched them die without comment or intervention. Because the local police had been unable or unwilling to protect the victims or bring the killers to justice, Truman wanted a law establishing federal jurisdiction over lynchings. Rankin, in leading the successful battle against the law and in favor of letting local communities "take care of their own," once again bellowed about states' rights and the Founders' original intent, extolling the virtues of segregation ("The Negroes have their own schools and they *want* their own schools"), and then uttering an inadvertent truth, intended as praise but which now reads like an indictment: "Nowhere else under the shining sun—nowhere—has the Negro ever received the treatment at the hands of the white people where he lived in large numbers as he does now among the white people of the South."

Rankin certainly was correct: With the possible exception of apartheid South Africa, no other place has treated black people so badly in the twentieth century as the states of the former Confederacy. Monte Posey remembers traveling with his mom to visit relatives in Louisiana when he was twelve years old, his first trip to the South, his first time crossing the Mason-Dixon Line, and finding himself shunted by the train conductors to the "colored" cars, the ones up front, where the smoke and soot were the worst. During his visit, he caught a glimpse of the beautiful, modern campus of the all-white Louisiana State University in Baton Rouge, then, just a few blocks away, he visited what he remembers as the "ramshackle nothing" that was then the "separate but equal" Southern University campus for blacks—another creation of the states' rights champions. "I was only twelve, but even I could tell something wasn't right," Posey recalls. "It left an impression, let's just say that: Anyone could see these two schools were not equal. But they sure were separate."

John Rankin was a racist and a thug, but he was a thug with power, the man who controlled all veterans legislation in the House of Representatives before, during, and after the war, with years of seniority and a strong base of support stemming from his championing of the New Deal rural electrification project and its famous Tennessee Valley Authority in 1933. That shining moment was followed by years of racist, anti-Semitic, pro-Nazi, Red-baiting demagoguery. Yet, for the most part, Rankin commanded the obedience of the American Legion, with its segregated posts and its willingness to do just about anything to win passage of its G.I. Bill.

Rankin also had support from the Veterans Administration, run by General Omar Bradley in the first two years after the war—the same general who would, as Army chief of staff a few years later, respond to Truman's 1948 executive order ending racial segregation in the military with outright insubordination. "The Army will not put men of different races in the same companies," he said, defying his commander in chief. "It will change that policy when the nation as a whole changes it."

To win over Rankin and ensure passage of the G.I. Bill, both the Legion and VA officials publicly supported his demand that locally appointed VA officials control the dispensation of benefits, rather than the centralized federal system the Roosevelt administration sought, thereby ensuring that the G.I. Bill would leave the Jim Crow South undisturbed and fully segregated. Rankin, in return, made certain that in the final bill the VA had sole domain over the G.I. Bill budget (with the exception of the U.S. Employment Service, which would provide job counseling, again through local rather than national auspices, and with VA oversight). The VA as a result greatly expanded its bureaucratic empire and budgetary powers—controlling the G.I. Bill meant, by 1947, it controlled 15 percent of the federal budget. All the agency had to do to acquire this extra power was become a witting vassal of American apartheid. The Veterans Administration then aided the segregationists' cause further by providing virtually no administrative control or review at the national level over how local G.I. Bill counselors treated black servicemen, and by hiring few black counselors anywhere in the country (and none in Rankin's state of Mississippi).

The results of this deliberate sabotage of America's first colorblind social program were predictable: The potential for the bill to jump-start civil rights, as African American activists had hoped it would do, ended up badly crippled.

Home loan benefits showed the most dramatic disparity between black and whites, as the explosion of home ownership in American society largely passed black veterans by. Again, this was part of Rankin's design—the VA was not allowed to make loans directly, as the Roosevelt administration had suggested, but could serve only as a guarantor, an official cosigner. Nothing compelled banks to make the loans in the first place. Most lending institutions of the era either created excessive barriers for blacks seeking home loans, or refused them outright for racial reasons, leaving many veterans unable to get a mortgage. And even the few institutions that would consider issuing the loans often rejected applications from black veterans on the basis of redlining—the practice of marking up areas of towns and cities as being too risky for mortgages because of high poverty and low real estate values. Never mind that the Veterans Administration essentially eliminated the lender's risk regardless of the location. As these were the only neighborhoods where most blacks could live in segregated America, black veterans were stymied once again. The famous Levittown suburb on Long Island, like many other postwar developments, did its part by refusing to sell to black veterans who otherwise would have qualified. And other areas had more ad hoc ways of dealing with the few black servicemen who managed to get a loan and move into a white neighborhood—the vets might find their homes vandalized or set ablaze, or find crosses burning in their yards.

Rankin's state of Mississippi provides an apt example of how this all played out: An *Ebony* magazine survey found that more than 3,000 VA home loans had been issued to veterans in Mississippi in the summer of 1947. In a state where fully half the population was black, only two of those loans went to black veterans.

This lopsided distribution of one of the G.I. Bill's most profoundly life-changing, society-transforming benefits was repeated to one degree or another nationwide. And so home ownership among white families quickly soared to two out of three, then more gradually reached its current zenith of three out of four. Home ownership rates for black and Hispanic families during the postwar housing boom years, however, hovered at or below 40 percent; and even today, while the children and grandchildren of white veterans enjoy the benefits of all that government-subsidized home equity, black and Hispanic home ownership rates remain stuck below 50 percent.

College enrollments under the G.I. Bill for black veterans provide a somewhat different picture: They did increase significantly over prewar levels, but unlike the huge gains in trade school enrollment the gains in black college attendance remained paltry compared to white veterans—black veterans had less than half the proportional increase in college enrollment that white veterans had. What gains there were in higher education and earning potential were concentrated in northern states, where black veterans attended integrated colleges and universities, although even there, quotas at many institutions limited enrollment (as they did for Jews and other minorities). In the South, however, where upward of 90 percent of black veterans who went to college ended up earning their degrees, segregation left them no option but to enroll in one of the hundred or so historically black colleges and universities in the country. These schools, set up under the separate-but-equal doctrine, at the time were small, chronically underfunded, unprepared for the huge influx of G.I. Bill students, and only provided limited courses of study (mostly focused on "preach or teach" options, as they were called at the time). None, for example, offered an engineering program immediately after the war—a profession in great demand at the time—and only a handful had postgraduate programs of any kind. Enrollments at those schools more than doubled through the G.I. Bill, but space was so limited that between 20,000 and 50,000 more black veterans were turned away for lack of space and because other whites-only Southern institutions would not accept them.

Apart from quotas, segregation, and over-full historically black campuses, many African American veterans had another good reason to forgo their G.I. Bill college benefits: insufficient academic preparation. The separate-but-equal elementary and high schools available to most black youths in the World War II era were not equal at all—black children simply were cheated when it came to the quality of teachers and schools (a problem America still has failed to resolve fully more than forty years after desegregation became the law of the land). Selective Service records on the educational levels of potential recruits in World War II reveal the unsurprising fact that, as a group, African Americans of draft age had completed fewer years of school and had higher illiteracy rates than white recruits. This is a matter of discrimination and deprivation across generations, rather than a fault of the G.I. Bill or its implementation per se; but it does help explain the VA statistics that showed a lower-than-expected college enrollment coupled with a marked preference for vocational training for black veterans who sought to use their veterans education benefits.

This did not have to be a negative—quite the contrary, as vocational training could have been an engine for huge economic gains for black veterans. Economists sometimes refer to the postwar era as "the Great Compression," because the disparity in earning power between blue- and white-collar workers grew smaller across society as a whole for the first time in history. Economic classes in America literally compressed as never before (a trend that lasted nearly three decades, then began to reverse with a vengeance in the seventies and eighties). In the postwar boom, skilled and semiskilled jobs that required no college degree—working for the phone company, an automobile manufacturer, an electric utility—were plentiful, paid well, offered an ever-growing array of benefits, and provided a ticket to the middle class for millions of Americans. That's why half of all veterans of World War II took advantage of this training either on the job or in vocational schools and institutes. Vocational training seemed a good bet for black veterans who wanted a better life and who could not go to college; the G.I. Bill still seemed to hold huge promise for them.

Once again, though, the promise was not kept. Rankin's poison pill made sure that whenever possible the locally appointed, white veterans officials in charge of vocational benefits and on-the-job training programs, particularly in the Jim Crow South, directed black veterans away from highly-paid, skilled work in the private sector, and toward menial, unskilled, low-wage positions. (How much of this is due to discrimination by the VA counselors, and how much is due to the employers' preferences, is not known, though it is clear that the Veterans Administration at that time made no effort to become an agent of change, preferring to facilitate and endorse existing employment practices rather than fight them.) Instead of coveted jobs at the phone company, black veterans were offered placement as Pullman porters, servicing white train passengers in luxury coaches where the only blacks allowed inside were the servants—twelve-hour days, six-day weeks, no room for advancement. Another survey of more than 6,000 Mississippi job placements by the VA in the fall of 1946 found that 86 percent of the skilled, professional, and semiskilled jobs went to white veterans, while 92 percent of the nonskilled and service positions went to black vets.

The situation was not completely bleak. Black-owned businesses and black veterans clubs in some cities joined forces to create on-the-job training and vocational programs that schooled veterans in a range of trades and industries, and these proved highly successful. These programs were part of a general nationwide expansion of vocational schools that began after the war to meet the increased demand from veterans of all races—and to cash in on millions of dollars in G.I. Bill payments suddenly available with few strings attached. The bill gave birth to an entire vocational education industry: Where there had been fewer than one hundred private vocational schools in the country before the war, there were more than 10,000 by 1950, providing training for everything from piloting an airplane to cooking a soufflé.

Some of these programs were excellent and highly specialized, perhaps the most famous of which was the Culinary Institute of America, which opened in 1946 with sixteen veterans (fifteen men and a former WAC) in a New Haven storefront. It expanded within a year to accommodate more than a hundred students, almost all attending on the G.I. Bill. The Culinary Institute of America soon became the top chef-training program in the country, a program that would not have existed without the G.I. Bill. Sixty years later, it has 2,000 students on its main campus in New York, with a second campus in California's wine country, and a tuition of about $20,000 a year—forty times what the G.I. Bill students paid in the years immediately after the war. These elite vocational programs, however, seldom offered places for nonwhite veterans in the immediate postwar years.

Many vocational schools at that time were segregated, and as the industry expanded rapidly and with little oversight, complaints arose about fly-by-night schools that provided little or no actual training. Instead, they existed merely to collect G.I. Bill–funded tuition or to allow veterans to collect a monthly stipend without providing any meaningful training. Black veterans were especially vulnerable to this sort of exploitation and, sadly, they were victimized by both white and black-run businesses and training programs. The lack of federal oversight Rankin and his allies built in to the bill had the unintended but entirely predictable additional consequence of allowing corruption and abuses to continue unfettered for years, costing taxpayers millions of dollars for educational programs that taught nothing. A two-year congressional investigation into charges of ineptitude, waste, and corruption at the Veterans Administration local offices and in various training and educational programs around the country led to a scathing report on VA failures and the closure of hundreds of schools. Programs for black veterans—some of them owned and operated by African Americans—appeared to have been among the most abusive, preying on those veterans most in need of help.

The G.I. Bill picture for World War II veterans of other ethnic backgrounds is not as clear or as well documented as the black veterans' experience, but it appears other groups fared somewhat better both during and after the war.

Asian Americans faced racial discrimination in the postwar era, but as a group they were not victimized by such formal systems of segregation, and there are ample anecdotal accounts of Asian

Americans throughout the nation attending college and purchasing homes with their G.I. Bill benefits, with far fewer difficulties than black veterans faced. Their wartime experiences were markedly different as well: Asian Americans in general were not segregated within the military, except for Japanese Americans, who, even as their families were locked up in internment camps during the war, volunteered to serve and were organized into a single unit, the 442 Regimental Combat Team. This unit, nicknamed the "Go For Broke" regiment, went on to become one of the most decorated in the war. Among its many heroes was a young lieutenant named Daniel Inouye, who lost his right arm in battle while single-handedly destroying two machine-gun nests that had his men pinned down, then crawling to within five yards of one of the powerful guns before silencing it with two grenades. After the war, Inouye used the G.I. Bill for college and law school, then in 1960 became the first Japanese American to be elected to the House of Representatives (from the new state of Hawaii). Two years later he won election to the U.S. Senate (where he served for many years with another Asian American G.I. Bill veteran, Spark Matsunaga). In 2005, Inouye began his eighth term in office and made national headlines as one of the Senate "Gang of Fourteen," a group of moderates from both major political parties who forged a controversial compromise on judicial nominations and the use of the Senate filibuster.

The half million Mexican Americans who served in World War II also had a very different experience than black servicemen, as they did not have to endure segregated units or institutionalized racism in the military. The relatively equal treatment they received while serving alongside white soldiers, sailors, and Marines—for many, a first in their lives—had a marked effect on Hispanics and Anglos alike, forging bonds and new attitudes that never had a chance to flourish before the war. Considered in proportion to their relatively small numbers in the military during World War II, no ethnic group received more Congressional Medals of Honor, the highest and rarest award for valor offered by the military, than Mexican American servicemen.

Of course, they still faced discrimination on an individual basis, and the harm that ignorance and prejudice could wreak during wartime proved immense, the case of Army Private Alex Miranda being just one example. As his unit prepared in England for the pivotal moment of the Normandy Invasion in 1944, Miranda was arrested for murdering his sergeant, a widely despised and bigoted tyrant who had been threatened by several of his men shortly before his death. No one actually saw Miranda, who had been drunk that night, commit the crime. But the official court-martial judge's opinion stated there was no reason to doubt his guilt. "It is fairly common knowledge that Mexicans are of principally Indian blood," the military judge wrote, in dismissing conflicting evidence in the case. "These latter are undemonstrative and uncommunicative, as well as being inclined to violence when drinking." And so, because everyone "knew" Mexican Americans were no different from Native Americans, and that booze turned them all into wild-eyed killers, Alex Miranda—Army volunteer, husband and father of a newborn daughter—was summarily executed, his body tossed into an unmarked criminal's grave in France, and his family left clueless about what had happened and why. Many years later, after researching this farcical evidence and uncovering admissions that witnesses against Miranda had been coerced by their commanders, Miranda's nephew petitioned the Pentagon to have his uncle posthumously exonerated. But the Pentagon refused to reopen the case.

Still, the war marked a turning point for many Mexican Americans who survived the conflict. And though they faced Jim-Crow-style sanctions in America's border states, particularly Texas, where signs in some restaurants announced that neither dogs nor Mexicans were welcome, the nation rallied behind Mexican American veterans early on when cases of abuse came to light. When a small-town funeral home refused the remains of one its native sons—Private Felix Longoria, killed on patrol in the Philippines—the incident blossomed into a national cause in which the whites-only policies of the citizens of Three Rivers, Texas, were held up for public scorn. *The New York Times* put the story on its front page, muckraking *Washington Post* journalist Drew Pearson denounced the town and its citizens as unpatriotic, and radio columnist Walter Winchell taunted in a national broadcast, "The great state of Texas, which looms so large on the map, looks mighty small tonight." Soon Texas's junior U.S. senator was intervening in the matter—future president Lyndon B. Johnson—and suddenly Three Rivers' townspeople decided to offer Longoria a hero's welcome, followed by a full military burial in Arlington National Cemetery. The publicity helped one of the Longoria family supporters, a physician and Hispanic veteran, Hector P. Garcia, to fund a network of advocacy centers for Mexican American servicemen, the American G.I. Forum, which provided, among other services, G.I. Bill counseling. The G.I. Bill provided the educational and professional training for a generation of Hispanic activists influenced by Garcia and the Longoria case. Three founders of the Mexican American Legal Defense and Educational Fund—Pete Tijerina, Albert Armendariz, and Ed Idar—all used the G.I. Bill for college or law school or both, and credited it, along with military service, with transforming their lives.

Black servicemen had every right to expect a similar transformation after the war. The National Association for the Advancement of Colored People, the National Urban League, and other black advocacy organizations repeatedly expressed the belief that the combination of wartime service and the G.I. Bill would launch a new age for America's black men and women. These organizations had encouraged African Americans to enlist and to serve their country, arguing that the war effort would unite the nation in a way that would make racial strife and animosity an anachronism. The Double V campaign, they called it, for victory against fascism abroad and victory against racism at home—a linkage that made eminent sense, given that race hatred and oppression, combined with a fervent belief in the ruling elite's racial superiority, were key elements of both Far Right fascism in Europe and reactionary segregationism in America. In many respects, the two were indistinguishable, the Ku Klux Klan, John Rankin's praise for it on the House floor notwithstanding, being one of America's, if not the world's, original fascist institutions. With passage of the G.I. Bill, the early champions of civil rights sensed victory within sight: An America that could defeat fascism in Germany, Italy, and Japan, it was said, could never allow it to endure at home, could it? "The outlook . . . is much brighter than it has been in the past half century," Julius Thomas, director of industrial relations for the Urban League declared triumphantly shortly after the war ended.

That optimism quickly faded as it became clear that Jim Crow and the poll tax had survived the war intact, and that the G.I. Bill would never be allowed to realize anything close to its full promise. Yet for all the setbacks and cheats and twisting of something good into something divisive, it also appears that, despite the best efforts of John Rankin and his cronies, the G.I. Bill gave many black veterans the things Rankin had feared most: the educational and economic tools they needed to do something about it.

Monte Posey's remarkable life story follows the arc of the G.I. Bill's own promising, contradictory, trying, and ultimately rewarding history. Not only did the bill transform his life (in ways its authors had intended, and in ways they did not), but it also set him on a path that let him help thousands of others overcome the same sort of discrimination and racism that almost derailed his own use of the G.I. Bill's benefits.

His great-grandparents were born slaves on an Alabama cotton plantation, the beginning of his known family history. Everything before that is lost. His paternal grandfather fled the South and settled in Illinois, where Posey's father, Anthony, was born. Posey's mother, Eva, born in Louisiana to children of slaves, was sent away at an early age after a white plantation foreman made threatening sexual advances. She, too, settled in Illinois, where she met and married Anthony Posey in 1925. Monte was born two years later in Chicago.

The Chicago Monte Posey knew as a child growing up in the Depression years was poor and mean, a city in which African Americans lived in a circumscribed area on the South Side, beyond which they were not permitted to live or even venture without risking harassment, beatings, or worse—unless, of course, it was to go to work as janitors or maids. You just didn't cross beyond 63rd Street, Posey recalls. He and his sister used to jokingly call their part of town the ghetto. As they got older, they realized it was no joke. They had no idea at the time that the original settlement of Chicago was founded and led by a free black man, Jean Baptiste Pointe du Sable, who established a multicultural, business-friendly trading town on the north bank of the Chicago River in 1773, a fact neither acknowledged by the white leaders of Monte Posey's Chicago, nor taught in any of its public schools, black or white. City officials did not recognize him as the settlement's founder until 1968.

Eva Posey worked as a seamstress, laboring with her hands every day, needle and thread and calloused, talented fingers, a trade she had learned as a girl before leaving the South. Her skill won her work from the affluent residents of Chicago's Hyde Park, fitting and tailoring their clothing. The pay was not very good, but her clients often expressed their appreciation by passing on their children's and their own fine clothes, many of the expensive garments barely worn more than once, often like new. Monte and his sister always looked like a million bucks, and what they didn't need, Eva Posey would pass on to friends in the neighborhood.

Tony Posey's story was very different. Unlike his wife and children, his race was not readily apparent, and while he did not ever claim to be white, he did not correct the misimpression if a potential employer reached that conclusion. It was the Depression, he later explained to his son, and a person did what he had to do to make sure his family had food and shelter—even if it meant enduring pain and humiliation. In Tony Posey's case, he endured it for decades.

The job wasn't much—he was a stock clerk for the old Rockwell Barnes Paper Company, where his duties kept him mostly in solitude in the basement of the plant. Though his education had ended with the sixth grade, he was bright, reliable, and industrious, and so was soon given the responsibility of opening the factory each morning. He had one sick day in thirty-seven years at the company.

There were no other black employees at the plant when he took the job, and he often heard racist jokes and insults among his co-workers. He never said anything, never took part in those conversations, and mostly stayed to himself, avoiding company picnics and parties, as they would involve appearing with his family, bringing his secret into the open and placing his job in jeopardy. The pain of this subterfuge ate at him, though only rarely would he talk about it. Sometimes he voiced his anguish at hiding his identity from his co-workers, but Tony Posey also told Monte of his service in the Army during World War I, how he had been treated with respect and without prejudice by the French citizens and soldiers he met during his time there, and how he held out hope that those enlightened attitudes would find their way across the Atlantic some day. In the meantime, both his father and mother commanded Monte and his sister to devote themselves to school, so that they would exceed their parents in education and make it to college—something they considered a prime defense against racism. If you have an education, his father told him, you will find a way out no matter what anyone says or thinks. "I want you and your sister to grow up and be somebody," his father said one evening over dinner.

These simple words left an unusually deep impression on the young Monte, who took his father's comment literally. "I heard this idea that someday I could be 'somebody,' and I realized that was tantamount to saying I wasn't somebody yet. I was nobody. I never forgot that."

Monte consistently ranked as the top student in his neighborhood elementary school, where he skipped a year and earned valedictorian honors when he graduated from the eighth grade. Nevertheless, his parents uprooted him from the all-black neighborhood schools, intent on providing him the best quality education they could, even if it meant "borrowing" an address to enroll him at a more affluent public high school in a white area. The school they chose was close to Northwestern University's campus, a beautiful area, as Monte remembers it, "the kind of place you'd want your kids to be." The school was top-notch, light years ahead of the decrepit neighborhood high school he had expected to attend. But he hated his years there. His experience with the other students was great—the only positive aspect of his time there he can recall—as he got along well with the white teenagers in his classes. He finally understood why his father so fondly recalled his time in France, even though it had been during the war: He had seen it really was possible for race to be irrelevant, for white people to be kind without condescending, to approach a group of white teenagers without a sense of dread and anger gnawing a hole in his stomach—they could just be kids together. Unfortunately, it also seemed clear to Monte that neither the parents, the neighborhood, nor the teachers shared that attitude. Even walking from the elevated train station to his school became a harrowing daily trial—people would stare or insult him as he hurried down the sidewalk, books under his arm. The faculty extended no welcome to the handful of black students at the school; with the exception of one biology instructor who tried to take Monte under her wing, not a single teacher at the school seemed the least bit interested in his development—or his lack of development, once his grades began dropping as he grew increasingly unhappy with his situation and lost his enthusiasm for study. He ended up graduating with only fair grades.

The one interest that sustained him through those four years of high school was aviation—he was passionately interested in airplanes and flying. "Flying became my dream. It's what kept me going, kept everything else bearable," he recalls. "That's where I felt alive. That's where I thought I could learn to be 'somebody.'"

His fascination with aviation was first sparked when his father took him to the 1933 Chicago World's Fair when he was seven. Italy's air marshal, Italo Balbo, arrived at the fair leading a fleet of twenty-four enormous double-hulled seaplanes, which flew in formation directly from Rome and splashed down spectacularly in Lake Michigan. At the fair, filled with all sorts of spectacular attractions, young Monte had eyes only for those seaplanes, gliding into the lagoon near the fairgrounds, enormous and powerful, graceful and elegant. "They were beautiful. I fell in love with them," he recalls wistfully.

Soon he began constructing airplane models, his bedroom filled with them. Then a friend's uncle took him to Harlem Airport in the Oaklawn area of South Chicago, a mecca of sorts for black pilots, famous the world over. The moment he saw that sod-covered field, Monte was hooked. He began spending all his spare time at the little airfield, learning to repair and fly airplanes, listening raptly to the older fliers. A pilot training program had been founded there by two black aviation pioneers, Cornelius Coffey and his wife, Willa Brown. Brown would be appointed by the White House in 1941 to head the Civil Air Patrol civilian pilot training program, a racially integrated service that helped supply military pilot recruits once the war began. Brown helped train more than two hundred pilots who went on to form the heart of the famous all-black Army fighter group, the Tuskegee Airmen. Monte had yearned to join the Tuskegee Airmen since he was fourteen, when he had first heard about the group of black pilots the Army had reluctantly commissioned under pressure from the

White House. (Eleanor Roosevelt showed up one day with a photographer to have her picture taken while flying with the chief pilot at Tuskegee Airfield—proving to the nation that "Negroes could fly." As absurd as it sounds, this was a huge moment that had enormous national impact, and one that permanently endeared the first lady to the black fliers.) Expected to fail, the Tuskegee Airmen exceeded all expectations but their own. They flew thousands of successful bomber escort missions over Europe in their P-51 Mustang fighters, their aircraft distinguished by vivid red paint on their tail sections. Bomber pilots specifically requested Red Tail escorts whenever possible, as the Tuskegee Airmen were the only fighter group that never lost a bomber to enemy interceptors. Their dog-fighting skills were so impressive that German pilots referred to them with grudging respect as *Schwarze Vogelmenschen*—the Black Birdmen—and avoided them whenever possible. Yet on the ground and on supposedly friendly soil, the black pilots were often harassed—one hundred of them were officially reprimanded for entering an officer's mess that they were entitled to use after returning from a combat mission. In time, though, their combat records and many citations for bravery muted the mistreatment and hastened the move to desegregate the military after the war.

In 1944, Posey turned seventeen and was finally old enough to pass the Army pilot tests and physicals and to begin his training. This started not at an Army base, as he had expected, but at the University of Wisconsin in Madison, one of the many colleges the military had converted to partial defense duty, where recruits and officers learned everything from cryptography to electrical engineering to preflight training. Posey also zipped through a roster of general academic courses designed to fill the gaps for young men and women with less-than-optimal high school careers behind them. This provided an introduction to college life for Posey—an idealized college life with challenging, interesting classes and professors. The campus was beautiful, he had his own room in a fraternity house taken over by the Army, he enjoyed his classes, and hung out with friends and fellow trainees at the student union in the evenings. If he had harbored any doubts about going to college before joining the Army, his time in Madison erased them.

The next stop in his training proved to be as dreadful a time in his life as Wisconsin was joyful—three months at Keesler Air Field in Biloxi, Mississippi, a coastal town then rife with illegal casinos, cops on the take, organized crime, and brutally enforced Jim Crow laws. He boarded a train in Wisconsin and sat wherever he wished; when it was time to get off, he was on a segregated train and walked into a segregated station, where the separate facilities were not just labeled "white only" and "colored," but separately for "white troops" and "colored troops." Everything was separate and unequal, Posey recalls, from the barracks, to the training, to the equipment, to the recreational opportunities (which, for black soldiers, did not exist).

Many instructors at Keesler were appalled that the Army would send them black pilot trainees, and epithets like "nigger" and "coon" were constantly in the air. Unlike the white soldiers, Posey and the other black trainees could not leave the base when off duty and could not go to the clubs on the base. It was a miserable existence. The only thing keeping him going was the knowledge that soon he would be sent to the Tuskegee base in Alabama, where his real training would begin, and where he knew there would be a sense of camaraderie completely missing at Keesler.

Then the war ended before he made it to Tuskegee and before his time in the cockpit could really begin. Soon word came down from Washington that no more pilots would be needed or trained. Active pilots who had accumulated many points from combat missions and time in service were discharged. Newcomers like Posey, whose enlistment periods were far from over, presented a problem, because they had been designated for aviation and could not simply be transferred anywhere. "They just didn't know what to do with us," Posey recalls.

He ended up transferred to Eglin Airfield in Florida, where he was assigned not as a pilot but as an aircraft mechanic, thanks to his experience back at Harlem Airport. The move brought a surprising twist to Posey's military career: Though the Army would remain officially segregated until 1948 (and would not integrate in earnest until the Korean War was well underway five years later), the aviation units that needed mechanics in 1945 were white. So Posey was assigned to one, officially on loan from a black aviation unit, but in fact part of one of the Army's first, if unofficial, integrated commands.

Steeling himself for the same sort of mistreatment he had received in Biloxi, Posey instead found he was accepted without problem or rancor at his new unit, where he was immediately given his own plane to crew and maintain. This was no small matter at the time—there was no precedent in the Army for putting the safety of white pilots in the hands of a black enlisted man. Even so, he had no interest in fixing airplanes if he couldn't fly them. The decision to accept an early discharge if he could attend college was an easy decision to make once the opportunity came along. He called his sister, who was already enrolled at the University of Illinois, and got her to put in an application for him.

"We were all disillusioned by then," Posey recalls. "I had joined to be with the black elite, to be a fighter pilot, in the wild blue yonder and all that. These were good guys in the program, high powered. My job was okay, I was treated well, but a lot of the other guys were stoking furnaces, sweeping up, doing menial jobs. We couldn't go anywhere in town—when I did, one time, I almost got arrested for sitting in the wrong seat. I was very happy to get out."

The University of Illinois had opened a unique campus in 1946, on the historic Navy Pier, to accommodate thousands of veterans in the Chicago area, pledging to accept all qualified students. More than 100,000 would pass through the college-on-a-pier before the school was moved to dry land in the sixties. Soon filled to capacity, the program offered two years of undergraduate courses, after which students could transfer to other university campuses to finish their studies. The pier was long and bitterly cold in the winter, making walks to class brutal. The howling winds off the lake rattled the windows of every classroom, and many rooms, particularly the engineering division at the end, were so cold the students had to wear their gloves and coats inside. A huge neon sign hung above the entrance.

Posey's first year went well, but the hectic city commuter campus was not at all like the bucolic atmosphere he had enjoyed in Wisconsin, and soon other considerations intruded on his plan for a degree in four years. He had reunited with a young woman he had dated in high school, and when they decided to marry, he felt he needed a full-time job rather than the small stipend he could get as a G.I. Bill student. So, guessing that a civil service job might offer more opportunities for him than the private sector, he took a test to join the Chicago Police Department.

Out of more than 4,000 applicants in 1947, he scored high enough on the test to join the first class of twenty-nine cadets sent to the police academy that year. When he was sworn in as a police officer at age twenty, he was one of only thirty-one African American officers in the entire Chicago Police Department. He continued attending college part time, mostly night school—another common route to higher education for veterans.

"It was sort of an honor to be a black policeman in those days, it was so rare. My dad loved that, because, to him, I was finally going to be someone."

Unsurprisingly, Posey drew assignments white officers didn't want—although Posey considered some of them of critical importance. All the black officers were given duty standing guard at the homes of black veterans who had just purchased houses in predominately white neighborhoods. G.I. Bill home loans were more readily available to black veterans in Chicago than in southern states, but just because the government eased some racial barriers didn't mean the attitudes they reflected had changed. The old lines that had webbed various Chicago neighborhoods in a kind of ethnic Iron Curtain—keeping Irish, Italian, Jews, and African Americans each in their own zones—would only be breached slowly and painfully. Insults, threats, cross burnings, arson, and gunfire frequently greeted black veterans when they moved into white neighborhoods.

One of Posey's first assignments was to report for duty every day for a week at the newly purchased home of a black veteran with a wife and small child. Halfway through his tour, Posey heard a noise at the back of the house. When he dashed around the house, he saw a fire blazing and a man running up a railroad embankment that ran along the rear of all the houses on the street. Posey shouted, fired some shots, but the intruder got away. Later, a man fitting the description Posey provided was arrested by other black officers. Posey identified him, but he was never prosecuted.

It was almost impossible to get charges filed for crimes committed by whites against blacks, Posey recalls.

He advanced through the ranks to plainclothes officer, charged with investigating felony crimes, but he found no opportunities to become a supervisor. He was passed over for promotion time and again; all supervisors were white, even in the black areas of town.

In 1953, he moved to California, where his sister had relocated a year earlier. She had been raving about life in Los Angeles—the people, the weather, the ocean—and when he saw advertisements seeking police officers in Los Angeles that seemed to promise far more opportunities than Chicago, he decided to make the move. The Los Angeles County Sheriff's Department offered him a job shortly after he applied.

Harsh realities dashed his high hopes on his very first day on the job, when he found the situation for black officers in 1950s Los Angeles was even worse than in Chicago. Although Tom Bradley (who would be elected Los Angeles' first black mayor twenty years later) served as a Los Angeles police lieutenant at the time Posey came to town, he was the only exception in an otherwise all-white command structure at the major police departments in the LA area, which were all rigidly segregated. Posey drew jail guard duty in his first year with the sheriff's department, the least desirable assignment available and one that white officers with his level of experience would not have had to endure except as a punishment. When a new assignment for genuine police work finally came through for him and other black officers a year later, Posey was disappointed again. He felt that midlevel supervisors did everything they could to foil orders from department brass to integrate sheriff substations that were being established at the time across the vast Los Angeles Basin. They would assign black officers to posts as far as possible from where they lived, hoping the long commutes, undesirable shifts, and unpleasant assignments would drive them to resign, or at least keep them "in their place." When Posey asked why this was being done, he recalls Assistant Sheriff Peter Pitchess—who would become sheriff in 1959—telling him, "The community is not ready for people like you. They might resent you being a law enforcement officer."

Posey knew then he had to leave the department. "This man who was being groomed to become sheriff was more concerned about the criminals than me," he still says in wonder. "They might be upset if a black officer arrested them. Can you imagine that?"

By then he and his first wife had divorced, and he resigned from the department after a mere two years. He took a job as an investigator for the state and resumed his college studies, finally earning a degree in sociology and criminology. Then, in 1960, he heard California was creating a new agency to combat discrimination, the Fair Employment Practices Commission, and that it needed experienced investigators. Posey, certain this was the job he had been waiting for all his life, immediately applied and won the position.

For civil rights activists and black professionals weary of fruitless battles against discrimination, California circa 1960 was one of the most exciting places in the country. A popular liberal governor, Pat Brown, had just taken office and committed the state to an unprecedented series of progressive projects: He promised to create the best public schools in the nation; double the budget of the University of California and open three new campuses; create the first state antipollution agency to combat smog; expand the freeway system to end traffic jams and connect rapidly growing suburbs; expand medical care of the poor; create a state minimum wage; and end racial discrimination in employment. These were the goals he campaigned on and reaffirmed in his 1959 inaugural speech, an agenda for Big Government and higher taxes that would sound like a recipe for political suicide today, but which evoked roars of approval from voters at the time. And their approval was reality based: On Brown's watch, California's public schools were the best in the nation, a world-class university education could be had by virtually any state resident at an affordable price, the freeways worked, and medical care for all improved vastly. And despite tax increases (via a progressive income tax that shifted a greater portion of the burden to the wealthiest individuals and corporations), the state's economy, businesses, industries, and employment all boomed. In the space of a few years, Brown had managed to implement, for Californians at least, a large chunk of FDR's vision for a second bill of rights, making the Golden State the envy of the nation.

One of his early major legislative accomplishments was establishing the Fair Employment Practices Commission, modeled on a New Deal agency by the same name that Roosevelt had created during the war, but which Congress subsequently killed. California's version of the agency differed in one significant way: It had teeth. It had the ability to go to court to compel employers to open their books and give up their records, then take them to court if they did not comply with antidiscrimination laws.

Poorly funded and undermanned, the agency nevertheless cowed major corporations that refused to hire qualified black applicants for positions other than janitorial duties. Based in San Francisco, Posey and eleven other investigators ranged up and down the state, investigating myriad complaints of discrimination. When Posey reached the stage of an investigation where a meeting with corporate officers was called to review his findings, he would often take one of the prominent business leaders Brown had shrewdly appointed to serve as commissioner. This would often defuse confrontations at the very outset. A majority of cases quickly settled without lawsuits once Posey and his commissioner made it clear that the evidence of discrimination was overwhelming, and that it would be far easier to fix things voluntarily than under court order. Because discrimination was endemic at employers all over the state at the time, the caseload was enormous and constant—and led to employment opportunities for thousands of African American and Latino workers who previously had been locked out.

One of Posey's early victories involved cracking the code of a major phone company that had hired few blacks and never promoted those whom it did hire. In examining the company's files on job applicants, Posey found a numerical code at the top of each file. He determined the numbers designated religion, ethnicity, and gender, secret notations that allowed the company to avoid hiring Jews, Catholics, blacks, Chinese Americans, and others whom corporate officers found objectionable, without the discriminatory information apparent on the paperwork. Once its secret practices were exposed, that company settled immediately and agreed to alter its hiring methods.

During his years at the commission, Posey met and married his second wife, Diana, a special education teacher and political activist. She and Posey bought a house with a G.I. Bill loan, raised two children together, and became involved in a variety of political causes and civil rights protests. "It was an exciting time for me," Posey says. "The world was changing."

In 1963, Governor Brown rammed a law through the legislature banning housing discrimination (five years before the federal government adopted a similar law), and Posey's agency assumed responsibility for enforcing it. He and his colleagues chose a case involving St. Louis Cardinals baseball great Curt Flood, a native of Oakland, as their kick-off. It was a classic discrimination case: A real estate agency had refused to sell to Flood because he was black. The publicity was intense and instantaneous, and it allowed the commission to demonstrate that even a star athlete like Flood could have trouble buying a house because of discrimination.

But Brown had overreached in his policies and underestimated the depth of the racial divide he had exposed with his housing code. White voters rebelled and repealed the antidiscrimination housing law barely a year after its enactment, and Brown's popularity tanked further in the wake of growing campus protests over the Vietnam War and the 1965 Watts riots in Los Angeles. He never recovered, and the man who had trounced Richard Nixon in 1962 in his first reelection bid lost badly four years later to a former actor named Ronald Reagan, who campaigned for governor on a law-and-order, antistudent, antigovernment, antitax platform, his victory and policies coinciding with the start of California's long, slow decline in national rankings for schools, highways, and other public works and services.

By then, Posey made a timely exit. In 1965, the federal government had created the Equal Employment Opportunity Commission to enforce portions of the new Civil Rights Act of 1964, and one of its new commissioners, an alumnus of the California commission, offered Posey a job as an investigator for the new agency. He promptly accepted.

The commissioners selected by the Johnson administration were powerhouses, particularly its first chairman, Franklin Roosevelt Jr., whose name recognition commanded instant attention whenever he got involved in a case. The former Chicago cop who ten years earlier had lacked the clout to get a racist charged with arson found himself sitting in orientation meetings with FDR Jr. as well as the former head of the Peace Corps, a Texas minister who was on a first-name basis with the president, and the future leader of the National Organization of Women. Speakers brought in to brief the new investigators included Senator Daniel Patrick Moynihan, the head of the NAACP, the head of the Urban League, the head of the G.I. Forum, and the labor leader who led the epic twelve-year fight to unionize the Pullman porters three decades earlier.

Posey traveled throughout the nation investigating complaints of employment discrimination, but much of his work involved cases in the South. In many areas, men and women who pursued formal complaints with the EEOC risked their livelihoods and lives, and the investigators faced constant danger as well when probing discrimination in the still-segregated South. Their cars were followed and vandalized. Posey's food was poisoned in one restaurant. In Onslow County, North Carolina, the plane carrying the investigative team from Washington was greeted by a large sign proclaiming, "The Greater Klans of America Welcome You." The Klansmen seemed to have been alerted to their arrival and were aware of all their movements. They found Klan literature tucked in their windshields, the restaurants refused them service, and unfriendly comments on the street indicated many people knew exactly who they were, despite attempts at secrecy. Eventually, Posey and his colleagues learned that a local FBI supervisor, who was privy to the team's movements in his area, was the brother-in-law of a major KKK leader.

"There was real fear in those communities in those days. It took a lot of courage for black people to stand up and pursue these complaints with us," Posey recalls. "We were worried for our own safety, but we got to leave when it was all over. They had to live there. It was very hard back then. The authorities in many of those communities were part of the problem. But we had subpoena powers, we had the journalists on our side back then. And we brought those people to task."

In the first years of the agency, the emphasis stayed on protecting victims of racial discrimination and getting employers to offer at least entry-level jobs to black and other minority applicants. Employers often refused to give up their records and sometimes destroyed them to stymie the commission. But then the Justice Department would get involved and the threat of civil suits and criminal charges loomed large. Most employers at that point voluntarily complied—not out of conscience, but through a simple cost-benefit analysis. The commission, Posey says, made sure it wouldn't pay to continue to discriminate. In later years, Posey was able to pursue cases involving the promotion and hiring of supervisors, not just entry-level employees. "But first we had to concentrate on just getting people in the door," Posey recalls. "You can't promote minorities if there are none in a company to begin with."

As the new agency grew, Posey left Washington to work out of newly established district offices in New York and San Francisco, where he was district director until his retirement. The agency expanded its emphasis on racial discrimination after several years, and Posey began pursuing sexual discrimination cases as well as race-based ones.

He was forced to leave the agency in 1975 because of a severe spinal injury he suffered in a car accident while working a case. By then, there had been a change in administrations, and it seemed to him his beloved commission had grown more interested in pushing papers than effecting change. He returned to college yet again to earn his masters degree at age fifty, and settled on California's Central Coast.

At age seventy-eight, Monte Posey marvels at the changes he has witnessed and helped bring about since his Chicago childhood. The segregated military he served in is long gone, replaced by a model of equal opportunity and racial integration. The G.I. Bill that changed his life for the better, even as it passed over many other African Americans, is in its current form far less generous, but it is also no longer a vehicle for discrimination. And while housing and employment discrimination certainly still exists, its most blatant forms have been eradicated. No more racist housing covenants. No more quotas. No more separate but equal.

The measure of progress is abundantly clear to Posey when he talks to his grandchildren about his experiences in life. They find it all unbelievable. "I say, 'Fifty years ago, you could not have gone to the college you're attending. You would not have been allowed in the door.' They just look at me like I'm crazy and say, 'What?' And that just tickles me, that what I lived through just sounds outlandish to them. They have never experienced it. I *love* that."

His youngest daughter, born when Posey was fifty, is a college instructor specializing in research on racial issues in education. She's always been a gifted student and is working on her doctorate at Berkeley; the pride in Posey's voice at her accomplishments is hard to miss. Posey's daughter shares something in common with her grandfather: Her race is not obvious. But where Tony Posey felt compelled by prejudice and economic desperation to hide who he really was, Linn Posey, two generations later, proudly identifies herself as a black woman, secure in who she is and in the knowledge that her opportunities in life will not be limited one whit.

That is a source of joy for Monte Posey, but there is a bittersweet aspect to it. He feels immense sadness for his dad—just talking about the pain his quiet, gentle father had to endure during his working life still brings tears to Posey's eyes. "The opportunities just weren't there for him. Things are different now, thank God."

He says he can close his eyes and see his father, all those long years ago, trudging off to work at the paper company, steeling himself for another day. Monte ached for him then, still does.

Something happened, though, while Posey was away in the Army. The paper company hired a black worker who, for some reason, outed Tony Posey, revealing his race to his employers. This turned out to be an immense relief once the shock had passed. His dad did not lose his job—he was, by then, a fixture, and things continued as they always had, except for one thing.

When Monte returned from the service, he visited his dad at work for the first time ever, in his dress uniform, and a proud father got to show off his son to all his fellow workers—a son, he announced, who was "really somebody."

☆ 9 ☆

What's inside?
Leaders and the G.I. Bill

The birth of a new science, the birth of inspiration, the birth of leadership: In Leon Lederman's view, each begins with a question, deceptively small, often childlike, yet profound in its implications.

"The question is always the key," the physicist with the impish smile and properly disordered white mane likes to say. "With the right question, you can figure out what everyone else is missing. With the right question, you can make the breakthrough . . . that wonderful moment when you know something no one else knows."

The question that first moved Lederman, that galvanizes him still, does indeed sound like something his five-year-old grandson would ask: *What's inside?*

It is the question that sent him at age eight racing down into the basement behind his big brother, Paul, begging to take part in the crazy chemistry and electrical experiments he'd concocted in the basement. *What's in that jar? What's inside that motor? How does the electricity get inside those wires?* He'd even do Paul's chores for him if it meant he could be the mad scientist's assistant in the dim dampness of their old cellar in the Bronx.

It's also the question that sent him off to college to study chemistry and physics, then, when the United States went to war, to join the Army and tear apart captured German radar devices—to see what was inside, what made them tick, and to build better ones for the Allies. His radars helped defend Pacific Navy bases from kamikaze attacks and to direct airlifts safely into a liberated Europe.

When he got home, it was the question of matter itself—the building blocks of the universe and everything within—that spurred him on, the G.I. Bill paying his way (and supporting his growing family) through graduate studies at Columbia University, where modern physics quite literally was invented, particle by particle, day by day. What's inside that piece of classroom chalk? Slice it down as far as you can, zoom in, past the molecules, past the atoms, inside the nuclei, inside the protons and electrons. Zoom in farther, and tell me, what's inside?

Lederman is one of a handful of men alive who have provided meaningful answers to that question, hunting down ghostly particles no one had ever found before, peeling back some of the stubborn secrets of what's inside everything, and winning a Nobel Prize and innumerable other awards along the way. His research has spurred a generation of physicists and inspired the work of a dozen other Nobelists. He directed the legendary Fermilab, presided over the largest particle accelerator in the world, and assembled a team of physicists whose discoveries are too numerous to list, who brought a hundred nations together on a grassy plain in Batavia, Illinois, to split the atom for peace.

And when it was time to retire from the rigors of daily research, he turned his powerful question elsewhere, devoting his energies to leading a campaign, still in progress, to improve public schools and the training of teachers. We need to know what's happening inside our public schools, he says, and why so few of our kids are interested in math and science. How can America continue to compete, much less lead the world, Lederman asks, if its young people don't understand what's inside? Or even that this is a question worth asking?

Leon Lederman—son of immigrants, child of the Depression, the first in his family to go to college—never set out to be a leader and never expected to become one. He was lured to science as a boy out of romance and adventure, after reading a children's book by Einstein that likened science to detective work, and a magazine account of a Nobel Prize winner in the 1930s who had to drag his machines up a mountain to capture cosmic rays. Chasing star particles up mountaintops sounded like the life for Lederman, though he never anticipated reaching the top of his profession.

And so he joined an extraordinary collection of thinkers and scientists returned from the war to lead a golden age in science and research, men who came home to invent lasers and computer chips, cancer-curing particle beams and MRIs, all the while peeling back the invisible realm of the subatomic layer by layer, coaxing mysteries into view. They were a quirky, diverse bunch, united by a passion to know—and by the fact that most of them were there because the G.I. Bill allowed them to be there rather than working "real" jobs. If he had been forced to hold down a job *and* pursue his graduate studies while supporting a wife and children, Lederman says, he almost certainly would have quit school—leaving a hole in modern physics that might not have been filled to this day.

This is one of the significant legacies of the G.I. Bill: It gave the nation a generation of leaders for Americans to revere—not just in science, but in medicine, architecture, law, government, and just about any other field that comes to mind.

The extraordinary wave of researchers and inventors, senators and presidential candidates, judges and councilmen, civil rights activists and space explorers did not simply spring into being because the war had been such a great and inspiring experience for them. This generation of leaders was nurtured as no other generation has been, before or since. Men of vastly different backgrounds, poor and rich, immigrants and bluebloods, liberals and conservatives, religious and agnostic, all found themselves on far more equal footing than ever before in the contest to see who would lead, which ideas would prevail, what direction the nation would take.

In this postwar world, Lederman, the child of a Jewish laundry worker, could become the leading physicist of his generation. The son of a South Dakota minister, whose salary was as often paid with a sack of potatoes as with dollar bills, could get a history degree, become a professor, then become a U.S. senator, and later be nominated for president. The child of a hotel magnate and the boy whose family was so poor they had to live in the basement while renting out the rest of the house could find themselves equals in running the federal government and in commanding the respect of a nation. This was really something new.

Until the G.I. Bill, America had always been led, with a few exceptions, by a wealthy elite, beginning with the Founding Fathers. Even the famously humble Abraham Lincoln, with his carefully cultivated log-cabin history, was born to a relatively prosperous working father and had become one of the richest lawyers in Illinois by the time he was elected president. Rags to riches, and even rags to president, has always been possible in America; it just didn't happen all that often. The G.I. Bill helped alter that equation, empowering a new brand of leaders to fill commanding positions in postwar America. The bill didn't just create an expanding new middle class—it opened up the ruling class, too.

And for better and worse, the nation we live in today is in large part their handiwork.

Two old men share a stage at the Smithsonian, veterans, war heroes, former senators, former presidential candidates. They are craggy and slowed by their eighty-plus years, but unbowed, their talent for oratory undiminished, effortlessly showing up the younger guys who have filled their Senate seats. One a Republican, one a Democrat, opposed in their views on almost everything, they have nevertheless been friends for decades, united by their service in the U.S. Senate, in the U.S. Army, in European combat six decades past—and in returning from war to find their lives, their prospects, and their country profoundly transformed.

"The biggest piece of legislation the country ever passed was the G.I. Bill," former Senator Robert Dole tells the gathering.

"It changed my life," former Senator George McGovern agrees without hesitation.

Of all the things they remember about the war, and all that they might wish to forget but cannot, this is what they choose to bring up almost every time they speak of the era: the G.I. Bill. For them it is the vast counterweight to a generation's sacrifice, the engine of countless good things in America, and of their own success and opportunities in life and work. Their tone, invariably, is one of quiet amazement, even now, at the accidental greatness of it—seasoned with just a hint of regret behind their words, perhaps even disappointment, when they gaze out at the horizon and spy nothing like it in sight for their grandchildren.

Long retired, they returned to Washington on Memorial Day 2004 for the dedication of the capital's first-ever National World War II Memorial, a monument sixty years in the making, and an opportunity for the nation to get reacquainted with two great leaders. The memorial itself is a ponderous, ungraceful affair, a modern Stonehenge of columns, fountains, and martial imagery, but the symbolism is huge and the veterans have come in droves, drawn not by how the memorial stands, but by what it stands for. The brief dedication ceremony, in which Dole delivered one of his finest, most gracious speeches, drew 140,000 to the National Mall.

Afterward, McGovern and Dole agreed to speak to the smaller gathering at the nearby Smithsonian, to ruminate on their experiences during and after the war, two of the nation's most prominent leaders with nearly a century of public service between them. Then they made the media rounds together, Democrat and Republican, liberal and conservative, opponent of America's most recent wars, and their dutiful if reluctant supporter.

"We're not the oddest of couples," Dole assures one audience, and it was true, their life stories have more parallels than differences—both of them uniquely American, and both uniquely a product of a time and a set of opportunities their successors can only envy.

Of the two, Dole's history as a wounded war hero is the more familiar to most Americans.

It was Dole whose family was so poor during the Depression that his mother and father decided to move everyone into the basement so they could supplement their income by renting out the upstairs rooms of their small frame home in Russell, Kansas.

2,000 yards off course. The sons of Army Chief of Staff George Marshall, Republican Senate Whip Leverett Saltonstall and Harry Hopkins, Roosevelt's closest aide, so invaluable he was sometimes called FDR's "deputy president," would all be killed in combat.

How then, Dole asks, could he do anything but join the fight? "It was our duty," he says simply. This does not sound quaint or old-fashioned when he says it. It sounds both humble and humbling.

In 1943, at age nineteen, Dole enlisted in the Army and rose to the rank of second lieutenant and platoon leader in the storied 10th Mountain Division. This division saw heavy, hard combat in the mountains of Italy near the end of the war and suffered substantial casualties—nearly a thousand killed and more than 4,000 wounded in less than four months. On April 14, 1945, Dole's platoon received orders to take a high point in the Italian foothills known only as Hill 914—a badly planned operation that required one squad to cross an open field rather than maintain cover in adjacent woods. The platoon sergeant had been ordered to lead the squad on this dangerous mission, but Dole insisted on doing it instead while the rest of the platoon provided cover fire. Trip wires, mines, and a hidden machine gun nest awaited Dole and his men. They never had a chance, as the innocent-looking pasture turned into a killing field. Eight of twelve men in Dole's squad died within minutes, with the rest wounded. When Dole's radio man went down and the young lieutenant crawled from cover to try to drag him to safety, a machine gun blast tore into Dole's back, shoulder, and right arm. After Dole lay there bleeding for hours, his sergeant was finally able to crawl beneath the stream of bullets and drag him to safety, though by then Dole was paralyzed, delirious, and near death. When he finally reached an Italian hospital, Dole's arm was a shattered, unrecognizable mess, his temperature spiking as high as 109 degrees, and the doctors assumed he would never walk again, if he survived at all.

Three weeks later, Germany surrendered. Heartbreakingly, the battle for Hill 914 had been for naught—it had no purpose or value beyond the lives ended and altered there. The Bronze Star for heroism and the two Purple Hearts pinned on Dole's crippled body provided small comfort to the bittersweet timing of peace.

Despite his pessimistic prognosis, after nine surgeries and more than three years of therapy and rehabilitation, Dole not only walked again, but he returned to college, though this time it was on the G.I. Bill instead of an athletic scholarship. Much of his rehabilitation came not from professional medical care but through sheer willpower, as Dole maintained a months-long regimen of repetitive, painful exercises with ropes and pulleys in the Dole family garage. One of Dole's inspirations was President Roosevelt, who had died two days before Dole was wounded—and who had spent years of effort and exercise just trying to get his toes to move after polio had left him paralyzed.

Though his recovery exceeded all expectations, Dole never regained the use of his right arm—leading to his long habit of clutching a pen in his right hand to disguise the disability. Forced to give up his dream of a career in medicine, he went to law school instead. Then he entered public service, beginning as a state legislator in 1953, followed by a stint as a county attorney. For most of the sixties he served as a congressman, and then in 1968 he won the first of five terms in the U.S. Senate, where he served as both minority and majority leader, establishing himself as one of the leading conservatives in the nation who nevertheless forged relationships with liberals and earned a reputation of ruling the Senate from the center. He championed the original Civil Rights Act, an important extension of the Voting Rights Act, and he coauthored the Americans with Disabilities Act—all important causes for liberal politicians, yet Dole frequently ranked them as his greatest legislative accomplishments.

A contradictory figure, he came to be known for both his humor and his darkly brooding moodiness, for choosing a life in the public eye even as he is loath to glance in a mirror because of his crippled arm, for being a dogged defender of Richard Nixon's scandalous presidency, yet a supporter of civil rights who worked with his ideological opposite, McGovern, to win passage of landmark disability and antihunger legislation. He's had three runs at the White House and one for the vice presidency with Gerald Ford; his last campaign was in 1996 as the Republican nominee against an incumbent Bill Clinton.

Dole resigned from the Senate to wage that final battle, then retired from politics when Clinton cruised to a second term. Typical of Dole, he immediately turned to the opponent he had criticized and asked for help in establishing the National World War II Memorial. Clinton not only provided that help, he awarded Dole the Presidential Medal of Freedom, the country's highest civilian honor, for his long years of public service. Dole's retirement did not remove him from the public eye, as he undertook such diverse activities as becoming for a time a very visible spokesman for the anti-impotency drug Viagra, and the establishment of the Robert J. Dole Institute of Politics, which has the difficult mission of restoring bipartisanship to the increasingly fractured American political process.

Dole has long been a fiscal conservative, yet he is an ardent fan of the G.I. Bill's immense largesse, certain that it made his recovery, education, and career possible instead of improbable. Without it, he asks, how does a Bob Dole come out of Russell, Kansas, to run the most exclusive club in America, the U.S. Senate? "It was a pretty good little law," he says. "Maybe we need something like it again."

George McGovern also believes his career in the Senate and run for the presidency were made possible in large part by his military service and the G.I. Bill. As he sits with Dole for yet another interview, McGovern reflects on why he and such men as Dole, Senator Daniel Patrick Moynihan, Senator Daniel Inouye, Senator Fritz Hollings, and a host of other members of the Greatest Generation were able to rise from humble origins to become national leaders:

"If, in fact, we were anything close to the greatest generation, it's probably the result of three factors.

"We were honed and toughened by the Great Depression for ten years prior to World War II. Nobody had a dollar. There weren't any rich people; we were all poor in the 1930s.

"And then the war itself—we believed in it. We had a clear mission, and we executed it. So that gave us a sense of self-confidence.

"The third thing . . . is the G.I. Bill of Rights. That's one of the most marvelous things the federal government has ever done, is to offer these 16 million people who fought in World War II a chance to go to any college of their choice. I went all the way through Northwestern University to a PhD in American history. It changed my life."

McGovern, the South Dakota preacher's son, went from university professor after the war to Congress and then the Senate for eighteen years. He ran for president as the Democratic nominee in 1972, the campaign that defined his career. Incumbent President Richard Nixon, mired in Vietnam and soon to be driven from office by the Watergate scandal, defeated McGovern in a landslide by successfully painting him as a dangerously radical peacenik for his opposition to the war in Southeast Asia. That cartoon portrait has stuck for decades, as McGovern's name, to this day, is used as a warning to Democratic politicians who consider embracing liberal or dovish ideas: *Don't pull a McGovern.*

The problem with this view, of course, is that McGovern was right. A decade before most anyone else in the national leadership, he understood the truth of Vietnam and, more importantly, was willing to speak it: that the war was an unmitigated disaster, a poisonous cauldron of bad policy, bad tactics, bad intelligence, a misuse of brave servicemen, the needless destruction of more than 2 million Vietnamese and 60,000 American lives, and an alliance with a corrupt and unpopular regime that was doomed to fail. As McGovern predicted, it finally ended badly, with a shameful retreat that Nixon insisted on calling "peace with honor," though it soon left a communist regime in total control of the country and our former allies in chains or in exile. That the war was a mistake is now overwhelmingly accepted as obvious and true by the vast majority of Americans, which obscures just how hard it was for McGovern to stand up and say so at the time. As a junior senator, McGovern had the courage to call for withdrawal and negotiations early in his first term in office, while his own party, in control of the White House and Congress, supported the war. He says that took more guts than flying his bomber in World War II. His South Dakota constituents overwhelmingly supported the war at the time, so he assumed his principles would end his political career. Apparently the voters liked his principles more than he had anticipated; he was reelected to the Senate for a total of eighteen years. President Lyndon Johnson, McGovern's fellow Democrat, banned him from the White House, and Nixon excoriated him ten years later as dangerously soft and out of touch. But McGovern wasn't radical, he was correct—and he paid the price because he was right before the country was ready to hear it. It cost him the presidency.

And for that, he says, he bears not a single regret. He still considers his candidacy an honorable mission, one that did not sacrifice truth for expediency, and he remembers his acceptance speech at the chaotic Democratic convention in 1972 as one of his best. The theme: "Come home, America."

This is another quality that seems common among the leaders of his generation—a lack of whining, of playing the victim. Perhaps it comes from seeing war or from living through Depression. Dole rarely speaks about his disability—he does his best to hide it—and instead has channeled his frustration at his injuries into championing legislation to help the disabled and protect them from discrimination. During the memorial dedication ceremony, he told one personal World War II anecdote, and it was perfect—not about fighting, not about glory or heroism or America's military prowess, nor was it about his final battle and recovery. It was about a lonely, hungry, homesick Kansas boy writing a letter home from the front:

> *"You can send me something to eat whenever you're ready," he wrote. "Send candy, gum, cookies, cheese, grape jelly, popcorn, nuts, peanut cluster, Vicks Vapor Rub, wool socks, wool scarf, fudge cookies, ice cream, liver 'n onions, fried chicken, banana cake, milk, fruit cocktail, Swiss steak, crackers, more candy, Life Savers, peanuts, the piano, the radio, the living room, the suite, and the record player and Frank Sinatra. I*

> *guess you might as well send the whole house if you can get it into a five-pound box.*
>
> *"P.S. keep your fingers crossed."*
>
> *In authoring that only slightly exaggerated wish list I merely echoed the longing of 16 million Americans whose greatest wish was for an end to the fighting.*

McGovern, too, has every right to whine, though he never does: While his opponent, Nixon, ran a shipboard snack shack and made a fortune playing poker during his World War II stint in the Navy, McGovern served as an Army bomber pilot who flew thirty-five dangerous missions over North Africa and Europe aboard the lumbering, difficult, freezing, and deafening B-24 Liberator. The airplanes had been manufactured so quickly and in such great numbers that they were deployed without heaters, without insulation for the noise, without windshield wipers. Pilots had to stick their heads out the window to see when the windshield was obscured. Half the pilots and crews McGovern flew with never made it home, as a full tour of duty meant flying thirty-five missions, while the average crew only made it to seventeen. His navigator and close friend never made it home, never made it to the seminary where he'd planned to become a Presbyterian minister. McGovern made it to the end of the war, then volunteered to fly extra missions delivering food and medicine to the European countryside, often to areas he had bombed just a few months before. He received the Distinguished Flying Cross for his bravery; he was twenty one years old when he commanded his first mission.

Yet in his failed bid for president, McGovern rarely mentioned his war experience. And he paid the price at the polls, falsely painted as a pacifist incapable of being a strong commander in chief, simply because he didn't think it was proper to trade on doing his duty during the war, risking his life many times over.

This, more than anything, separates leaders who never saw combat from those who have, and the World War II generation from their successors. There is no talk by either of these men of being a war leader, no strutting about in uniforms and flight suits, no talk of accumulating "political capital," no embrace of the notion of "preemptive war"—all hallmarks of the man who was commander in chief when the World War II Memorial brought Dole and McGovern to town. Neither Dole nor McGovern has ever parsed the meaning of the word "is," as President Bill Clinton famously did when his truthfulness was called into question. Both men believe the blood of young Americans should be offered up only as a last resort, and their definition of leadership keeps returning to the ideas of duty and sacrifice and honor. Dole took heat for championing civil rights when many Republican leaders wanted to forge ties with Southern Democrats who favored segregation; McGovern took heat for opposing a war when other Democrats feared advocating peace implied weakness. Both men say they chose to persevere because it was their duty to do so, even though both were politically weakened in the process. "You make sacrifices," Dole says simply. "That's part of the job."

"Many of you were plucked off the farm and college campuses, never having thought about defending your country," one interviewer observes after the memorial dedication. She marvels that so many young people would voluntarily go to war, and at how different and distant those days seem from contemporary America, where the military is desperate for recruits, and many supporters of America's war in Iraq have little interest in fighting there themselves.

"You know, I didn't feel there was any other choice," McGovern answers. "We were attacked at Pearl Harbor. The next day it was declared war on the United States. So we had no recourse except to get into service. I couldn't wait to sign up. We went to Omaha, ten of us from my little college. We didn't know whether to join the Army or the Navy. One of the guys picked up a rumor that if you went to the Army Air Corps recruiting station, they would give you a free meal ticket to a downtown cafeteria in Omaha. So on the strength of that unsubstantiated rumor and a ticket that was worth about a dollar, all ten of us joined up as Army Air Corps pilots."

McGovern shares two anecdotes about his war experience on the day of the dedication, and like Dole's touching letter home, McGovern's are anything but glorious. The first involved a regret he had lived with for many years, his only regret in thirty-five successful bombing missions against Nazi strongholds. McGovern's air group had been assigned the job of bombing an enormous and well-defended munitions plant that Germany had constructed in Czechoslovakia. His plane, the *Dakota Queen*, nearly got shot down over the target, antiaircraft rounds taking out two of its four engines. McGovern managed to complete the bombing run and turn his crippled plane home, but then the crew told him one of the bombs was jammed in the rack, rattling around above the bomb-bay doors, fully armed. If he tried to land, the plane would almost certainly blow up. So he dropped out of formation as the crew members frantically tried to loosen the huge explosive. Suddenly, it dropped free, and to McGovern's horror, he watched it explode in the middle of a farm in the Austrian countryside, a peaceful civilian landscape out of the fighting zone, shattered by this errant bomb at high noon. McGovern was devastated. On the very same day that he learned his first child had been born back home, he feared he had just wiped out an innocent farm family sitting down to lunch. He carried the guilt of this around for decades, certain he could have done something different, something better.

Many years later, he recounted the incident on Austrian television during a lecture trip. An elderly man called in after the broadcast and announced that he was the farmer McGovern had accidentally bombed, that he had seen the plane coming that day and hid in a ditch with his family. He wanted McGovern to know that everyone came through unscathed. And he added that he had despised Hitler, and that he had told his family that if having the farm bombed somehow speeded up the end of the war, it was all right. The memory still has the power to awe McGovern, and he says quietly, "I got redeemed after all those years." If anything crystallizes the difference between his G.I. Bill generation of leaders and their successors, it is this anecdote. In an era in which politicians believe their success rests on never admitting error and never saying I'm sorry, the story a genuine war hero wants America to hear on Veterans Day is an admission of regret and redemption.

His other story is no less poignant, and he says it changed his life's direction. This one took place on a troop ship entering the harbor in Naples. Italy had been devastated by the war. People were starving. As his ship approached the dock, McGovern could see children, dozens of them, lined up on the pier yelling in broken English: *Baby Ruth, Butterfinger, Hershey Bar!* McGovern and the other G.I.s started rummaging around for some treats to toss to the kids, but the captain said no, don't throw anything to them. The day before, the same thing had happened and the soldiers started throwing candy from the ship to the dock. Some of the bars fell in the water and the kids were so hungry and desperate they dived in after them. Other kids just fell in the frantic scramble.

Twenty-five children drowned in all that day, over a few candy bars. "That was my first introduction to human hunger," McGovern says quietly. "And I have been interested in that hunger issue ever since."

He has made that a signature issue throughout his career, most recently with the United Nations. In 2001, he was appointed to serve as the UN global ambassador on world hunger, tirelessly working to establish school lunch programs for 300 million of the world's most desperately hungry children, and organizing conferences on the connection between world hunger and AIDS. AIDS medicine does not work without adequate nutrition, and so hunger has helped the epidemic to spread.

Given his history, it is not surprising that McGovern also became a prominent critic of America's first war of the twenty-first century, the Iraq War, his prescience about Vietnam and his background as a combat pilot giving him a unique platform. "I had thought . . . we never again would carry out a needless, ill-conceived invasion of another country that had done us no harm and posed no threat to our security," he wrote in an impassioned essay in *The Nation.* "I was wrong in that assumption."

Yet McGovern also proudly and approvingly pointed out that one of his granddaughters, at age nineteen, joined the Air Force Academy, saying, "Well Grandpa, it's what you did."

As the day of the war memorial dedication slowly draws to a close, the last media interviews conclude, and the two old men prepare to go their separate ways, McGovern turns to Dole with a comment about Iraq. If Bob Dole were president, McGovern suggests, this war would not have happened, not without consulting fully with Congress, not without bringing in other nations, not without making sure it was both the right thing to do and the only thing to do—like the war both men fought together so long ago. Dole, ever the loyal Republican, has supported the Iraq War and the president who launched it, but on this day he does not disagree with his old friend McGovern.

"It's a tough call," he says diplomatically. "It's not like World War II."

The leaders who emerged after war service and schooling under the G.I. Bill are the easiest to spot in the governmental realm, from President Kennedy and the first President Bush to Supreme Court Justice Stevens and Chief Justice William H. Rehnquist. There was a time when it seemed every other senator and congressman was an ex-serviceman, along with the leading journalists who covered them, including David Brinkley and John Chancellor.

The impact extended far beyond Capitol Hill, as the veterans flocked to other branches of government as well: Deke Slayton flew B-25s in the war, got his aeronautical engineering degree on the G.I. Bill, then led NASA's astronaut teams for two decades. Donald Arabian returned from the war, attended college, and became a program chief for the Gemini, Apollo, and Skylab space programs. Veteran Francis Madden led the engineering team that produced the first generation of spy satellites for the CIA; in one 1960 launch, the Corona satellite revealed more details about Russian missile capabilities than all previous spy-plane efforts combined. James L. Goddard left the Army, got his medical degree, then served as director of the Center for Disease Control and then commissioner of the Food and Drug Administration, where he took on the pharmaceutical industry and forced the recall of hundreds of unsafe drugs. Navy veteran John McLucas obtained several advanced degrees after the war and went on to serve as head of the Federal Aviation Administration and secretary of the Air Force. A little-known Marine named Dale Bumpers, son of an Arkansas storekeeper, came home, finished college, and became governor of his state (and later a U.S. senator). He was joined by a dozen other G.I. Bill vets occupying governors' mansions across the country, in Georgia, Alabama, New York, Texas, and Pennsylvania, for three consecutive administrations.

With a few obvious exceptions—the few who grew up in wealth and privilege—most of these men have credited the G.I. Bill with giving them the opportunity to further their educations and to choose a career in public service.

For the leaders in the postwar world of scientific research, the same holds true.

"Just about everyone had been in the war," Leon Lederman recalls. "Nobody had any money. Before the war, we used to joke about being poor. Unemployment was so high, we didn't worry about being practical in choosing a major. We'd say, 'What are you going to be unemployed in?' I'd say, 'Physics, how about you?' After the war, well, it was different. We knew there would be jobs. Things were taking off in a big way. But we had the G.I. Bill that let us finish our studies. That $90 a month was very welcome."

Lederman's is a classic G.I. Bill success story: A poor child of immigrants, he grew up listening to his Russian-Jewish parents extol the virtues of education. They made sure he could go to a good public school and surrounded him with books. It was a blow when his older brother, Paul, had to leave school to help with the family laundry business, but Leon's marching orders remained clear: Study hard. Go to college. Be somebody. His mother's highest hopes were that he might be lucky enough to become a dentist.

Lederman, however, had other fields in mind. First drawn to chemistry by a kindly college student who worked as a lab assistant at his high school, Lederman eventually fell in love with physics because, he claims, it is simpler to be a "particle guy" than a "molecule guy."

"Have you ever seen a DNA molecule? Now that's complicated!" Habitually irreverent, he adds that the kids he knew in physics were more popular and played basketball better, "so the choice was easy." He contends his greatest ambition was to be a stand-up comic, but his jokes were never good enough except for physicists, among whom, Lederman asserts, he is one of the few capable of even telling a joke without blowing the punchline.

While still uncovering the secrets of German radars in Europe near the end of the war, Lederman heard that Columbia University had just launched a top-notch physics program. He had managed to get his bachelor's degree through a crash Army program just before heading off to basic training, so he decided Columbia would be the perfect place for grad school. When the war ended and Lederman shipped out for home, he got in a cab as soon as the ship docked and he went directly to Columbia, in uniform, his duffel bag over his shoulder, so he could file his application in person. A few weeks later he was accepted.

At that time, Columbia was one of two centers for the new field of particle physics, the other being on the West Coast, at Berkeley, in the program created by Manhattan Project mastermind J. Robert Oppenheimer. The Columbia program was run by I.I. Rabi, a Nobel Prize winner and physics legend, a friend to General Eisenhower, who would soon become president of the university, and the genius behind the construction of what was then the most powerful atom-smasher in the world.

It was here that Rabi's team of graduate students had begun to unlock the secrets of particle physics, while down the hall Charles Townes and his colleagues were inventing the laser, for which they would later share a Nobel Prize. Both Townes and Rabi offered the bright and personable Lederman spots in their programs. "It was like pressing your nose against the window of a candy shop," Lederman recalls. "There were so many choices."

He ultimately chose Rabi and particle physics because, he jokes, it was such a new field he would know nearly as much as his professors at the start. It is only half a joke: The opportunities for discovery seemed everywhere, as understanding of elementary particles was still rudimentary at the start of Lederman's career, and the prospects of finding answers to the question, What's inside? were legion.

His first major discovery started with Chinese food. He had completed his graduate studies and was on the faculty, teaching and doing research. The Columbia physicists went out for melon soup and other Asian treats on a regular basis, sharing Chinese dishes and talking physics for hours. The discussion one Friday night in 1957 turned to symmetry, the notion that every particle has a mirror image, a parallel world of sorts (the electrons of our world versus the positrons of its mirror world—matter and its reflection, antimatter). Because it was aesthetically pleasing and seemed to make sense—Why would the universe prefer one type of particle over another?—most scientists assumed symmetry existed. And the question that came up that night was so obvious that no one could believe it hadn't been asked before: Is symmetry real? Is the assumption true? Lederman realized that the recently completed Columbia accelerator and some additional new equipment gave them everything they needed to test the validity of nuclear particle symmetry.

They raced back to the lab and chased away a graduate student in the middle of an experiment for his thesis and started setting up the experiment. On Monday evening, they fired up the accelerator and started gathering the data, and by three in the morning Tuesday—Lederman insists these things always happen at three A.M.—Lederman and his colleagues knew something no one else in the world knew. The law of symmetry was wrong. This discovery was a shock, it upended the scientific world, and yet it explained so many things that had eluded physicists up to that point, such as why there is a universe at all. If particles enjoyed perfect parity, they would have canceled one another out at the moment of the Big Bang, leaving nothing. Instead, one set of particles—what we call matter—had a slight advantage over antimatter. The moment of creation was, in essence, lopsided.

"That one gave us some sweaty palms," Lederman recalls. "It was quite a thrill."

He shared the Nobel Prize for an experiment several years later in which he and two colleagues were the first to detect two kinds of neutrinos—mysterious ghost particles with no charge, little or no mass, and the ability to pass through almost all objects. Their existence had been assumed for years because there was no other way to explain nuclear reactions, not even the reactions that make the sun shine, because the energy produced was never equal to the energy put into the reaction, a violation of fundamental laws of physics. Either the most basic rules were wrong, in which case the universe made no sense, or energy was being robbed, siphoned off in the form of some sort of particle no one could see.

Using a powerful beam of charged particles and an innovative type of accelerator, Lederman and his partners finally detected and measured the elusive neutrino. Their findings explained why the sun can shine and why the universe seemed to be missing so much material that, mathematically, should have been floating around in space. It was there after all, in the form of neutrinos. The discovery unleashed whole new areas of physics, with new lines of research still going on forty years later.

Lederman became director of the accelerator lab the following year, then finally left his beloved Columbia in 1979, when he became director of the Fermi National Accelerator Laboratory, where he supervised construction of the world's first superconducting particle accelerator, the most powerful such device for the next three decades. The lab has been at the center of discoveries in particle physics ever since, as well as being a key participant in the invention of the World Wide Web. One of the first handful of Web pages in the world was Fermilab's, when the Web consisted of nothing more than links among the world's five preeminent particle physics laboratories. Fermilab itself is an international hub, with scientists from all over the world living on its campus, their children playing together while chattering in a dozen different languages. Years ago, in the midst of the cold war, one of the first foreign teams invited to experiment at Fermilab was from the Soviet Union, putting Lederman in the position of scientist and diplomat. The Russians lived there in Batavia, on the sprawling campus where a herd of buffalo roams—signifying Fermilab's place on the frontiers of science—and their children attended the local schools. They went home different people, Lederman says, leaving behind lasting relationships in an era where these things did not happen so easily.

After retiring as Fermilab's director for ten years (but still maintaining his home on the campus), he served as president of the American Association for the Advancement of Science, then seemed ready to settle into the life of a professor emeritus and conference speaker. No more sleeping on the cold, hard floors of accelerator labs, no more three A.M. discoveries, no more tiptoeing home to avoid waking the kids (Lederman has three).

Except that he was not ready to retire. There was too much to do.

In this, he echoes the sentiments of former Senators Dole and McGovern and so many others of their generation, men who feel they have too much to do to ever quite call it quits. Here again, Lederman brings up the notion of duty, of giving something back to the next generation—and of instilling in children that sense of wonder that drove him into science, because he says they are related. Neither involves getting rich, which he bemoans as the main motivation for career choices among today's college kids—and which is why he believes science in America is on the decline. The children of the Depression didn't worry about doing science to get rich; they assumed that wouldn't happen no matter what they did, and so they chose to follow their passions and their sense of duty. And then the G.I. Bill was there to give them educations and homes and a secure middle-class life. Americans held science in great esteem in the decades after the war, and government supported it generously, though this proved to be more a function of the Cold War competition with the Soviets than a quest for knowledge.

In the twenty-first century, in Lederman's view, America has become an antiscience nation. The number of American students seeking graduate degrees in science and engineering has diminished year after year, with enrollments—and America's high-tech dominance—long propped up by foreign students, who began in 2001 to look elsewhere for educational opportunities. Other nations have strengthened their research universities, and other governments with money to burn—China among them—have begun to spend lavishly on science and research facilities, even as the U.S. cuts funding for science and makes it increasingly difficult for foreign students to attend American schools. Fewer than a third of U.S. undergraduate students pursue science or engineering degrees, compared to nearly twice that number in China and Japan. Lederman believes America risks losing its global edge in innovation and technology unless these trends are reversed.

"People have got to understand we are facing a crisis," Lederman says. "We cannot compete, we cannot maintain our quality of life if we lose our scientific prowess. We need leadership on this, but there is no national strategy. The problem is, our brilliant Founding Fathers left education to local communities. They never imagined education could be more important than military prowess—but it is."

Lederman has testified twice in Congress so far, without much success, advocating for the creation of a corps of highly trained teachers in math and science. He believes children are natural scientists. They always ask why: why the sky is blue, why the sun can make you hot even though it's far away. They ask, *What's inside?* But, as Lederman sees it, this curiosity is quashed in elementary school, where far too many teachers lack the skills or the time to encourage questioning and discovery. Once that happens, far too many American children lose interest in math and science. So far Lederman has established a teacher training program and lobbied successfully for the creation of a state school for gifted math and science students in Illinois, and at eighty-three, he has hopes of exporting those ideas nationwide.

"It's hard. There's a lot of antiscience out there these days, whether it's against evolution or global warming. To turn that around takes leadership."

And since no one else seemed to be doing it, Lederman, with his Nobel Prize and his jokes and his passion for what's inside, decided to take up the cause, one more battle to fight and perhaps in so doing, making a difference.

A dozen other schools like the Illinois Mathematics and Science Academy have opened up around the country, and Lederman sees this as a miniature but encouraging attempt to replicate the G.I. Bill investment—nurturing education in science with a bit of extra spending and attention, in order to reap bigger dividends later on.

"We are so shortsighted as a country not to see that this ought to be a national priority, something huge. Because one of these kids will some day cure a terrible disease or do something else incredible, and then they will be able to tell their grandchildren that they never would have had the opportunity without this wonderful government program, this special school. My generation had the G.I. Bill, and look what it brought us. It's time to do that for the next generation."

Epilogue

Kilroy's Not Here: The Future and the G.I. Bill

With both the war and the romance that helped carry him through it ended, Allan Howerton threw himself into college life at the University of Denver. The G.I. Bill paid his way, as it did for all the other vets crammed into the dorms and frat houses and the constantly expanding rows of Quonset huts. Still, he pulled a year's worth of night shifts as an ambulance driver, that Depression boy's work ethic permitting no less.

For Howerton, there was an element of the surreal to this transition, which is probably why the G.I. Bill's official title included the phrase "servicemen's readjustment." That was the euphemism for how he and millions of other veterans had to get reacquainted with civilian clothes and not using four-letter words as casual greetings and not ducking and covering every time something dropped or crashed or backfired. Here he was in Denver, signing up for a course in comparative economics, buying textbooks, drinking beer with friends, and arguing about Truman versus Dewey. A year earlier, Howerton had been lining the frozen sides of his foxhole in Belgium with old sheets of salvaged wallpaper, which is how he kept himself from noticing how much it looked and felt like he was lying in an open grave as the shells arced overhead.

Now here he was on a leafy, sun-drenched campus, relishing his studies, his work with the international relations department, and his activism with the new American Veterans Committee, with its mission to build a better, safer, more just nation, and its unique, doomed slogan, "Citizens First, Veterans Second." If he didn't talk much about his war experiences, if he found he couldn't commit to a relationship, if the trauma of seeing most of those around him wounded or killed caught up with him sometimes—well, he wasn't all that different from half the guys on campus. After the darkness of the past four years, the world seemed new again, full of promise, and despite the oddness of the transition from cramming yourself into a foxhole to cramming for an international law exam, Howerton felt a surge of optimism about the future with every stroll across the Denver campus.

Ben Cherrington, head of the international relations department at the university, was busily launching UNESCO and bringing nationally recognized speakers to the campus to describe a future like nothing the world had ever seen. The new United Nations, still an untainted vision, seemed to Howerton and his fellow veterans to hold enormous promise for world peace and prosperity. The very name inspired confidence and intimated victory over totalitarianism—during the war, the term "United Nations" had been used interchangeably with "Allies." Wasn't this what we had fought and died for—the triumph of democracy? The Marshall Plan, meanwhile, had revealed America to be generous in victory, another source of pride for Howerton, and he found himself becoming a committed internationalist. He revered Cherrington as a gracious, optimistic gentleman, an old-fashioned liberal who believed the United States was destined to lead the world through international cooperation—a brand of idealism that combined strength with compassion, steely determination with democratic virtue. To Howerton, this was irresistible. After all he had lived through and all he had seen, after America and the Allies had beaten the forces of hatred, fascism, and barbarism, Howerton was amazed to find that he retained the capacity for idealism.

World War II had just claimed the lives of three out of every hundred people on earth. This generation was going to build a better world. Howerton felt certain of it.

The G.I. Bill's legacy, as unforeseen at its inception as it is widely venerated sixty years later, is far more than it was meant to be, yet far less than it could have been.

Born out of a mixture of fear, patriotism, and pork-barrel politics, it nonetheless provided the architecture of an accidental America, one that democratized higher education, made home ownership a majority experience, and built a level of prosperity, comfort, and technical prowess unrivaled in world history. The G.I. Bill cost taxpayers a fortune, as Congress had anticipated, yet it made an even greater fortune for the nation's citizens and its treasury—developments no one had even remotely anticipated. And so the G.I. Bill justly joins the Bill of Rights, the Civil Rights Act, and the Morrill Land Grant College Acts, as one of a handful of landmark and transformative legislative achievements, though perhaps the only one whose most far-reaching impacts were largely unintended. So pervasive were the bill's benefits that they have come to be taken for granted, as if they had evolved on their own, a birthright, an inevitable part of the epic American enterprise. But these benefits were not inevitable. Widespread home ownership and college education and middle-class America were not inevitable. Before the war, many of America's leaders in government and industry did not even consider such things desirable. They took root because of the single most sweeping grant of government largesse to a select group ever undertaken in the history of mankind.

The result, a triumph of Big Government, has long been hailed by conservatives and liberals alike as an epochal achievement, worthy of emulation. And so it should be.

And yet, seldom acknowledged though undeniably true, the G.I. Bill fell short. Not only did it unnecessarily shortchange women and minorities, it shortchanged America's future by failing to ensure that its greatest gifts would be passed on fully to later generations. The bucks, quite literally, stopped with the Greatest

Generation. Many of the doors the bill opened remain open, of course, and the financial security many of the veterans achieved could be passed on within families. Still, today's young people, veterans and nonveterans alike, simply do not enjoy anything close to the advantages that the World War II G.I.s received—not in health care, not in home ownership, not in education, not in jobs, not in income. This is the untold tragedy of the G.I. Bill: the opportunities lost amid the many opportunities obtained.

There is a complex of reasons for this, the most obvious being the immense changes in the military since World War II.

There is, of course, still a G.I. Bill (as opposed to *the* G.I. Bill). Veterans of every conflict that followed World War II, beginning with Korea, as well as the veterans of peacetime, have enjoyed theoretically similar benefits. However, each generation of warriors has seen those benefits grow more miserly. The G.I. Bill as it exists today is no longer a significant force for change or advancement in society at large, and even within the military it has become a frequent source of disappointment.

This shortcoming is most obvious when it comes to education benefits. World War II veterans received a free education at any college, trade school, or vocational institute that accepted them, whether it was the Culinary Institute of America or Harvard University or the Sorbonne. Tuition, books, and room and board were fully covered, along with monthly stipends for living expenses, without need of additional student loans, grants, or scholarships. None of this cost veterans of World War II a cent; they earned it by virtue of their military service during the war, regardless of whether they saw combat (as did about 6 million veterans) or not (about 10 million). Because the draft and the war reached so deeply, most of a generation of men—those born in the 1920s—ended up eligible.

The modern G.I. Bill offers no stipend for living expenses and has fallen far behind the actual cost of a college education; accounting for inflation and the rising costs of tuition, the benefit's buying power is far less than what World War II veterans enjoyed. The maximum benefit requires a veteran to be "fully vested"—which means he or she had to contribute $1800 in payroll deductions during service. In return, they receive an education allowance spread over four years that could not cover a single year at an Ivy League or other top-tier private school. The benefits cover only about 60 percent of the average cost of tuition and fees at public universities, which puts a four-year degree out of reach for many veterans, particularly those with families to support. The average state university bill for tuition, room, and board was about $1700 a month in the U.S. in 2005. The most the G.I. Bill would offer that same year was a bit over a thousand a month. The Department of Veterans Affairs has reported that as a result of the growing gulf between what the modern G.I. Bill provides and what college actually costs, only 8 percent of veterans have taken full advantage of their higher-education benefits since 1985.

Similarly, the subsidized mortgage benefits that made it so easy for World War II veterans to become homeowners have not kept pace with housing prices. Indeed, World War II veterans, by any measure, benefit by benefit, were more generously compensated than any generation of veterans before or since. Lawmakers have turned back most proposals to increase the benefits in later decades. For veterans of the Iraq War launched by President George W. Bush in 2003, the situation has grown worse, as about half the combat duties—and a majority of the casualties—were initially absorbed by National Guardsmen called up to active duty. Members of the National Guard receive only a third of the G.I. Bill benefits that regular troops receive, and no benefits at all once they leave the service. So in real terms, the benefits offered America's men and women in uniform, even in time of war, are a pale shadow of what World War II veterans received.

Policy makers have not been nearly as generous with subsequent generations of veterans for a variety of reasons, not the least of which is that the veterans' lobby and veterans' vote, once a force with the power to make or break congressmen and presidents, has lost much of its unity and clout. Harry Colmery, the American Legion lobbyist, in reflecting on events after World War I, famously warned Congress in 1944, "Except for England, this is the only country where the men who wore uniforms did not overthrow the government on either side of the conflict." This was considered a sound reason to treat the 16 million veterans of World War II very well. No such worries of unrest and revolt have jolted Congress into action since then. The Korean War G.I. Bill benefits, just a handful of years after the end of World War II, profited from that proximity and came close to the original, but it has been downhill since then.

And so the age-old pattern of mistreatment of veterans, so thoroughly renounced during World War II, resurfaced with a vengeance for the 3 million men who saw combat in Vietnam. Saddled not only with doing their duty in an unpopular, losing, and ultimately pointless war, the Vietnam veterans returned to a tightfisted shadow of the old G.I. Bill, receiving scant help for their readjustment difficulties, which ranged from post-traumatic stress to homelessness to exposure to cancer-causing chemicals. This poor treatment was, to be fair, a bipartisan effort, with blame to share all around, though it accelerated markedly when President Ronald Reagan took office and slashed veterans' benefits as part of his systemwide cutting of social welfare programs. Veterans have found themselves increasingly marginalized since then, a trend that, paradoxically, accelerated after the 9-11 terrorist attacks and the launch of the war in Iraq, when "support the troops" became the mantra of most every politician. Public criticism of the paucity of veterans' benefits was once considered an expression of support for the troops—there were extensive media exposés of veteran mistreatment during the height of World War II, and similar coverage of the plight of Vietnam vets in the seventies and eighties. But in the twenty-first century, post-9-11 world, such criticism has often been branded unpatriotic, a supposed vehicle for undermining national unity and military morale (not to mention recruiting efforts). Using that same logic, even that most basic of veterans' benefits—the military funeral—has been hidden from public view in the twenty-first century. The Pentagon, beginning with casualties in the wars in Afghanistan and Iraq, has banned the once traditional, cathartic ritual of media coverage of flag-draped caskets returning home, while the president, again reversing many years of tradition, has avoided the funerals of fallen servicemen and women. It is as if the veterans—and the subject of what benefits they do and don't receive—have become invisible, the grand vision of the G.I. Bill shrinking into insignificance.

Beyond the diminished specific benefits for veterans, there is a larger, fundamental shift: The current G.I. Bill has lost its capacity to transform the nation as a whole; it simply lacks the firepower of the original bill. This is a function not of the legislation itself, but of the changing military and the unique circumstances of World War II, and it would be true even if G.I. Bill benefits were every bit as generous in their reach in the twenty-first century as they were in 1945. Most of an entire generation went to war in the 1940s, in a military that, demographically, looked like America thanks to the draft and the need for immense numbers of men under arms. Gifting 16 million soldiers, Marines, and sailors with such far-ranging benefits meant directly improving the lot in life of one out of eight Americans; factor in the indirect benefits to spouses, children, and other dependents, and it becomes something closer to one in five. Then add, at the very least, an equal number of nonveterans who benefited from a G.I. Bill's domino effect—the lowered barriers to college, the rapid growth of vocational and on-the-job training programs, the boom in affordable suburban housing, the booming economy. In those sorts of numbers lie the power to transform society.

By contrast, the G.I. Bill benefits of the twenty-first century reach, at most, 1 percent of the population at any given time, a natural function of a smaller, all-volunteer military in which the political and wealthy elite have, since Vietnam, generally avoided service. The impact is too small to cause the slightest ripple in America's vast economy.

Another important reason the G.I. Bill's legacy is less than it might have been lies in the simultaneous deaths of Franklin Delano Roosevelt and his New Deal. The G.I. Bill was seen by the New Dealers as a start, not as an end in itself. Had FDR lived to see the end of the war and to pursue his proposal for a second economic bill of rights, he would have insisted that the health, education, and employment benefits veterans received be extended at least partly to war workers, and then to all Americans. His forgotten proposals for universal health care are perhaps the clearest example of this wasted potential, as they would have been an extension of the full medical coverage enjoyed by World War II vets and their dependents. In the twenty-first century, re-creating the health care system is a daunting prospect, but in 1945 it was tantalizingly within reach. Without Roosevelt to advocate government's role in the health care equation, those who advocated free-market approaches prevailed. And while the resulting mix of private insurance and public coverage for the poor and elderly has worked for many years, it has never been able to provide full coverage for Americans—45 million remained uninsured in the year 2006. The U.S. system has ended up costing far more than the single-payer systems Europe and Canada chose, with the U.S. saddled with poorer outcomes, lower overall patient satisfaction, higher infant mortality rates, and shorter life expectancies (a category in which the U.S. is forty-eighth in the world, not only behind such advanced nations as Germany, the United Kingdom, Canada, Italy, France, and Switzerland, but also Aruba, Macau, Guam, and Jordan). Meanwhile, the largest government-run medical care system in the United States—the Veterans Health Administration—underwent major reforms in 1995, and since then has become a model of efficiency, economy, and quality that consistently outperforms the private sector. Demand for VA medical services, once shunned by veterans, has since doubled, hinting at what a national health care program could have looked like.

Like his health-care proposal, FDR's proposals for a guaranteed living wage, full employment, and education grants—coupled with a large-scale program of national service—had the potential for extending G.I. Bill–like benefits to most citizens while engaging them in service to their country. Late in the war, public opinion polls showed a majority of Americans supported the idea of a program of national service, even after it seemed clear the Allies were headed to victory. Of course, even if FDR had lived to champion them, these proposals could well have gone down in defeat—the New Deal coalition was splintering, and the Cold War conservatives were on the march. But in that moment of public optimism, in a country flush with victory, just beginning to boom economically, with a president it trusted and a government that seemed to work, the American people just might have decided to accept a G.I. Bill for everyone.

Without FDR, it would fall to the Greatest Generation to make that call. And here lies the final reason why the G.I. Bill's legacy has, so far, not been passed on: The World War II veterans' attitudes, policies, and politics, once they assumed power, differed enormously from their predecessors, and were marked by a distrust of government and an abhorrence of Big Government programs, notwithstanding that its members benefited so handsomely from the granddaddy of all government programs.

To their credit, the veterans of World War II never labeled themselves the Greatest Generation—that fell to younger admirers, with the term achieving prominence through the books of news anchor and author Tom Brokaw. Most World War II vets readily agree that America has seen a number of great generations: the nation's first generation, with such towering figures as Washington, Jefferson, Hamilton, Franklin, and Adams, as well as the generation of Lincoln, which saw the end of slavery, the preservation of the Union, and the creation of the land grant colleges. The generation that led the country through World War II and its aftermath—Roosevelt, Truman, Marshall, Eisenhower—and which invented the G.I. Bill and the Marshall Plan, is also among the greatest the country has seen. And while these men are sometimes lumped in with the G.I. Bill generation, they actually preceded it.

The members of the Greatest Generation were little more than kids at the time of the war—they sacrificed, they did their duty, they did what the men running the country at the time told them to do, and it was their blood and courage and lives that were on the line. It is their graves that fill the nation's military cemeteries—and that continue filling them, at the rate of 1,200 a month by the year 2005, as old age gradually claims them. Their sacrifice and bravery is rightly honored. But they were not the leaders of the nation at the time of the war.

And this points to a critical difference that, perhaps, suggests an explanation for the G.I. Bill's and the war veterans' disparate legacies: The men and women of the Roosevelt generation were adults during the Depression. They knew, most of them at least, some measure of poverty and desperation and joblessness. They had lived through the Gilded Age and its robber barons, then they saw it all come apart, and many harbored great distrust of corporate America as a result, while seeing government, particularly the federal government, as an ally. The idea of government as a force for good in the world was not anathema to this generation. The next generation, however, experienced the Depression as children. They grew up despising both poverty and the notion of being "on the dole"—accepting a welfare hand-out was for them a source of deep shame. They weren't old enough to have lost their jobs to the Depression as their fathers did; the oldest of them went to work at the end of the hard times, as things got better, and many didn't enter the full-time adult workforce until after the war, with jobs plentiful and the G.I. Bill giving veterans a leg up. Their first impressions of government were informed not by the New Deal and a chance to work; they were more influenced by the draft board

and then the Army or Navy or Marine Corps and by following orders and living in fear. And when they returned home, they soon took up countering the threat of Communism—the ultimate triumph of a government over the individual—as their main political cause, their attitudes about Big Government further poisoned by the accusations leveled by Joseph McCarthy.

When the Greatest Generation began to assume the mantle of leadership, their legacy included a couple of inspiring presidents—Kennedy and Reagan—and one who resigned in disgrace. Their noblest legacies include the Civil Rights Act, the end of the Cold War, the War on Poverty, and passage of the Clean Water and Clean Air Acts. But it also includes a long tolerance of segregation, forty costly years of Cold War and threatened nuclear Armageddon, the shame of McCarthyism, loyalty oaths, and blacklists of innocent men and women, and the tragic, pointless war in Vietnam—a debacle ended not by the Greatest Generation, but by its children's outraged protests.

It was during the G.I. Bill generation's reign, and particularly under the leadership of its most beloved president, Ronald Reagan, that the legacy and accomplishments of the G.I. Bill itself began to lose ground. It was Reagan, beginning in California and then taking his message nationwide, who convinced a majority of American voters—most of them of his generation—that the greatest force for evil in the country was government. "The nine most terrifying words in the English language," Reagan told his countrymen, "are, 'I'm from the government and I'm here to help.'"

Selling this message to the G.I. Bill generation should have been tough, but World War II vets, who understood better than most the value and cost of making sacrifices for their country,

somehow never saw themselves as also being the most privileged generation in history, the flip side of their sacrifices. Somehow they could not see that buying a home with no money down and mortgages lower than rent, or that going to Yale or Berkeley or Cal State–Long Beach for free—except it wasn't free, it was paid for by taxpayers—was just another form of the government assistance they had come to despise and oppose. It was a wonderful form of assistance, one that offered them skills and paths to better lives, rather than simply a wad of cash from the welfare state, but it was assistance—socialism—nonetheless. Did they deserve those benefits for their war service? Absolutely. Did Vietnam veterans deserve the same, too? Or Desert Storm veterans? Or women who risked death working at the Redstone Arsenal or test-flying Liberator bombers during World War II? How about the first-grade teacher who turns down a high-paying corporate career path because she loves to teach and has a gift for it? Do they deserve the same consideration for their service and sacrifice to country? Whether the answer is yes or no—and it's certainly open to debate—the fact is that only the World War II veteran has ever received such sweeping benefits.

But that had happened long decades before, a distant memory of a government program that worked. At the time, Reagan's message had much more immediate power and appeal: The government, with its misguided, costly programs, the Great Society that Lyndon Johnson had poured billions into with precious little to show for it, was blamed for the mess known as the 1970s. Reagan won election in a landslide, and he fulfilled his promise. Subsidized housing, education funding, college grants and loans, school lunch programs, medical care for the poor, even veterans benefits

for younger military men—all were drastically cut under Reagan's presidency and have faced periodic cutbacks ever since. He cut taxes, too, as promised, beginning a decades-long transfer of the nation's wealth to its wealthiest citizens; since Reagan, the incomes of workers at the bottom of the pay scale have stagnated, while the richest Americans have experienced staggering gains. The concentration of wealth in the twenty-first century has accelerated to Gilded Age standards: In 1980, when Reagan took office, the average chief executive officer of a major company earned forty times the salary of the average manufacturing employee; twenty years later, that ratio had become 475 to one. (By contrast, at the beginning of the twenty-first century, that same ratio in Britain was twenty-four to one; in France, fifteen to one; and in Sweden, thirteen to one.)

With that, the great leveling of incomes the G.I. Bill had brought about—so that truckers, factory assemblers, telephone linemen, and other blue-collar workers could enter the middle class—began to reverse, the Great Compression unraveling. Sixty years after the original G.I. Bill, the middle class began to contract. The rapid expansion in home ownership stalled. College became so expensive it lay out of reach for growing numbers of eligible students. The minimum wage in the U.S. at the start of the twenty-first century remained the lowest in the developed world, while the number of citizens living beneath the poverty line in the U.S. ranked among the highest. The nation that once raised taxes without a fuss to finance a monumental war and to pay for the G.I. Bill in the 1940s has reduced taxation so much that by the year 2005, even during a time of war, immense natural disasters, and in the face of massive deficits, tax rates reached their lowest level in the history of postwar America, and the lowest in the Western world.

And for the first time, polls of Americans in the early twenty-first century show that they expect the standard of living their children will experience when grown up will likely be lower than their parents'. An article of faith of the American dream, that the next generation will always do better, has been lost.

ALLAN HOWERTON'S time at the University of Denver was as much about healing as it was about learning, as much about getting over being a G.I. as it was about using the G.I. Bill. Of the two hundred men who served in Company K, 335th Infantry, 84th Division, he was one of eighteen who lived through the Battle of the Bulge and six other major engagements without being wounded or killed. Forty-two of his comrades died. When he came home and found his way to Denver, he considered himself blessed, hale and hearty. In truth he would later realize, he was "torn up inside." It took time for that to change.

He found it best to fill up his time—with studies, with extracurriculars, with several doomed romances, anything to avoid idleness and introspection and memory. One of his passions soon became the American Veterans Committee, the most popular and activist veterans organization on college campuses at the time. Its progressive ideals attracted all sorts: ordinary G.I.s, black veterans—it was the only integrated veterans organization at the time—and celebrities, including the famous *Stars and Stripes* editorial cartoonist Bill Mauldin, the future star of *Sunset Boulevard* William

Holden, and a then-liberal film actor with political aspirations named Ronald Reagan.

At the time, the committee had become a popular alternative to the American Legion and Veterans of Foreign Wars, particularly for veterans who viewed themselves as Left-center. The unusual slogan, "Citizens First, Veterans Second," set it apart from the other service organizations whose political apparatus existed in large part to garner benefits exclusively for veterans. The American Veterans Committee, mirroring FDR's position before the war ended, argued that the best course for society were measures that benefited all citizens, those that promoted the four freedoms Roosevelt had spoken of so eloquently in his 1941 State of the Union speech, his last in peacetime: freedom of speech, freedom from want, freedom of worship, and freedom from fear and tyranny. The organization flourished briefly, with Howerton serving as its Denver chapter president for a year, at a time when it commanded meetings with the governor of Colorado. Howerton even earned a spot as a delegate to the state's Democratic Convention in 1948 (where he tried, unsuccessfully, to pledge the Colorado delegation to maverick Supreme Court Justice William O. Douglas for president). The organization fell apart after the American Communist Party attempted to take it over—a bid that failed, but which left a fatal taint in that era of Red-baiting and fervent anti-Communism.

Howerton pulled back from politics after that, earned his bachelors degree in international relations, worked for a time for United Airlines, then got his masters degree in 1952. His goal was to join the diplomatic corps, hopefully to be posted abroad. After VE Day, he had been assigned to the occupation army in Germany, giving him a chance to appreciate Europe outside his wallpapered foxhole. It had left him wanting more. He imagined himself returning to an embassy job and rising through the State Department ranks, finding a way to make a difference, still the committed internationalist.

He did well on the civil service tests and was accepted as a management intern for six months of training in Washington. Then he waited on the list of applicants for foreign service. And waited. The State Department, at that time under constant investigation for disloyalty by McCarthy's Senate committee, was paralyzed. Hiring ground to a standstill. Finally, when a job opened in the U.S. Office of Personnel Management—the hiring body for the federal government and the Civil Service Commission—Howerton took it, just temporarily.

He ended up working his entire career there, overseeing hiring for executive positions and rising to head various statewide branches of the office, as well as several different posts in Washington. When things finally loosened up at the State Department, he decided against moving, realizing he had a promising career where he was. It wasn't what he had originally intended, but he was good at it.

He married in 1958, finally ready to share his life. He

and Joan have three children and now, in retirement, six grandchildren. All his kids went to college, one an artist, another specializing in merchandizing, the third a mathematician—the ripple effect of the G.I. Bill blessing the next generation. Now living in Alexandria, Virginia, he has been general manager of a cooperative television station, he's managed local political campaigns, volunteered in his community, and traveled (finally) throughout Europe. He's also written two books: a nonfiction account of his own and his Army unit's experiences in the war, and a fictional account of the postwar era set on a college campus packed with veterans on the G.I. Bill.

The writing projects have led him to reflect on that era and to compare it to the United States of the twenty-first century. It is not a comparison he particularly enjoys, but he brings to it the perspective of a combat veteran, a G.I. Bill student, a World War II amateur historian, and a man with deep convictions about the country he loves. He gives his own generation little slack.

> *I guess I feel that the World War II generation is responsible for some of the dilemmas we now confront. It was a "greatest generation" as to the way it met the challenges presented by the war. But we did not do well afterwards as to the "four freedoms" and other goals for which the war was fought. We overdid the Cold War, and it left us with this vast national*

> *security state and the problems which are closing in on us globally. Our generation failed, I think, to produce statesmen up to the job of managing the post–World War II challenges.*
>
> *FDR's call for national service reminds of how far this country has gone in the opposite direction . . . When I attended DU the world and the country seemed full of promise, even amid the rough patches such as the McCarthy era and the upcoming Cold War. Today, I see the opposite—a living standard that cannot be sustained and a political class in both parties reluctant to take on the challenges that confront us. That is not a happy scenario. I hope I am wrong.*

If there were ever a time for something like the original G.I. Bill to come along again, it would seem that America is ready—and certainly in need. Is such a thing even possible?

Politicians talk about it often enough, tying one project after another to the idea of a "new G.I. Bill" for education, for housing, for school vouchers, or for any number of other pet causes. The notion of recreating the G.I. Bill (or appropriating its rosy legacy) in some form or another is appealing, at least as political rhetoric. Yet no one has ever made a serious attempt to replicate it for society at large, even though it is the only model for a social-welfare program that has ever really worked, and worked well.

Some economists and lawmakers have argued that replicating the G.I. Bill is simply impossible, as its setup was (fortunately) unique in history. First, there was massive global economic depression. That was followed by a world war, 60 million deaths, and more than 10 trillion dollars in costs (2006 dollars)—not counting the cost of reconstruction. America had to convert its economy to serve the war, raise a military of 16 million men, and send 19 million women to work. And then it survived the war unscathed, more prosperous than ever—while every other major nation involved had been devastated. The pump, so to speak, was primed for the G.I. Bill's success—it was the right legislation at the right time. But those planets aren't going to align again, and only a madman would wish them to do so.

This argument has merit. And yet, the allure of the "greatest legislation" is irresistible. Could there be a new G.I. Bill with the same sort of reach and transformative power as the original, without a depression, without a world war, without an army of 16 million, without any G.I.s at all?

President Bill Clinton has suggested as much. He considered the G.I. Bill the most successful social program the country has ever undertaken, one he felt could be replicated. In his view, its success was not nearly as dependent on the war as many have thought. Clinton pinned its success instead on what he saw as its fundamental reliance "on the American values of work and responsibility."

"It offered not a handout, but a hand-up," Clinton argued in a speech commemorating the fiftieth anniversary of the bill. "The veterans of World War I got a handout, and they deserved it. But it was sixty dollars and a train ticket home. The veterans of World War II got a ticket to the American dream . . . We cannot even calculate how much our nation has been enriched."

Clinton sought to recapture that greatness with a program he dubbed AmeriCorps, a national service program he developed to recruit a hundred thousand students to tackle community service jobs in exchange for modest college tuition, health care, and child-care benefits. It was open to all—as opposed to a program specifically targeting the poor, or urban youth, or any other specific group. As an experiment to test the waters of national service, it was a modest success, but it fell far short of its model, the World War II G.I. Bill, both in the benefits it offered and the numbers it recruited. One critic derided it as a "make-work program for privileged kids." But it is the closest the country has come so far to fulfilling FDR's twin notions of national service and a second bill of rights focused on economic justice and opportunity.

AmeriCorps may be a small gesture compared to the G.I. Bill it attempts to emulate, but Clinton was right about one key aspect. Duplicating the G.I. Bill first requires understanding its enduring success and the reason why it has been more positively viewed than traditional welfare programs: It was inclusive, not exclusive. That is the essential difference. Anyone, rich or poor, urban or rural, blue collar or white collar, could benefit. There was no means test, which Americans despise, and it gave the appearance of being completely self-directed, which Americans love—the individual G.I., not the government, picked the college, the neighborhood, the job, the vocational school, the paint color of the garage. Clinton engaged in a bit of spin in his explanation, for the G.I. Bill was both a handout and a hand-up. It worked because the cash it distributed was almost incidental. Its true power came in directing the largesse into the beneficial realms of education, home ownership, and the creation of responsible, productive citizens with firm stakes in their communities and country. Truly a hand-up.

With that understanding as the guiding light, there is no practical reason why the original G.I. Bill could not be duplicated on a similar scale in the twenty-first century, with national service replacing (or in addition to) military service as the prerequisite for eligibility. There are enormous political and budgetary reasons why it would not or could not be done, but the truth is, there are no practical barriers. It is a matter of political and national will: If a president and Congress took a look at FDR's sixty-year-old economic bill of rights and national service plan, and said, *Hey, that sounds pretty good after all, let's do it,* it certainly would not cost any more to get started than the $400 billion (as of early 2006) that the war in Iraq has cost, and probably a good deal less, with far more tangible benefits. And the values at its core—encouraging peacetime service to the nation while giving something back to Americans willing to serve society—are values the nation needs and should welcome. What better way to do that than modeling it on the one government program everyone loves, the G.I. Bill? From Bob Dole and George McGovern, to Arthur Penn and Monte Posey, veterans whose lives were changed by the bill all believe that something like it—something as big and as generous and as transforming—is needed today.

What would it look like? Starting out small, but building up to a national service corps numbering in the millions, it would train young people, then assign them to tours of duty—as teaching assistants, legal aides, peer counselors, literacy instructors, math tutors, patient advocates, lifeguards, nursing-home aides. It could resurrect the old Works Progress Administration and Civilian Conservation Corps ideals and use the national service manpower to build homes for the needy, reinvigorate national parks, clean up blighted neighborhoods, rebuild areas devastated by natural disasters, eradicate graffiti. For some, this might involve living frugally for a time, perhaps with the same dearth of creature comforts military men and women currently accept as a matter of course. (All those military bases decommissioned since the 1980s could come in quite handy for this purpose.) The good works that could be attempted with this sort of manpower are endless, as is the need.

What would the incentives be for volunteering for national service? They would mirror the original G.I. Bill's: In return for agreeing to postpone college for one to two years (or perhaps going part time while in national service), young people would receive generous college tuition aid, access to expanded, VA-style health care, and home-loan subsidies waiting for them once they finished school. Colleges would have to do their part. They would have to offer cut-rate tuition for national service corps members, perhaps in exchange for other incentives, such as preference for research grants and federal contracts. Members of the military could be incorporated into this broader national service program, perhaps on an equal footing, or perhaps in addition to their existing benefits.

It would be huge, and hugely expensive to do it right. But one thing the G.I. Bill has proved is that this form of assistance, unlike others, more than pays for itself over time. The numbers, truly, are staggering.

Considering college benefits alone, Congress's Joint Economic Committee made a detailed cost-benefit analysis in 1988. Updating the findings with 2006 dollars, this study revealed that the cost to the government of sending every G.I. to college who wanted to go after World War II amounted to 51 billion dollars. The return on that investment was found to be 260 billion dollars in increased economic output from those educated G.I.s—their average incomes were that much higher than their peers. Another 93 billion in extra taxes paid on that income rolled in. That's a gross profit of

353 billion dollars. Seven dollars earned for every dollar invested is a pretty good return.

There is every reason to assume that similar returns on investment would be achieved once again by empowering a new generation to enter national service, then go to college, master various professions, own homes in greater numbers, and ultimately be healthier (at a lower cost) because of better health care. Along the way, the middle class would be strengthened and in time expanded anew; public schools would enormously benefit from an army of teaching aides who would lower the student-teacher ratios; and young Americans would become reacquainted with the concepts of service to society, unity of purpose, and sacrifice for country—a far milder form than marching to combat, but sacrifice nonetheless. These are values the Greatest Generation understood and accepted in its youth. In an era in which barely 1 percent of the population is willing to serve in the military, even during a war launched with a majority of Americans' support, these would seem to be values the country would do well to rediscover.

A few weeks before he died in 2003, former Senator Paul Simon of Illinois, a crusading liberal on social causes but long a fiscal conservative, wrote at length about his belief that a new program modeled on the G.I. Bill was essential for continued national prosperity and security. He lamented that President Bush in 2001 had pushed through Congress a ten-year, $1.35 trillion tax cut, and suggested that just a small portion of that money could have been set aside to create a new G.I. Bill for a new generation. He eloquently summarized the reasons for doing so:

> If you ask the question—*Who is the world's superpower today?*—the answer is easy. The United States. But ask a

second question, *Who will be the world's skill power twenty years from now?* The answer is not clear. We must build a more skilled work force. Every economic study suggests that we must invest more in education or we will harm the nation. Wages of unskilled workers have been dropping slowly since 1973. The economist Lester Thurow writes, "To return to a world of rising real wages for most Americans, a massive program of reskilling and reeducating the bottom 60 percent of the work force would be needed."

Then Simon closed with this thought: "We should do it."

"YOU will find me a skeptic, sort of, as to the idea of 'The Greatest Generation,'" Allan Howerton muses. "It was a marvelous marketing slogan for Tom Brokaw and will likely become a part of the American legend. But any truth in it is due, I think, to two things: the draft and the G.I. Bill.

"The draft brought everybody from the most illiterate to the PhD into the same foxhole for a common shared experience and purpose. Then the G.I. Bill made it possible for the survivors to accomplish good things for themselves, their families, and their country. Only these things, I think, give the slogan any claim on reality."

Acknowledgments

For sharing their stories and time, I wish to acknowledge and thank the veterans of World War II whose cooperation and kindness made this book possible: Allan Howerton, Robert Booth, Bill Thomas, Bill and Vivian Kingsley, Dr. Richard and Jean Koch, Arthur Penn, Josette Dermody Wingo, Monte Posey, Leon Lederman, and Senator George McGovern.

Thanks must also go to the faculty and staff of the University of Denver for their hospitality and invaluable assistance, particularly Steven Fisher, associate professor and curator of special collections at the university's Penrose Library; Robert E. Stencil, professor of astronomy and director of DU observatories; and Professor J.J. Johnston of the Department of Business Ethics and Legal Studies.

A Note on Sources

A number of books, articles and Web sites concerning the G.I. Bill, its historical context, and American war veterans were mentioned in the preceding chapters, or may be of interest to readers. These include:

www.EdwardHumes.com, for additional resources on the G.I. Bill and veterans history.

Dear Captain, et al.: The Agonies and the Ecstasies of War Memory, Allan Wilford Howerton, Xlibris Corporation, 2000.

Mother Was a Gunner's Mate, Josette Dermody Wingo, Naval Institute Press, 1994.

The God Particle: If the Universe is the Answer, What is the Question, Leon Lederman, Houghton Mifflin Company, 1993.

With Eyes on the Stars, Harold (Hal) B. Secrist Jr., self-published at the University of Denver, 1999.

Holy Land: A Suburban Memoir, D.J. Waldie, W.W. Norton & Company, 1996.

When Affirmative Action Was White, Ira Katznelson, W.W. Norton & Company, 2005.

"'The Only Good Thing Was the G.I. Bill': Effects of the Education and Training Provisions on African-American Veterans' Political Participation," Suzanne Mettler, *Studies in American Political Development,* 19 (Spring 2005).

"I Saw the GI Bill Written," David Camelon, *The American Legion Magazine,* in three parts, September, October, November 1949.

Preparing for Ulysses: Politics and Veterans during World War II, Davis R.B. Ross, Columbia University Press, 1969.

"A G.I. Bill for Today," Paul Simon, *The Chronicle of Higher Education,* October 31, 2003, online edition, www.chronicle.com/free/v50/i10/10b01601.htm

"The G.I. Pamphlet Series," www.historians.org/projects/GIRoundtable/index.html

"Women Veterans Historical Collection," University of North Carolina, Greensboro, library.uncg.edu/depts/archives/veterans

US House of Representatives' history and commemoration of the G.I. Bill, veterans.house.gov/benefits/gi60th/title.html

American Wars Fact Sheet, Department of Veteran Affairs, www.va.gov/pressrel/amwars01.htm

Black Mountain College Project, www.bmcproject.org

"Patriotism is Non-Partisan," George McGovern, *The Nation,* April 11, 2005, www.thenation.com/doc/20050411/mcgovern

Index

Index

Index

Index